Problems created by the civil nuclear energy industry will require increased international attention during the 1980s. The international community now relies mainly on the 1970 Treaty on the Non-Proliferation of Nuclear Weapons and safeguards administered by the International Atomic Energy Agency to keep the peaceful exploitation of nuclear energy from contributing to the spread of nuclear weapons. As more nations acquire reprocessing or enrichment facilities—which can produce the explosive component of nuclear weapons—the need for additional forms of international cooperation becomes more pressing.

What international measures might be taken to reduce incentives to acquire national reprocessing or enrichment facilities? This book seeks to answer that question by examining how nuclear fuel supplies can be assured and how alternatives to national storage of spent nuclear fuel can be provided. It also considers means of channeling the development of reprocessing capacity, controlling separated plutonium, and achieving a consensus on the terms of trade in sensitive nuclear materials, equipment, and technology. Possible institutional changes—a nuclear fuel bank, a commodity agreement for uranium, a plutonium storage system, and multinational fuel cycle facilities—are explored in some detail.

Joseph A. Yager, a senior fellow in the Brookings Foreign Policy Studies program, is the editor of *Nonproliferation and U.S. Foreign Policy* (Brookings, 1980). Ralph T. Mabry, Jr., a member of the research staff of the Brookings Foreign Policy Studies program when he worked on this study, became counsel to the Overseas Private Investment Corporation in 1979.

Jacket Design: Carol Crosby Black

JOSEPH A. YAGER

with the assistance of Ralph T. Mabry, Jr.

International Cooperation in Nuclear Energy

THE BROOKINGS INSTITUTION

Washington, D.C.

Library of Congress Cataloging in Publication data:

Yager, Joseph A., 1916–
    International cooperation in nuclear energy.
    Includes bibliographical references and index.
    1. Atomic energy—International cooperation.
2. Atomic energy policy—International cooperation.
3. Atomic energy industries—Security measures—
International cooperation.   I. Mabry, Ralph T.
II. Brookings Institution.   III. Title.
HD9698.A2Y34   333.79′24   81-1414
                              AACR2

ISBN 0-8157-9676-5
ISBN 0-8157-9675-7 (pbk.)

1 2 3 4 5 6 7 8 9

Foreword

THE DANGER that the peaceful exploitation of nuclear energy might contribute to the spread of nuclear weapons has long been recognized. Until recently, the 1970 Treaty on the Non-Proliferation of Nuclear Weapons and the safeguards administered by the International Atomic Energy Agency were widely viewed as adequate responses to this danger. The treaty committed most nations (though with several important exceptions) to oppose the further proliferation of nuclear weapons, and the safeguards were designed to give timely warning of any diversion of nuclear materials from peaceful to military use.

Confidence in the timely warning of a nuclear material diversion was justified as long as the enrichment and reprocessing facilities capable of making the explosive component of nuclear weapons were confined almost exclusively to countries that already had such weapons. But the acquisition of such facilities by states that do not possess nuclear weapons is creating a new situation—one that calls for new forms of international cooperation to control the development of nuclear energy.

This study considers a broad range of cooperative measures and evaluates their potential contribution to the goal of checking the spread of nuclear weapons and their consistency with the continued exploitation of nuclear energy for peaceful purposes. Some of the measures are already under consideration by concerned governments and international organizations. Others may be considered in the future.

Joseph A. Yager is a senior fellow in the Brookings Foreign Policy Studies program. Ralph T. Mabry, Jr., a member of the same program when he worked on this study, became counsel to the Overseas Private Investment Corporation in 1979.

vii

Abram Chayes, Philip J. Farley, John E. Gray, and J. Robert Schaetzel served as consultants on the project and commented on successive drafts of the study. Steven Raymund provided research assistance. Jeanane Patterson and Ann Ziegler served as project secretaries. The study was edited by Jane Freundel Levey; its factual content was checked for accuracy by Clifford A. Wright. The index was prepared by Florence Robinson.

The authors benefited from the generous advice and assistance of many persons in the United States and abroad. They express their appreciation for comments on drafts to Justin L. Bloom, Warren H. Donnelly, Alan Hanson, Kurt Juul, Katherine Hope Larson, Frederick McGoldrick, Patrick W. Murphy, Sigurd O. Nielsen, Manfred Popp, Eleanor B. Steinberg, John Steinbruner, and Walt H. Wolf.

In March 1980, at the invitation of the Rockefeller Foundation, the Brookings Institution held an international conference at the foundation's study and conference center in Bellagio, Italy, to discuss the issues considered in this study. A draft of the study was distributed to participants before the conference and various points made at the conference are reflected in the text of this volume. A summary of the conference proceedings constitutes appendix C.

This study was financed by the U.S. Department of Energy and the Fritz Thyssen Foundation. The Fritz Thyssen Foundation also helped cover the expenses of the conference, as did the Alfred P. Sloan Foundation.

The views presented in this study are those of the authors and should not be ascribed to the persons or organizations whose assistance is acknowledged above, or to the trustees, officers, or other staff members of the Brookings Institution.

BRUCE K. MACLAURY
President

November 1980
Washington, D.C.

Contents

Appendixes

Index   221

Tables

International
Cooperation
in Nuclear Energy

Glossary

AFR	Away from reactor
FBR	Fast breeder reactor
GWe	Gigawatt(s), electric
HWR	Heavy water reactor
IAEA	International Atomic Energy Agency
INFCE	International Nuclear Fuel Cycle Evaluation
IPS	International Plutonium Storage System
LEU	Low-enriched uranium
LWR	Light water reactor
MWe	Megawatt(s), electric
NNPA	Nuclear Non-Proliferation Act of 1978
NPT	Treaty on the Non-Proliferation of Nuclear Weapons
RNFCC	Regional nuclear fuel cycle center
SWU	Separative work unit

Introduction

THE international development of nuclear energy for peaceful purposes has always carried with it the risk of spreading nuclear weapons because the explosive component of nuclear fission weapons and the fuel used in nuclear power plants are derived from the same substances. Moreover, the technology required to exploit nuclear energy for peaceful purposes inevitably gives its possessors some of the knowledge needed to produce nuclear weapons. These uncomfortable facts reflect unchanging attributes of the physical universe. Mankind must be prepared to live with them for the rest of human history. It has been doing so for only a third of a century.

The record during this brief period—merely the dawn of the nuclear age—has been mixed. Since the destruction of Hiroshima and Nagasaki in August 1945, no nuclear weapons have been used in war. Efforts to check the spread of nuclear weapons, however, have been only partly successful.

The U.S. attempt to put the nuclear genie back into the bottle immediately after the end of World War II failed when the Soviet Union rejected the Baruch Plan.[1] The Soviets pushed forward with their own nuclear weapons program and successfully tested a nuclear explosive device in 1949. The British followed in 1952, the French in 1960, and the Chinese in 1964. Membership in what is inappropriately referred to as the nuclear weapon club remains at five, unless one counts India with its so-called

1. The Baruch Plan called for the abolition of nuclear weapons and for giving an international agency exclusive authority to conduct intrinsically dangerous operations in the field of nuclear energy. The plan was based on U.S. Department of State, *A Report on the International Control of Atomic Energy*, prepared for the Secretary of State's Committee on Atomic Energy by a Board of Consultants (Government Printing Office, 1946), especially pp. 31–43.

peaceful test explosion and Israel with its "bombs-in-the-basement" as associate members.

A total of five, or possibly seven, nuclear weapon states cannot be viewed as a great victory for advocates of nuclear disarmament. But at the same time, the number falls far short of the unchecked proliferation of nuclear weapons that many observers have feared. Why nuclear weapons have spread so slowly is hard to say. Plausible explanations for the decisions of individual countries not to acquire nuclear weapons can be found,[2] but general causes are elusive.

Two largely fortuitous circumstances may, however, provide much of the answer. First—for a variety of reasons—civil nuclear energy, and with it nuclear technology, has not spread as rapidly as was expected. And second, some countries that could have developed nuclear weapons have lacked a sufficient incentive to do so. As will be seen, both of these circumstances are changing in ways that could favor the spread of nuclear weapons.

Some credit for checking nuclear weapon proliferation goes to the international regime set up for that purpose,[3] but how much is not clear. The Treaty on the Non-Proliferation of Nuclear Weapons (NPT)[4] formalized a broad international consensus against the further spread of nuclear weapons. The system of safeguards administered by the International Atomic Energy Agency (IAEA) provides some assurance that civil nuclear programs are not being used as a cover for the development of nuclear weapons. And the informal constraints on the export of sensitive nuclear facilities and technology agreed to by the members of the London nuclear suppliers' group make it more difficult to assemble the essential components of a nuclear weapons program. The present system may not, however, be able to cope with the new problems emerging in both the developing and the industrialized countries.

The number of developing countries that have the technological capabilities and the industrial base required to make nuclear weapons is large

2. For example, see the country case studies in Joseph A. Yager, ed., *Nonproliferation and U.S. Foreign Policy* (Brookings Institution, 1980).

3. The present regime consists principally of the Treaty on the Non-Proliferation of Nuclear Weapons and the safeguards administered by the International Atomic Energy Agency. See chap. 2 and app. A for more complete descriptions.

4. 21 U.S.T. 483.

and increasing.[5] By unfortunate coincidence, some of these countries feel less secure militarily than they did only a few years ago, and their interest in at least exploring the merits of nuclear weapons has grown. The causes of their insecurity vary, but the loosening of the alliance system constructed by the United States in the 1950s and doubts concerning the value of U.S. security commitments created by the failure in Vietnam must be viewed as contributory or reinforcing factors.

In the industrialized world, civil nuclear industries have matured to the point where a number of countries have built, or plan to build, enrichment or reprocessing plants or both. Those countries that are not already nuclear weapon states will in this way acquire the means of making the explosive component of nuclear weapons. This development is intrinsically important and also sets a precedent for developing countries that have embarked on ambitious civil nuclear energy programs. A new class of states is on the point of emerging, first in the industrialized world, and slightly later among the more advanced developing countries: the "near-" nuclear weapon state. This development threatens to undermine the effectiveness of the established international nuclear regime.

The safeguards administered by the IAEA pursuant to the NPT or other international agreements are not designed to impose physical obstacles to the diversion of nuclear material from civil to nonpeaceful uses, but only to detect such diversion in time for interested powers to take effective countermeasures. The present international nuclear regime, it must be emphasized, does not impose any legal obstacles to the construction of reprocessing and enrichment plants.[6] But nonnuclear weapon states adhering to the NPT must put these plants (and all other nuclear activities) under IAEA safeguards. Presumably diversion of nuclear materials from safeguarded enrichment or reprocessing plants would be quickly detected, but whether this would constitute timely warning is doubtful.

Some observers, particularly in the United States, have concluded that the impending spread of reprocessing and enrichment facilities under

5. See Albert Wohlstetter and others, *Moving Toward Life in a Nuclear Armed Crowd?* prepared for U.S. Arms Control and Disarmament Agency (Los Angeles, Calif.: Pan Heuristics, 1976), especially pp. 13–18.

6. The informal constraints agreed to by members of the London nuclear suppliers' group make it difficult for nonsupplier nations to build plants, but a country circumventing those constraints would not be acting illegally.

national control (especially the former in the near term) poses a serious problem, and that new and possibly radical measures must be taken to channel the growth of civil nuclear energy in ways that do not make the proliferation of nuclear weapons more likely. This conclusion has by no means gained universal acceptance. Many observers outside the United States remain unconvinced that a new problem, calling for drastic international action, actually exists. Some people regard the spread of nuclear weapons as inevitable. Others believe that the present international nuclear arrangements can cope adequately with changes in the civil nuclear energy industry. In their view all that needs to be done is to give full support to the NPT and improve the technical efficiency of safeguards. Still others see little or no connection between the development of civil nuclear energy and the spread of nuclear weapons. (It is a fact that no country now possessing nuclear weapons acquired them by diverting material from civil nuclear facilities.) They argue that the way to keep more countries from acquiring nuclear weapons is to reduce their incentives for doing so. They view efforts to control nuclear technology, facilities, and materials as misdirected and futile.

There is some merit in each of these positions. Certainly, it would be foolhardy to claim that no more nations will acquire nuclear weapons. Similarly, no one can question the wisdom of trying to adapt the present international nuclear system to changing conditions. And without doubt, prospects for checking the spread of nuclear weapons will not be good, as long as some nonnuclear weapon states see strong reasons for acquiring them. But granting all of this, a compelling case remains for regarding the impending spread of reprocessing and enrichment facilities as a serious problem. There can be little doubt that easy access to the explosive component of nuclear weapons removes an important inhibition against crossing the nuclear threshold—the fear that a move to develop nuclear weapons would be blocked by timely diplomatic or other action by other powers.

This study, having accepted the existence of the problem of near-nuclear weapon states, considers how the international community might best respond. Checking the spread of nuclear weapons is not, however, taken as an overriding goal to which all other considerations must give way. The fundamental problem is instead to reconcile two partially conflicting objectives: increasing energy supplies and reducing the risk of further nuclear weapon proliferation.

CHAPTER ONE

Trends in Civil Nuclear Energy

THIS CHAPTER provides a framework for the analysis of specific problems of nuclear energy policy in later chapters. But before examining the present status and future prospects of the civil nuclear energy industry, it is useful to review briefly the unique characteristics of nuclear power as a means of generating electricity.

The Nuclear Fuel Cycle

Today's civil nuclear energy programs take advantage of the fact that a naturally occurring isotope of uranium, U^{235}, is fissionable.[1] When atoms split, or fission, energy is released in the form of heat. The heat is used to make steam, which drives turbines and generates electricity in the same way as conventional power plants use steam produced by burning oil, coal, or gas.

Fission occurs both spontaneously and when an atom of U^{235} is struck by a neutron emitted by the fission of another atom of U^{235}. Sustained fission, which is necessary for power plant operations, depends upon the

1. Plutonium (the isotope Pu^{239}) and another isotope of uranium (U^{233}) are also fissionable and can be used as nuclear fuel. They do not yet, however, play any appreciable role in civil nuclear energy programs. Neither Pu^{239} nor U^{233} occur in nature. Pu^{239} can be formed by irradiating U^{238} in a reactor; U^{233} can be formed by irradiating thorium.

5

continuous steady production of neutrons by collisions of neutrons with atoms of U^{235}. If too many neutrons escape from the reactor core without colliding with atoms of U^{235}, or are absorbed by other materials, the process cannot continue. If too many neutrons do collide with atoms of U^{235}, the rate of fission escalates and causes an uncontrolled release of energy.

Sustained fission can be achieved by bringing together the right amount of fissionable material (U^{235} in today's power reactors) and by moderating the speed of neutrons emitted by fission. If the speed is reduced, the probability of a fission-producing collision with an atom of U^{235} is increased. Light water reactors (LWRs) use ordinary water, which is an effective moderator, but absorbs a relatively large number of neutrons. As a consequence, LWRs must use low-enriched uranium in which the proportion of U^{235} has been raised to between 2 and 4 percent. Heavy water reactors (HWRs) use water which contains deuterium, a heavy and rare isotope of hydrogen. Because this moderator absorbs fewer neutrons, HWRs can use natural uranium, which contains only about 0.7 percent of U^{235}. Reactors with graphite moderators can use natural or low-enriched uranium.

Nuclear reactors are the central element of the civil nuclear energy industry. They are supported by other facilities, however. The functions performed by these facilities and by the reactors themselves are known collectively as the nuclear fuel cycle.[2]

The nuclear fuel cycle has two phases: the front end, which includes all activities involved in obtaining and preparing fuel for insertion in a reactor; and the back end, which embraces the various things that may be done with spent fuel after it has been removed from a reactor. Unless otherwise indicated, the following brief description of the nuclear fuel

2. For more detailed explanations of the nuclear fuel cycle see *Nuclear Proliferation Factbook,* prepared for the House Committee on International Relations and the Senate Committee on Governmental Affairs, 95 Cong. 1 sess. (Government Printing Office, 1977), pp. 161–68; Nuclear Energy Policy Study Group, *Nuclear Power Issues and Choices* (Ballinger, 1977), pp. 389–405; Stockholm International Peace Research Institute, *The Nuclear Age* (Cambridge: MIT Press; Stockholm: Almqvist and Wiksell, 1974), pp. 46–62; U.S. Central Intelligence Agency, *Nuclear Energy,* ER 77-10468 (August 1977), pp. 1–20; and Anthony V. Nero, Jr., *A Guidebook to Nuclear Reactors* (University of California Press, 1979).

cycle refers to facilities associated with the operation of today's dominant LWRs.

The Front End of the Fuel Cycle

The fuel cycle begins with the mining of uranium ore in either an open pit or an underground mine. The uranium content of the ore is typically quite low (0.2 percent or less of U_3O_8). The ore is therefore concentrated by mechanical and chemical processing in a mill near the mine. The product of the mill is known as yellowcake and has a U_3O_8 content of 75 to 85 percent.

Most of the uranium in yellowcake consists of the isotope U^{238}; only 0.7 percent is the fissionable isotope U^{235}. The process of raising the percentage of U^{235} to the level required for LWR fuel is known as enrichment. To prepare natural uranium for enrichment, the yellowcake is sent to a conversion plant. There, the U_3O_8 is purified and converted to uranium hexafluoride (UF_6), which is shipped to an enrichment plant. For many years, the only commercial method of enrichment was gaseous diffusion, which involves forcing UF_6 (which is a gas at relatively low temperatures) through a series of membranes. At each stage, a slightly higher percentage of U^{235} than U^{238} passes through. Another method, gaseous centrifuge, is also coming into use. It, too, uses UF_6 in gaseous form, and depends on the difference in the mass of the two isotopes of uranium to achieve an increased concentration of U^{235}. Both processes separate the UF_6 feed gas into two streams: a product stream with the desired enriched percentage of U^{235}, and a leftover, or tails, stream whose content of U^{235} is normally assayed at 0.2 to 0.3 percent.

The enriched UF_6 is not directly usable as reactor fuel. It must be sent to a fuel fabrication plant where it is converted to uranium dioxide (UO_2). The oxide is shaped into pellets, which are inserted in tubes that are usually made of a zirconium alloy and are referred to as fuel cladding. The resulting rods are grouped in fuel assemblies, ready for insertion into reactors.

The front end of the LWR fuel cycle, therefore, consists of five stages: mining, milling, conversion, enrichment, and fabrication. The front end of the HWR fuel cycle skips enrichment, but depends upon another technologically complex process, the production of heavy water.

The Back End of the Fuel Cycle

When spent fuel is removed from a reactor, it is quite hot in a radio-active as well as a thermal sense. Because it is highly radioactive, spent fuel must be stored under water in a pool at the reactor for at least six months. If necessary, it can be stored in this way for much longer periods.

Storage of spent fuel at reactors has limits, however. Additional interim storage space away from reactors (AFR) can be built, but eventually spent fuel must be either disposed of permanently or reprocessed. Permanent disposal is the last step in what is known as the once-through fuel cycle. Reprocessing spent fuel would yield plutonium and residual uranium, both of which could be recycled as reactor fuel, thereby closing the fuel cycle.

Permanent disposal of spent fuel is designed to prevent reentry of its radioactive components into the biosphere. No non-Communist government has yet approved a means of permanently disposing of either spent fuel or the high-level radioactive wastes remaining after reprocessing spent fuel. The method most likely to be approved deposits spent fuel and high-level wastes deep underground in stable geological formations.

Reprocessing is controversial because the plutonium extracted from spent fuel can be used in nuclear weapons. The U.S. government, in particular, has urged that the decision to reprocess spent fuel be deferred. Many other governments with civil nuclear energy programs favor reprocessing as a means of recovering valuable fuel assets and facilitating the final disposal of nuclear waste.

Opinions differ on the economics of recycling plutonium and residual uranium in today's reactors. The cost of reprocessing and preparing the recovered plutonium and uranium for recycling may exceed the savings in newly mined uranium and enrichment services. Reprocessing and recycling plutonium will, however, be necessary when fast breeder reactors (FBRs), under development in several countries, begin operation later in this century or early in the next. The FBRs breed more fuel in the form of plutonium than they consume, an advantage that can only be realized by reprocessing.

If a country decides in favor of reprocessing and recycling, spent fuel is sent to a reprocessing plant in which uranium, plutonium, and unusable fission products are chemically separated. Only about 0.8 percent of the residual uranium will be U^{235}, so it must be re-enriched for use in LWRs.

This entails sending it first to a plant for conversion to UF_6, and then to an enrichment plant, after which it goes to a fabrication plant for conversion to uranium dioxide (UO_2). The plutonium goes directly to a fabrication plant, where it is converted to plutonium dioxide (PuO_2) unless it is already in that form. The uranium oxide and plutonium oxide are mixed and formed into sintered pellets for insertion in fuel tubes. The result is known as mixed oxide fuel.

The back end of the fuel cycle, therefore, can follow different paths. The once-through cycle involves storage at the reactor, probably also AFR storage, and final disposal. The closed cycle involves storage at the reactor, AFR storage, reprocessing, final disposal of nuclear wastes, and recycling of recovered plutonium and residual uranium. Recycling, of course, requires retracing part of the front end of the fuel cycle.

Existing and Projected Fuel Cycle Facilities

Generating capacity dictates the requirements for other fuel cycle facilities, and will be discussed before the other parts of the fuel cycle. Because good information on plans for the civil nuclear energy industry in most Communist countries is not available, the following deals largely with non-Communist areas.

Nuclear Generating Capacity

Estimating future nuclear generating capacity has always been difficult. Most past estimates tended to be high because they did not fully anticipate the political and economic difficulties that have retarded the growth of the civil nuclear energy industry. At present, two conflicting considerations make judging the future of the industry especially difficult. On the one hand, public fears concerning the safety of nuclear reactors could seriously curtail the building of new nuclear power plants. On the other, sharp increases in the price of oil and doubts about the reliability of conventional supplies of energy make the development of alternative energy sources, including nuclear power, more attractive.

Under these circumstances, any estimates of future nuclear generating capacity must be speculative at best. Table 1-1 presents two recent estimates of nuclear generating capacity in non-Communist areas in 1985,

Table 1-1. *Nuclear Generating Capacity in Non-Communist Areas*
Gigawatts, electric

Area	1978, actual	1985, estimated		1990, estimated		1995, estimated	
		A	B	A	B	A	B
OECD Europe	32.9	73	100	93	166	120	224
United States	50.0	89	100	130	157	153	200
Canada	4.7	10	12	13	20	17	33
Japan	11.0	17	26	25	45	35	70
Other countries[a]	2.2	15	19	28	45	45	92
Total	100.8	204	257	289	434	370	619

Sources: Figures for 1978 are from "World List of Nuclear Power Plants," *Nuclear News* (February 1979), pp. 59–77. Case A estimates are from the "low-mid" forecast of the U.S. Department of Energy, April 1980. Case B estimates are the low projections from International Nuclear Fuel Cycle Evaluation, *Fuel and Heavy Water Availability: Report of Working Group 1,* INFCE/PC/2/1 (Vienna: International Atomic Energy Agency, 1980), pp. 44–47. Figures are rounded.
a. Developing countries plus Australia, New Zealand, and South Africa. None of these has nuclear power plants today. South Africa will probably begin producing nuclear power in the mid-1980s and may have 4.3–5.6 GWe of generating capacity by 1995 (in case B; case A does not break out South Africa separately).

1990, and 1995. The lowest (A) is a forecast of the U.S. Department of Energy, prepared in March 1980. The other (B) is the lower of two estimates developed by the International Nuclear Fuel Cycle Evaluation, and published in February 1980 on the basis of work completed in May 1979.[3]

The fact that the divergence among these estimates is greater in 1990 than in 1985 and greater in 1995 than in 1990 is not surprising. Capacity that is to come on line by 1985 must already be under construction, and plans must be well advanced for capacity that is to be completed between 1985 and 1990. What may happen after 1990 can be only a subject for speculation.

Even if the lower of the two estimates presented in table 1-1 is used, the future contribution of nuclear power to meeting total energy requirements can be quite substantial. Table 1-2 shows that the nuclear generat-

3. INFCE also produced a high estimate of future nuclear generating capacity that does not appear to be realistic. Under this estimate, nuclear generating capacity in non-Communist areas would reach 807.7 gigawatts, electric (GWe) by 1995, 30 percent greater than the low INFCE estimate and over twice the DOE estimate of 370 GWe. See International Nuclear Fuel Cycle Evaluation, *Fuel and Heavy Water Availability: Report of Working Group 1,* INFCE/PC/2/1 (Vienna: International Atomic Energy Agency, 1980), p. 47.

ing capacity projected by DOE (case A) could produce 5.3 percent of the total energy requirements of the non-Communist nations in 1985, 6.4 percent in 1990, and 7.0 percent in 1995. In these calculations, the projections of total energy consumption are of course as important as the estimates of nuclear generating capacity. Forecasts of energy consumption depend on the validity of a number of key assumptions, including those with respect to rates of economic growth, the relationship between economic growth and energy consumption, and the price of energy—especially the price of oil.

The geographical distribution of nuclear generating capacity also figures in the problems considered in this study. As table 1-1 suggests, nuclear generating capacity is expected to expand much more rapidly in developing countries than in industrialized countries. Nevertheless in 1995, roughly 85 percent of total capacity will still be in the latter countries.

In 1978, 63 percent of the nuclear generating capacity in non-Communist areas was in nuclear weapon states—the United States, France, and the United Kingdom.[4] By 1995 the nuclear weapon states may still have 47 to 56 percent of generating capacity.[5]

The number of countries with nuclear power plants is growing, especially in the developing areas. In 1978 nineteen non-Communist countries had operable nuclear power plants. Of this number, only five (Argentina, India, South Korea, Pakistan, and Taiwan) were developing nations. By the end of the century, eighteen more countries could acquire nuclear generating facilities, including twelve developing nations. By no means are all of the latter group certain to act on their expressed interest in nuclear energy.[6]

Table 1-3 presents operable nuclear generating capacity and capacity under construction in Communist countries in mid-1979. Over three-

4. "World List of Nuclear Power Plants," *Nuclear News* (February 1979), pp. 59–77.

5. The U.S. Department of Energy estimates that by 1995 France may have 41 to 46 gigawatts, electric (GWe) of nuclear generating capacity and the United Kingdom, 15 to 17 GWe. Taking the lower end of these ranges and adding the 153 GWe estimated for the United States gives a combined capacity of 209 GWe in 1995 in case A for the three non-Communist nuclear weapon states. In case B, the three nuclear weapon states are estimated to have 293 GWe of nuclear generating capacity.

6. The entry of Brazil, Mexico, and the Philippines into the civil nuclear energy club appears likely. Uncertainties of varying degree affect the other developing countries that have indicated an interest in building nuclear power plants.

Table 1-2. *Estimated Primary Energy Consumption and Percentage of Consumption Provided by Nuclear Power in Non-Communist Areas, 1985, 1990, and 1995*

Consumption in millions of barrels of oil per day equivalent

Area	1985			1990			1995		
	Total[a]	Nuclear (case A)[b]	Percent nuclear	Total[a]	Nuclear (case A)[b]	Percent nuclear	Total[a]	Nuclear (case A)[b]	Percent nuclear
OECD Europe	27.4	2.0	7.3	29.4	2.6	8.8	32.8	3.3	10.1
United States	40.9	2.5	6.1	45.2	3.6	8.0	49.5	4.2	8.5
Japan	9.8	0.5	5.1	11.9	0.7	5.9	15.7	1.0	6.4
Other OECD	6.8	0.3	4.4	7.5	0.4	5.3	8.8	0.5	5.7
Other countries[c]	22.6	0.5	2.2	30.1	0.8	2.6	40.7	1.3	3.2
Total	107.5	5.7	5.3	124.0	8.0	6.4	147.5	10.3	7.0

Source: U.S. Department of Energy, April 1980. Figures are rounded.

a. The key assumptions used by the Department of Energy in forecasting total consumption were that the world price of oil would be $27 a barrel in real terms throughout the period and that the economies of the non-Communist countries would grow at an average annual rate of 3.4 percent.

b. Case A is DOE's low-mid forecast.

c. Includes Yugoslavia. No other Communist countries are covered.

Table 1-3. *Nuclear Generating Capacity in Communist Countries, June 30, 1979*

Megawatts, electric

Country	Operable	Under construction	Total
Bulgaria	880	880	1,760
Czechoslovakia	990	880	1,870
East Germany	1,390	1,320	2,710
Hungary	0	1,760	1,760
Rumania	0	1,040	1,040
USSR	11,475	13,320	24,795
Yugoslavia	0	615	615
Total	14,735	19,815	34,550

Source: "World List of Nuclear Power Plants," *Nuclear News* (August 1979), pp. 69–87.

fourths of the operable capacity and two-thirds of the capacity under construction are in the Soviet Union. Despite the success of its nuclear weapon program, China does not yet have nuclear power plants.[7] Although good information on planned capacity is not available, the importance of nuclear energy in the Communist nations will almost certainly continue to grow.[8]

In most parts of the world, the light water reactor is dominant and will remain so for some time. In 1978 LWRs accounted for 86 percent of nuclear generating capacity in non-Communist areas. The Organisation for Economic Co-operation and Development estimates that the share of LWRs may increase to 90 percent by the year 2000.[9] Heavy water reactors contributed about 5 percent of capacity in 1978, and may rise to 7 or 8 percent by the end of the century. Fast breeder reactors will probably not be built in any numbers until the next century.

A comparable estimate of the distribution of reactor types in the Communist countries is not available. Outside the Soviet Union, however,

7. China has agreed in principle to buy two 900-MWe power plants from France. *Wall Street Journal*, October 20, 1980.

8. At a meeting in Warsaw in June 1979, Comecon leaders reportedly endorsed plans to expand nuclear generating capacity to about 150 GWe by 1990, or roughly ten times the capacity existing in 1979 (*Nuclear News* [August 1979], p. 52). Whether this goal is attainable appears open to question. The "low" INFCE estimate of nuclear generating capacity in centrally planned countries in 1990 is 98 GWe.

9. Nuclear Energy Agency, Organisation for Economic Co-operation and Development, *Nuclear Fuel Cycle Requirements and Supply Considerations, through the Long-Term* (Paris: OECD, 1978), p. 71.

almost all nuclear power plants in existence or under construction have light water reactors. The only exception is a 110-megawatt, electric (MWe), gas-cooled, heavy water reactor in Czechoslovakia. Rumania has ordered a 600-MWe pressurized HWR from Atomic Energy of Canada, Ltd.

The pattern in the Soviet Union is somewhat different. Sixty percent of power reactor capacity, existing or under construction, is accounted for by LGRs (light-water-cooled, graphite-moderated reactors). The remaining capacity is in LWRs (36 percent) and FBRs (4 percent).[10]

The Soviet Union is pushing the development and use of fast breeder reactors. The first FBR power station began operations in 1973, but has been forced to operate below its rated capacity because of an accident in 1974.[11] The second FBR is scheduled to begin operations in 1980.[12]

Front End Fuel Cycle Facilities

Two of the five stages in the front end of the LWR fuel cycle, conversion and fabrication, appear to pose no serious problems. Present capacities of conversion and fabrication plants are adequate and should keep pace with future demand. But questions have arisen concerning the future adequacy of supplies of natural uranium and enrichment services.

NATURAL URANIUM PRODUCTION. The adequacy of prospective natural uranium supplies can be measured in two ways: annual requirements can be compared with attainable annual production capabilities; or cumulative requirements over a period of years can be compared with the uranium deposits (commonly called resources) that may be available within specified cost ranges. In the second approach, requirements can be defined either as the estimated fuel needs of nuclear power reactors during a stated period, or as the lifetime requirements of reactors in being during the same period. However they are defined, estimates of production, resources, and requirements are fraught with uncertainties and should not be considered predictions, but merely rough indications of what the future may bring.

A comparison of annual uranium requirements and attainable annual production capabilities in thousands of metric tons through 1990 is quite

10. *Nuclear News* (August 1979), pp. 69–87.
11. *Washington Post,* October 5, 1978.
12. *New York Times,* January 14, 1980.

Table 1-4. *Estimated Attainable Uranium Production Capabilities in Non-Communist Areas, 1980, 1985, and 1990*

Thousands of metric tons

Country	1980	1985	1990
Australia	0.6	12.0	20.0
Canada	7.2	14.4	15.5
France	3.4	4.0	4.5
Namibia	4.1	5.0	5.0
Niger	4.3	10.5	12.0
South Africa	6.5	10.6	10.4
United States	20.9	34.1	44.2
Other	3.0	7.4	7.6
Total	50.1	98.0	119.2

Source: OECD Nuclear Energy Agency and IAEA, *Uranium: Resources, Production and Demand* (Paris: OECD, 1979), p. 23.

encouraging (estimates of actual production and consumption in 1977 are shown for comparison):

	1977, actual	1985, attainable (estimated)	1990, attainable (estimated)
Annual production	29	98	119
Annual requirements			
Case A	23	31	44
Case B	23	39	66

The above estimates of attainable production are based on table 1-4. They assume the presence of sufficient economic incentives for uranium producers to expand output, including the orderly growth of nuclear power, the absence of market perturbations, and a favorable economic climate. The two estimates of annual requirements are drawn from table 1-5. Assumptions were no recycle of plutonium or residual uranium and a tails assay (which determines how much natural uranium is needed to produce a given quantity of enriched uranium) of 0.2 percent.[13]

A comparison of estimated uranium resources and cumulative requirements over the remainder of the century is also favorable. Reasonably

13. Explicit assumptions concerning the future price of uranium are not commonly made in estimating attainable production or requirements. By implication it is assumed that the price will be sufficient to cover total costs plus a return on capital invested. Since demand is quite insensitive to price, at least in the short- and mid-term, a more exact assumption concerning price is not needed in estimating requirements.

Table 1-5. *Estimated Uranium Requirements in Non-Communist Areas, 1977–2000*

Thousands of metric tons

Requirements	1977[a]	1985[b]	1990[b]	1995[b]	2000[b]
Annual[c]					
Case A	23	31	44	56	n.a.
Case B	23	39	66	94	136
Cumulative					
Case A	23	n.a.	332	n.a.	n.a.
Case B	23	n.a.	499	n.a.	1,520

Sources: Actual requirements in 1977 are from OECD Nuclear Energy Agency and IAEA, *Uranium: Resources, Production and Demand* (Paris: OECD, 1977), p. 33. Case B estimates of both annual and cumulative requirements in 1990 and 2000 were developed by the International Nuclear Fuel Cycle Evaluation and published in the 1979 edition of *Uranium: Resources, Production and Demand*, p. 36 (LWR-dominated, single-type strategy). Estimates for annual requirements in 1985 and 1995 for case B were calculated by interpolation. All estimates for case A were calculated on the assumption that the relationship between uranium requirements in cases A and B would be the same as that between nuclear generating capacities in those two cases.
    n.a. Not available.
    a. Actual.
    b. Estimated.
    c. All estimates of uranium requirements assume a tails assay at enrichment plants of 0.2 percent U^{235} and no recycle of plutonium or residual uranium.

assured uranium resources in thousands of metric tons, plus estimated additional resources, available at a forward cost of \$130 per kilogram (see table 1-6), can be summarized as follows:[14]

	Cost less than $80 per kilogram	Cost $80–130 per kilogram	Total
Reasonably assured	1,850	736	2,586
Estimated additional	1,480	966	2,446
Total	3,330	1,702	5,032

Total uranium resources would therefore appear to be more than three

14. "Reasonably assured resources" are known mineral deposits. "Estimated additional resources" are extensions of well-explored deposits, little-explored deposits, and undiscovered deposits believed to exist along a well-defined geological trend with known deposits. See OECD Nuclear Energy Agency and IAEA, *Uranium: Resources, Production and Demand* (Paris: OECD, 1979), p. 13.

Costs are forward costs: the capital and operating costs not yet incurred that will be required to produce a kilogram of uranium. Corresponding market prices are higher. Uranium producible at a forward cost of \$80 per kilogram (or \$30 per pound of U_3O_8) might sell at \$40–60 per pound of U_3O_8. See Uranium Resource Group, National Research Council, *Problems of U.S. Uranium Resources and Supply to the Year 2010: Study of Nuclear and Alternative Energy Systems,* Supporting Paper 1 (Washington, D.C.: National Academy of Sciences, 1978), p. 1.

Table 1-6. *Uranium Resources, January 1, 1979*
Thousands of metric tons

	Reasonably assured resources		Estimated additional resources	
Country	Cost less than $80 per kilogram	Cost $80–130 per kilogram	Cost less than $80 per kilogram	Cost $80–130 per kilogram
Australia	290	9	47	6
Canada	215	20	370	358
France	40	16	26	20
Namibia	117	16	30	23
Niger	160	0	53	0
South Africa	247	144	54	85
Sweden	0	301	0	3
United States	531	177	773	385
Other	255	53	127	86
Total	1,855	736	1,480	966

Source: OECD Nuclear Energy Agency and IAEA, *Uranium: Resources, Production and Demand* (Paris: OECD, 1979), pp. 15, 18–19.

times the requirements under case B, the higher of the two requirements cases presented in table 1-5.

Committed requirements in the year 2000 (that is, the lifetime requirements of all reactors that are expected to have been put into service between 1977 and 2000) are a different story. Under case B, committed requirements could reach 3.4 million tons,[15] or about two-thirds of estimated resources and 800,000 tons greater than reasonably assured resources. No comparable estimate exists for case A, which extends only to 1995. The situation could, however, be significantly better or worse than these figures suggest.

The estimates of nuclear generating capacity on which case B is based could be too high. Moreover, much of the world has not yet been explored intensively for uranium, and more deposits presumably will be found. In 1978, a panel of experts estimated that speculative uranium resources in non-Communist countries, exploitable at a forward cost of $130 per kilogram of uranium or less, total between 6.6 and 14.8 million metric tons.[16]

15. INFCE, *Fuel and Heavy Water Availability*, p. 13.
16. OECD Nuclear Energy Agency and IAEA, *World Uranium Potential: An International Evaluation* (Paris: OECD, 1978), p. 10. "Speculative resources" refers to uranium "that is thought to exist mostly on the basis of indirect evidence and geological extrapolations, in deposits discovered with existing exploration techniques" (ibid., pp. 165–66).

On the other hand, the payoff is yellowcake at the mill, not ore in the ground. Whether future exploration for uranium will succeed in converting all estimated additional resources plus a substantial amount of speculative resources into reasonably assured resources by the year 2000 is still an open question. Nor can it be assumed that the large investments in mining and milling facilities will be made that are necessary for actual yellowcake production to keep pace with estimated requirements. The problem is only partly economic. Political and environmental problems can also interfere with the exploitation of uranium resources.

ENRICHMENT SERVICES. As the following estimates suggest, sufficient commercial enrichment capacity, in millions of separative work units (see table 1-7), should exist in the non-Communist countries to meet their annual requirements[17] at least through 1995:

	1978	1985	1990	1995	2000
Capacity	13	40	63	79	...
Requirements					
Case A	14	20	29	37	...
Case B	14	26	40	62	88

Under case B, enrichment capacity would have to be expanded substantially during the last years of the century, if estimated requirements are to be satisfied. The need for additional capacity would be reduced, however, by the amount of enrichment services made available to non-Communist countries by the Soviet Union. Under case A, excess capacity would persist for some time after 1995.[18]

The distribution of enrichment capacity in 1978 and that estimated for 1990 differ in two important respects (see table 1-7). First, the U.S.

17. Requirements in 1978 are from OECD Nuclear Energy Agency, *Nuclear Fuel Cycle Requirements,* p. 29. Estimates of requirements in 1990 and 2000 under case B are from INFCE, *Enrichment Availability: Report of Working Group 2,* INFCE/PC/2/2 (Vienna: IAEA, 1980), p. 115. (The relevant reactor strategy is L1a: once-through LWR cycle, low nuclear growth, and current technical characteristics.) These estimates of requirements are consistent with the estimates of nuclear generating capacity (case B) presented in table 1-1. Estimates for requirements in 1985 and 1995 under case B were calculated on the assumption that each gigawatt of generating capacity requires roughly 100,000 SWUs annually. All estimates for case A were calculated on the same assumption. All requirements estimates assume a tails assay of 0.2 percent.

18. Estimates of the future situation in the market for enrichment services are complicated by the uneven impact of rising electricity costs on gaseous diffusion and centrifuge plants. Some diffusion plants that are heavy users of electricity could conceivably become uncompetitive and be forced to close.

Table 1-7. *Plant Capacities Available for Commercial Enrichment*
Millions of separative work units per year

Area	1978	1980	1985	1990	1995
United States	12.7	10.5	25.6	29.6	34.4
France[a]	n.a.	6.0	10.8	20.8	20.8
Urenco[b]	0.3	0.5	2.5	10.0	17.5
Japan	0	*	0.4	2.5	5.5
Brazil	0	0	0.2	0.2	0.2
South Africa[b]	0	0	0.2	0.2	0.2
Subtotal	13.0	17.0	39.7	63.3	78.6
USSR[c]	2.4	3.9	3.4	2.4	2.4
Total[d]	15.4	20.9	43.1	65.7	81.0

Source: INFCE, *Enrichment Availability: Report of Working Group 2*, INFCE/PC/2/2 (Vienna: IAEA, 1980), pp. 74–75.

n.a. Not available.

* Less than 0.05.

a. The figures for 1980 and 1985 are estimates of the capacity of the Société Européenne d'Usine de Diffusion Gazeuse (Eurodif), and the figure shown for 1990 is an estimate of the combined capacities of Eurodif and Compagnie de Réalisation d'Usine de Diffusion Gazeuse (Coredif).

b. Capacity for Urenco in 1995 is estimated to be 17.5–20.0 million SWUs. Capacity for South Africa in 1985, 1990, and 1995 is estimated to be 0.2–0.3 million SWUs. In all cases, the lower end of the estimated range has been used.

c. The ability of the Soviet Union to supply commercial enrichment services is unknown. The figures shown are necessarily rough estimates. The U.S. Central Intelligence Agency estimated in 1977 that the Soviet Union had allocated on the order of three million SWUs of annual capacity to Western customers. (U.S. Central Intelligence Agency, *Nuclear Energy*, ER 77-10468 [August 1977], p. 37.)

d. The estimates of future capacity include existing, committed, and planned capacity as of May 1979. Thirty-eight percent of the capacity projected for 1995 and 49 percent of that for 2000 is in the planned category.

share of total enrichment capacity in non-Communist countries in 1978 was still over 97 percent. By 1990, the U.S. share is projected to fall to 44 percent, despite a large expansion of U.S. enrichment facilities. Second, in 1978 almost all enrichment capacity was in nuclear weapon states. The exception was about half of the capacity of the British-Dutch-West German Urenco, located in the Netherlands (the other half was in the United Kingdom). By 1990 enrichment plants may exist in five non-nuclear weapon states—the Netherlands, West Germany (Urenco plant), Japan, Brazil, and South Africa—with a capacity representing perhaps one-tenth of the total capacity in non-Communist areas.

Back End Fuel Cycle Facilities

The back end of the nuclear fuel cycle is much less developed than the front end. Most of the spent fuel that has been removed from power reactors thus far in the nuclear age is still stored in pools next to reactors.

Little storage space exists elsewhere, and, as was previously noted, the means of final disposal of spent fuel (and high-level waste from reprocessing) remains to be determined.

A 1,000-MWe light water reactor, operating at a 70 percent load factor, discharges spent fuel containing about 35 metric tons of heavy metal annually—mostly depleted uranium, but also including about 220 kilograms of plutonium. The 74 gigawatts, electric (GWe) of LWR capacity that existed in 1977 gave rise to roughly 2,200 tons of spent fuel, which suggests an average load factor lower than 70 percent.[19]

Very little spent oxide fuel from LWRs is being reprocessed today.[20] The Compagnie Générale des Matières Nucléaires (Cogema) plant at La Hague, France, has reached an annual capacity of only 100 metric tons of heavy metal. The British Nuclear Fuels, Ltd. (BNFL) Thermal Oxide Reprocessing Plant (Thorp) at Windscale, England, is still under construction. The plant built at Mol, Belgium, by the international consortium, Eurochemic, has been shut down for several years and in any case has an annual capacity of only about 75 tons. India has a 200-ton plant, West Germany has a 35-ton plant, and Japan has a 210-ton pilot plant.[21] As the result of a government decision, no commercial nuclear fuel is reprocessed in the United States.[22]

This situation could change dramatically in a few years (see table 1-8). The major projected developments are the continuous expansion of capacity in France, completion of Thorp in the United Kingdom (which could occur shortly after 1985), and the construction of reprocessing plants in Italy, Japan, and possibly West Germany by 1990.

Completion of all of the capacity shown in table 1-8 by the dates indi-

19. OECD Nuclear Energy Agency, *Nuclear Fuel Cycle Requirements,* pp. 36, 71, 74.

20. The BNFL plant at Windscale, England, has been reprocessing spent magnox fuel from British reactors (mostly in the United Kingdom, but also in Italy and Japan) for many years. Magnox fuel must be reprocessed, because the cladding of the fuel rods deteriorates in storage. The annual capacity of the magnox reprocessing plant is 1,500 to 2,500 metric tons of heavy metal. The Indians operate a small (30 tons per year) plant to reprocess HWR spent fuel at Trombay.

21. The information on reprocessing presented here is based on OECD Nuclear Energy Agency, *Reprocessing of Spent Nuclear Fuels in OECD Countries* (Paris: OECD, 1977), and INFCE, *Reprocessing, Plutonium Handling, Recycle: Report of Working Group 4,* INFCE/PC/2/4 (Vienna: IAEA, 1980).

22. Work on the partially completed 1,500-ton plant at Barnwell, South Carolina, has been suspended indefinitely.

Table 1-8. *Estimated Annual Capacities of Uranium Oxide Fuel Reprocessing Plants, 1985, 1990, and 2000*
Metric tons of heavy metal per year[a]

Country	1985	1990	2000
Argentina	0	0	500
Belgium	75	75	75
France	1,600	2,500	2,500
West Germany	35	500	1,435
India	200	200	200
Italy	0	500	500
Japan	210	1,710	1,710
United Kingdom	0	1,200	1,200
Total[b]	2,120	6,685	8,120

Source: INFCE, *Reprocessing, Plutonium Handling, Recycle: Report of Working Group 4*, INFCE/PC/ 2/4 (Vienna: IAEA, 1980), pp. 274–75.
a. When a range was given by the source, the lower end of the range was used.
b. The Brazilian pilot plant with an annual capacity of 3 tons of heavy metal that is scheduled to begin operations in the early 1980s is not included.

cated is by no means certain, however. Strong public opposition has already forced the indefinite postponement of the construction of a 1,400-ton West German plant.[23] Moreover, the United States and possibly other fuel-supplying nations could make some new capacity uneconomic by blocking, or imposing onerous conditions on, the reprocessing of fuel they have supplied. On the other hand, some small reprocessing plants may be built that are not reflected in the table. Brazil plans to build a pilot reprocessing plant with West German assistance. Pakistan is trying to complete a plant of uncertain size to reprocess HWR spent fuel on the basis of French plans, even though France no longer appears willing to provide technical assistance and key components.

The projected expansion of reprocessing capacity will almost certainly not keep pace with spent fuel arisings. Even if the relatively conservative estimate of nuclear generating capacity in 1990 issued by DOE (case A, table 1-1) is used, reprocessing capacity in that year could fall short of LWR spent fuel arisings by a substantial margin.[24] A recent estimate put cumulative spent fuel arisings in 1990 at something over 100,000 tons.

23. *New York Times*, May 17, 1979.
24. If generating capacity in 1990 is 289 GWe and if 90 percent of that capacity is LWRs, LWR capacity would be 260 GWe. At 35 tons per gigawatt of capacity, spent fuel arisings then come to about 9,100 tons, or 2,400 tons more than the reprocessing capacity that may exist in 1990.

Eighty percent of that amount of spent fuel, it was further estimated, would not have been reprocessed, but would remain in storage at reactors or elsewhere.[25]

How much, if any, of the plutonium extracted from spent fuel will be recycled as fuel for the present generation of reactors is uncertain. The separated plutonium is more likely to be held for use in breeder reactors when they begin service late in this century and early in the next.

The distribution of reprocessing plants between nuclear weapon states and nonnuclear weapon states will probably change markedly from 1985 to 1990. In 1985 the only large reprocessor of oxide fuel from LWRs will be France, a nuclear weapon state. Small plants will exist in Belgium, India, Japan, and West Germany. By 1990 there may be five major reprocessors (France, West Germany, Italy, Japan, and the United Kingdom), only two of which (France and the United Kingdom) are now nuclear weapon states. Small reprocessing plants will continue to exist in Belgium and India.

Conclusions

How rapidly nuclear generating capacity will grow during the remainder of the century cannot be estimated with any degree of confidence. But an increase in both the absolute and relative importance of nuclear power is virtually certain. Even under fairly conservative assumptions, nuclear generating capacity in non-Communist countries may triple between 1978 and 1995. In the latter year, nuclear power plants may produce about 7 percent of all the energy consumed in non-Communist countries.

Providing fuel for nuclear power plants should not be a problem at least through 1990. The attainable annual capacity of the uranium mining industry during the 1980s exceeds anticipated requirements for natural uranium by a wide margin. Projected enrichment capacity during the 1980s also is much greater than estimated needs.

Uranium resources appear more than sufficient to meet the requirements of power reactors for the remainder of the century. Whether resources are adequate to provide fuel for the lifetimes of all reactors put in

25. INFCE, *Reprocessing, Plutonium Handling, Recycle,* p. 30.

service by the year 2000 is less certain. In any event, a sustained explor-atory effort and large investments in mining and milling facilities will be needed to convert resources in the ground to natural uranium fuel. Large investments in new enrichment capacity may be necessary to meet the increased requirements of the late 1990s.

The future development of the back end of the nuclear fuel cycle re-mains uncertain. Spent fuel arisings are currently much larger than re-processing capacity and will probably continue to be larger for many years. Means of disposing of spent fuel permanently have not yet been determined. Under these circumstances, spent fuel is accumulating in pools at reactors. Additional storage capacity for spent fuel away from reactors will clearly be needed.

Some reprocessing of spent fuel has already taken place and more will occur in the future. Most of the plutonium extracted from spent fuel will probably be held for use in fast breeder reactors when they begin opera-tions late in this century and early in the next. In the interim, stocks of separated plutonium will increase.

Whatever the rate of growth of the civil nuclear energy industry and however the problems of the back end of the fuel cycle may be resolved, the geographical distribution of fuel cycle facilities will change during the next two decades. Nuclear generating capacity will grow more rapidly in developing nations than in those already industrialized. The near-monopoly of the United States in the provision of enrichment services is at an end, and large new enrichment capacity is being developed else-where, especially in Western Europe. By its own choice, the United States has withdrawn from the field of reprocessing, and that activity will be dominated by Western Europe.

From the nonproliferation point of view, several developments require international attention. The prospective growth of stocks of both sep-arated and unseparated plutonium (in spent fuel) has already been noted. The anticipated spread of enrichment and especially reprocessing facil-ities to more countries that do not now possess nuclear weapons also poses problems.

CHAPTER TWO

Improving the Present International Nuclear Regime

As WAS NOTED in the introduction, the present international regime for nuclear energy was not designed to deal with the problem of near-nuclear weapon states. The present arrangements evolved during a period when one nuclear weapon state, the United States, enjoyed a virtual monopoly of commercial enrichment services and when little reprocessing of spent fuel from civil power reactors had taken place. The nonproliferation aspects of the present regime were created primarily to detect diversion of nuclear materials from the once-through fuel cycle[1] in nonnuclear weapon states that did not possess their own reprocessing or enrichment facilities.

Although the present international nuclear system was not established to deal with the near-nuclear weapon problem, it must be taken into account in devising additional measures addressed specifically to that problem. The possibility that the present regime can be improved must also be considered.

The existing international regime for nuclear energy has two major and interrelated components: the Treaty on the Non-Proliferation of

1. The once-through fuel cycle is not closed. Spent fuel is not reprocessed to extract plutonium and residual uranium for recycling as reactor fuel.

Nuclear Weapons (NPT) and the safeguards administered by the International Atomic Energy Agency (IAEA).[2] Each will be reviewed separately.

The IAEA and Safeguards before the Nonproliferation Treaty

Both the establishment of safeguards over civil nuclear energy facilities and the creation of the IAEA can be traced to President Dwight D. Eisenhower's "Atoms for Peace" address before the United Nations General Assembly on December 8, 1953. This address marked the abandonment of the policy of secrecy with respect to nuclear technology followed by the United States since the end of World War II. Eisenhower's main proposal was to withdraw some of the fissionable materials in military stocks for peaceful industrial use and to establish an international agency to control the use of such materials. Nothing came of the idea of diverting military stocks of fissionable materials to peaceful uses. The "Atoms for Peace" address, however, did lead to international cooperation in nuclear energy and to the establishment of the IAEA.

In 1954 the U.S. Congress amended the Atomic Energy Act of 1946[3] to authorize the president to enter into agreements with other countries for cooperation in the field of civil nuclear energy. Congress specified that no such agreements could be executed in the absence of formal guarantees that any materials or equipment transferred by the United States would not be used for the development of nuclear weapons or for any other military purpose. Pursuant to this authority, the United States entered into cooperative agreements with twenty-seven countries in 1955.[4] These early agreements did not provide for on-site inspection of nuclear facilities by outside authorities, but they did contain guarantees against the transfer of nuclear materials to third parties and a pledge by recipients to maintain such safeguards as would be necessary to assure the physical security of nuclear materials and equipment. Later U.S. agreements also included the right of on-site inspection.

2. 21 U.S.T. 483. Appendix A, on which this section is based, gives a detailed account of the present regime and its origins.

3. 68 Stat. 919.

4. *Atoms for Peace Manual: A Compilation of Official Materials on International Cooperation for Peaceful Uses of Atomic Energy*, S. Doc. 84-55, 84 Cong. 2 sess. (Government Printing Office, 1955), p. 370.

After prolonged negotiations the statute of the IAEA was opened for signature on October 26, 1956. The statute contained only the faintest echo of Eisenhower's proposal that an international agency take custody of a pool of demilitarized nuclear material. Instead it concentrated on the establishment of safeguards to detect the diversion of nuclear materials or equipment for military purposes and on the provision of assistance in the development and application of the peaceful uses of atomic energy.

The statute required safeguards with respect to all IAEA technical assistance projects. In addition the application of safeguards was authorized when requested by the parties to other arrangements (such as those arising from bilateral agreements for cooperation). The extent to which the emerging civil nuclear energy industry would be covered by international safeguards, therefore, depended largely on voluntary requests by national governments. The IAEA was given no power to impose safeguards except on its own projects.

The statute did, however, spell out the rights and responsibilities of the IAEA when safeguards were applied to its own projects or, by request, to other arrangements.[5] These rights and responsibilities included those to: examine and approve the design of nuclear facilities; require the maintenance of operating records to assist in ensuring accountability for nuclear materials; approve the means of chemical processing of irradiated materials; and send inspectors into recipient states to determine whether undertakings against military use of nuclear materials equipment or facilities have been met.

The framework for a system of safeguards created by the statute was given greater specificity by the IAEA in subsequent bilateral and multinational agreements and in a series of information circulars (in effect, administrative regulations). On February 25, 1965, an information circular, INFCIRC/66, was issued providing the basis for all IAEA safeguards agreements. As amended, INFCIRC/66 still sets the standard for safeguards agreements which are not concluded pursuant to a country's obligations under the nonproliferation treaty.[6]

National governments were at first slow to put civil nuclear facilities

5. See article XII.A, IAEA, *Statute* (Vienna: IAEA, 1973).
6. Reproduced in Benjamin Sanders, *Safeguards Against Nuclear Proliferation*, Stockholm International Peace Research Institute Monograph (Cambridge: MIT Press; Stockholm: Almqvist and Wiksell, 1975), app. 4, pp. 95–111.

under IAEA safeguards. The United States, which then dominated the field of nuclear energy, was reluctant to give up the direct control provided by bilateral agreements. In time, however, the United States came to see advantages in assigning the safeguard function to an international agency and converted its bilateral agreements to trilateral ones, with the IAEA becoming the third party.

The Nonproliferation Treaty and Full-Scope Safeguards

The Treaty on the Non-Proliferation of Nuclear Weapons was negotiated over a period of years in the Eighteen Nation Disarmament Committee (later renamed the Conference of the Committee on Disarmament) under the cochairmanship of the United States and the Soviet Union.[7] The treaty was opened for signature on July 1, 1968, and became effective on March 5, 1970.

The essence of the NPT is expressed in five brief articles. Article I commits nuclear weapon states not to transfer nuclear weapons and not to assist nonnuclear weapon states in acquiring such weapons. Article II commits nonnuclear weapon states not to acquire nuclear weapons. Article III requires that nonnuclear weapon states accept IAEA safeguards on all of their nuclear activities. All parties are obligated by article III to require the application of safeguards to any source or special fissionable material they transfer to a nonnuclear weapon state. Article IV guarantees the right of all parties to engage in peaceful nuclear activities and commits them to cooperate in the development of nuclear energy for peaceful purposes. Article VI obligates all parties "to pursue negotiations in good faith on effective measures relating to cessation of the nuclear arms race at an early date and to nuclear disarmament, and on a treaty on general and complete disarmament under strict and effective international control."

Three nuclear weapon states (the United States, the Soviet Union, and the United Kingdom) and 111 nonnuclear weapon states have ratified the NPT.[8] Two nuclear weapon states (France and China) and two states

7. See Mason Willrich, *Non-Proliferation Treaty: Framework for Nuclear Arms Control* (Charlottesville: Michie, 1969), especially pp. 61–64. For complete text of the treaty, see Willrich, app. A.

8. *International Atomic Energy Agency Bulletin,* vol. 22 (August 1980), pp. 100–01.

in a borderline status (India and Israel) have not.[9] Nor have several states with significant existing or potential technical capabilities in the field of nuclear energy. In the latter category are Argentina, Brazil, Chile, Colombia, Egypt, Pakistan, South Africa, and Spain.

Of the nonnuclear weapon states ratifying the NPT, seventy-eight had negotiated safeguard agreements with the IAEA by May 1, 1980. Sixty-eight of these agreements were in effect on that date. Ten had been approved by the IAEA board of governors and were awaiting entry into force.[10]

Safeguard agreements entered into pursuant to the NPT follow requirements set forth in INFCIRC/153,[11] April 20, 1971, rather than INFCIRC/66/Rev.2 that applies to agreements between the IAEA and countries that have not adhered to the treaty. The safeguard systems described by these two information circulars differ significantly. The NPT system (INFCIRC/153) applies safeguards to all nuclear activities in a given country. The non-NPT system (INFCIRC/66) need not be comprehensive because under it safeguards are applied to particular material, equipment, or facilities designated by the parties to the agreement. The non-NPT system tends to be facility specific. The NPT system, consistent with the language of article III, attempts to keep track of all nuclear materials. Despite these differences, the purposes of NPT and non-NPT safeguards are the same: to detect the diversion of nuclear material from peaceful uses to the manufacture of nuclear weapons or explosive devices, or to any other military purpose.

Avenues for Improvement

The present international system for nuclear energy has two obvious advantages. First, it formally commits a large majority of the nations of the world to preventing the further spread of nuclear weapons. And second, it provides some assurance that safeguarded civil nuclear facilities will not be used in weapons programs. These advantages are of considerable value and should not be lightly cast aside. Any new or improved

9. France has declared that it will behave as if it had ratified the NPT.
10. *IAEA Bulletin*, vol. 22 (August 1980), p. 100.
11. Reproduced in Sanders, *Safeguards Against Nuclear Proliferation*, app. 3, pp. 73–95.

international system to control nuclear energy should be built on what is already in place.

Nevertheless, the present system has a number of deficiencies. It falls short of being geographically comprehensive, and it does not seek to influence the spread of sensitive nuclear facilities. The present regime also has only a marginal influence on incentives to acquire nuclear weapons, but that shortcoming must be blamed on the general international order rather than on the special arrangements for nuclear energy.

Efforts to improve the system have sought either to fill gaps in its coverage or to supplement it by establishing constraints on the transfer of sensitive materials, equipment, and technology.[12] Modest progress has been made in both directions. Prospects for further progress are at best fair.

Wider Coverage

The ideal way to round out the present nuclear regime would be to induce all countries to adhere to the NPT. Unfortunately, however, adherence to the NPT may have reached its high-water mark. The two holdouts among the nuclear weapon states, France and China, are unlikely to change their positions. The same must be said of most of the more important nonnuclear weapon states that have refused to sign and ratify the NPT. A few converts may be made (Spain appears to be one possibility), but the problem facing treaty supporters in future years may be how to prevent defections rather than how to gain adherents.

Resentment over the nonproliferation treaty's discrimination between nuclear weapon and nonnuclear weapon states has not subsided and even may have grown. Many nonnuclear weapon states feel that the nuclear powers have failed to honor their side of the bargain, which was to pursue nuclear disarmament in good faith and to make nuclear technology available. These complaints were vigorously expressed at the second NPT review conference in the summer of 1980.

In Latin America the Treaty of Tlatelolco provides an alternative to the NPT. Parties to this treaty agree not to acquire nuclear weapons or to permit the stationing of such weapons in their territories. They further

12. The IAEA and some member governments are making efforts to improve the technical effectiveness of safeguards, but that subject lies outside the scope of this study.

agree to accept IAEA safeguards for their civil nuclear energy facilities. Protocol I binds outside powers responsible for territories in the treaty area to apply the treaty to those territories. Under protocol II, the nuclear weapon states agree to respect the nuclear-free status of the treaty area.[13]

The Treaty of Tlatelolco was opened for signature on February 14, 1967. All of the twenty-four Latin American republics except Cuba have signed it. Of the twenty-three signatories, only Argentina has not ratified it, although it has indicated intentions to do so. The treaty is in effect for twenty of the twenty-two countries that have ratified it. Brazil and Chile, however, have not waived the requirement of article 28, which states that the treaty will enter into force only after its ratification by all of the Latin American republics and ratification of protocols I and II by the non-Latin American countries to which they apply.

Bringing Argentina and Brazil under the Treaty of Tlatelolco is especially important, since they are the most advanced Latin American countries in the field of nuclear technology and neither appears likely to ratify the NPT. Assuming that Argentina will in fact ratify the treaty, waiver of the requirements of article 28 by both it and Brazil would clearly be the best way way of bringing the treaty into force for these two key countries. Obtaining ratification of the protocols by all of the countries concerned appears feasible, but there is little reason to hope that Cuba will adhere to the treaty itself, unless pressed hard to do so by the Soviet Union.[14]

Extending the coverage of the Treaty of Tlatelolco to Brazil and Argentina would be a significant achievement, but it must be noted that in one respect that treaty falls short of the NPT. The NPT binds non-nuclear weapon states not to acquire either nuclear weapons or "other nuclear explosive devices." The Treaty of Tlatelolco explicitly permits "explosions of nuclear devices for peaceful purposes." The practical effect of this potential loophole would, however, be small if the IAEA

---

13. The treaty and protocols are reproduced in William Epstein, *The Last Chance: Nuclear Proliferation and Arms Control* (Free Press, 1976), pp. 299–315. For a discussion of the treaty's status see William H. Courtney, "Brazil and Argentina," in Joseph A. Yager, ed., *Nonproliferation and U.S. Foreign Policy* (Brookings Institution, 1980).

14. The Netherlands and the United Kingdom have ratified protocol I, and France and the United States have promised to do so. All five nuclear states have ratified protocol II. In 1978 the Cuban foreign minister said that Cuba would not adhere to the treaty unless the United States gave up its base at Guantanamo.

continues to insist on including a ban on nuclear explosive devices in its safeguard agreements.

Even though prospects for getting additional countries to renounce the acquisition of nuclear weapons are at best fair, it might still be possible to extend the geographical coverage of IAEA safeguards. The NPT includes a provision that has the effect of extending safeguards to facilities in countries that have not adhered to it. Under article III(2) of the NPT, each state that is a party to the treaty "undertakes not to provide: (a) source or special fissionable material, or (b) equipment or material especially designed or prepared for the processing, use or production of special fissionable material, to any non-nuclear-weapon State for peaceful purposes, unless the source or special fissionable material shall be subject to the safeguards required by this article." This provision could not, however, be relied on eventually to create a situation in which all nuclear facilities everywhere would be safeguarded. In the absence of other constraints, nonnuclear weapon states that are not parties to the NPT could acquire unsafeguarded facilities by building them themselves.

There are relatively few unsafeguarded nuclear facilities in nonnuclear weapon states today. The largest number is in India, whose unsafeguarded facilities consist of three reactors, two reprocessing plants, and two fuel fabrication plants. The other unsafeguarded facilities are in Israel (a large research reactor and a pilot reprocessing plant), South Africa (a pilot enrichment plant), Spain (a power reactor operated jointly with France), and Egypt (a small research reactor).[15] There may also be an unsafeguarded research reactor in North Korea.

The number of unsafeguarded facilities in non-NPT, nonnuclear weapon states could increase as some of these states increase their indigenous technological capabilities. Two major nuclear suppliers, Canada and the United States, have responded to this situation by trying to get their customers that do not possess nuclear weapons to accept safeguards on all of their nuclear facilities, that is, full-scope safeguards.[16] On December 22, 1976, the Canadian government announced that reactors and uranium would not be exported to nonnuclear weapon states that had not ratified the NPT or in some other way accepted full-scope safeguards.[17] A similar U.S. policy was established in the Nuclear Non-Pro-

15. *IAEA Bulletin,* vol. 19 (October 1977), p. 2.
16. See app. B for a review of the export policies of the major suppliers.
17. *New York Times,* December 23, 1976.

liferation Act of 1978 (NNPA).[18] Australia, which promises to be a major exporter of uranium, will not sell uranium to nonnuclear weapon states that have not ratified the NPT.[19]

Section 401 of the NNPA (amending section 123 of the Atomic Energy Act of 1954) states that all new agreements for cooperation with nonnuclear weapon states must require such states to accept full-scope safeguards. Section 404(a) directs the president to renegotiate existing agreements for cooperation to include this and certain other provisions of the NNPA. Section 306 (amending section 128 of the 1954 act) in effect overrides existing agreements for cooperation by making the acceptance of full-scope safeguards a condition of continued U.S. export of "source material, special nuclear material, production or utilization facilities, and any sensitive nuclear technology to non-nuclear-weapon states." The president is empowered to exempt specific exports from this provision, if he finds that blocking them "would be seriously prejudicial to the achievement of United States non-proliferation objectives or otherwise jeopardize the common defense and security." Congress, however, reserved the right to override the president by concurrent resolution within sixty days.

It is too early to judge how effective Australian, Canadian, and U.S. efforts to promote adherence to the nonproliferation treaty or acceptance of full-scope safeguards will be. The United States has found the policy an embarrassment in its dealings with India, which has relied on the United States for low-enriched uranium to fuel two of its power reactors. Since India has shown no signs of agreeing to full-scope safeguards, the United States faces the prospect of granting a series of exceptions to the general rule set forth in the NNPA, or damaging its relations with India.

Only the Soviet Union among the other nuclear supplier nations has in most cases followed a safeguard policy comparable to those of Australia, Canada, and the United States.[20] Countries that have not adhered

18. 22 U.S.C. 3201.

19. See statement by Prime Minister Malcolm Fraser in the Australian *House of Representatives, Parliamentary Debate,* vol. 105 (Canberra: Australian Government Publishing Service, 1977), pp. 1700–05.

20. The Soviet Union has required its customers in Eastern Europe to adhere to the NPT, and appears to have imposed the same requirement in the sale of a reactor to Libya. In selling heavy water to India, the Soviet Union required that all Indian reactors (but not all other nuclear facilities) be safeguarded. See Gloria Duffy, "Soviet Nuclear Exports," *International Security,* vol. 3 (Summer 1978), pp. 83–111.

to the NPT can therefore avoid the necessity of accepting full-scope safeguards by dealing with other suppliers.

Constraints on Trade

The present international regime for nuclear energy could be strengthened by agreements or informal understandings that would make more
specific the general constraints on trade established by the NPT.[21] Such
agreements or understandings could be among all interested countries,
both suppliers and importers, or among suppliers alone.

The latter approach was adopted in the early 1970s when representatives of several nuclear supplier nations began to meet, at first secretly,
to coordinate their export policies. Although this group, which came to
be known as the exporters' committee, met in Vienna where the headquarters of the IAEA are located, the committee had no formal links with
the IAEA. The director general of the IAEA, however, implicitly gave the
committee his blessing when he publicly described its purpose as "to develop arrangements that will ensure that all major exporting countries
interpret their [NPT] obligations in a uniform way and do not try to get
commercial advantage by cutting corners on safeguards."[22]

The committee succeeded in developing uniform procedures for the
transfer of nuclear materials and technology, including a trigger list of
items that would not be transferred without being placed under IAEA
safeguards. On August 22, 1974, a number of nuclear supplier countries
sent two memorandums to the director general of the IAEA that set forth
the results of the committee's work.[23] These memorandums were distributed by the IAEA as INFCIRC/209/Add.2.[24]

The 1974 memorandums have not been withdrawn by the governments
concerned, but they have been superseded by the more comprehensive

---

21. The relevant part of the NPT is Article III(2), which requires the application
of safeguards to certain categories of nuclear material and equipment. See Willrich,
Non-Proliferation Treaty, app. A.

22. Sigvard Eklund, IAEA director general, quoted in *Nuclear Industry* (November–December 1972), pp. 63–64.

23. The supplier countries included Australia, Denmark, Canada, West Germany, Finland, the Netherlands, Norway, the Soviet Union, the United Kingdom,
and the United States.

24. These documents are reproduced in app. 1 of Sanders, *Safeguards Against
Nuclear Proliferation.*

guidelines adopted in January 1978 by what has come to be known as the London nuclear suppliers' group. At the initiative of the United States, representatives of a number of major nuclear suppliers began a series of meetings in London with the objective of coordinating national policies on the transfer of sensitive nuclear technologies. The initial participants were Canada, France, the Soviet Union, the United Kingdom, the United States, and West Germany. Japan and Italy also attended as threshold exporters of nuclear equipment. At the insistence of France and the Soviet Union, the meetings were at first held secretly.[25]

The group gradually expanded to include fifteen nations: Belgium, Czechoslovakia, East Germany, the Netherlands, Poland, Sweden, and Switzerland joined the eight countries involved from the beginning.

On January 11, 1978, the director general of the IAEA received identical letters from the fifteen members of the London nuclear suppliers' group transmitting three documents: guidelines for nuclear transfers, trigger list referred to in the guidelines, and clarifications of items on the trigger list.[26] These documents are known collectively as the London suppliers' guidelines.[27]

The guidelines are quite complex and not easily summarized. Two sets of principles are set forth: those that should be followed in transferring items on the trigger list and certain additional principles not explicitly linked to the trigger list. Both sets of principles apply only to transfers to nonnuclear weapon states. The trigger list includes (with certain specified exceptions) source and special nuclear materials; reactors and equipment for reactors; deuterium and heavy water, and plants for their production; nuclear grade graphite; and reprocessing, enrichment, and fuel fabrication plants.

The guidelines specify that recipients should be required to place items on the trigger list under IAEA safeguards, provide effective physical protection for them, and pledge that they would not be put to any "uses which

25. A considerable amount of information about the meetings, however, appeared in the press, particularly in the *New York Times*.

26. The Australian government later wrote the IAEA director general that it was willing to adhere to these documents.

27. The three documents are reproduced in app. D of *Nuclear Power and Nuclear Weapons Proliferation: Report of the Atlantic Council's Nuclear Fuels Policy Working Group,* vol. 2 (Washington, D.C.: Atlantic Council of the United States, 1978), pp. 63–74. These documents were distributed by the IAEA as INFCIRC/254.

would result in any nuclear explosive device." Recipients of enrichment facilities or technology should be required to agree not to use such facilities or technology to acquire the capability of enriching uranium to more than 20 percent U^{235}. Recipients should further provide assurance that items on the trigger list would be retransferred only subject to the conditions applied to the initial transfer.

In addition the supplier nations agreed to "exercise restraint in the transfer of sensitive facilities, technology and weapon-usable materials." Suppliers also agreed to encourage multinational participation in enrichment or reprocessing facilities as an alternative to national plants and to "promote international (including IAEA) activities concerned with multinational regional fuel cycle centers." In a paragraph whose tortured language suggests an effort to bridge divergent positions, the guidelines declare that "suppliers recognize the importance . . . of including in agreements on supply of nuclear materials or of facilities which produce weapon-usable material, provisions calling for mutual agreement between the supplier and the recipient on arrangements for reprocessing, storage, alteration, use, transfer or retransfer of any weapon-usable material involved."

The agreement of fifteen supplier nations on the 1978 guidelines was a major diplomatic achievement. In contrast with the 1974 guidelines, those agreed on in London in 1978 paid more attention to sensitive nuclear facilities. They also applied to transfers to all nonnuclear weapon states, rather than just to those that are not parties to the NPT. The 1978 guidelines further seek more explicit assurances against the acquisition of nuclear explosive devices and provide criteria for the physical protection of transferred nuclear material and equipment. And finally, the 1978 guidelines contain an elaborate provision on the replication of transferred items that has no counterpart in the 1974 guidelines.[28]

The 1978 London suppliers' guidelines, therefore, represented a considerable advance in making the responsibilities of suppliers under the NPT more explicit. The scope for commercial competition at the expense

28. The 1978 guidelines specify that the IAEA safeguards requiring physical protection and banning explosive uses should apply to any reprocessing, enrichment or heavy-water production facility using technology directly transferred by a supplier nation. Moreover, for a period of twenty years there would be "a conclusive presumption that a facility of the same type utilized transferred technology."

of nonproliferation goals was reduced and some inhibitions created against the spread of reprocessing and enrichment facilities. At the same time, the 1978 guidelines have serious deficiencies. They are one sided and do not reflect the views of nonsuppliers. They do not call for the application of full-scope safeguards, although some supplier nations supported this action. They do not address the problem of the dissemination of sensitive nuclear technologies through academic training or practical working experience. And perhaps most important, the 1978 guidelines, like those of 1974, are entirely voluntary. They are not legally binding, and any participating nation can withdraw its support at any time.

The key question is whether the 1978 guidelines are the end of a process that began in Vienna in the early 1970s with consultations in the exporters' committee, or only a way station on the road to a new international system for nuclear energy. One theoretically conceivable means of carrying the guidelines a step farther does not appear promising. An effort to convert the guidelines into a formal agreement would almost certainly fail. Moreover, the long-run value of such an agreement is questionable. The nonsupplier nations would bitterly resent such a move as a further intensification of the discrimination inherent in the NPT and at least potentially a violation of their rights under article IV to share in the benefits of peaceful nuclear technology. Some of these nations would be further stimulated to develop their independent capabilities in the field of nuclear energy. The possibility of broad international agreement on nuclear issues would be reduced, and the risk of a further spread of nuclear weapons might well be increased.

An alternative, but also difficult, approach is to try to reach a consensus among both suppliers and importers on the rules of trade in nuclear materials, equipment, and technology. This approach has in principle two major advantages over efforts to coordinate the policies of only the nuclear supplier nations. First, it is not intrinsically discriminatory. And second, it does not rely on the transitory technological superiority of today's supplier nations.

On the other hand, achieving a broad international consensus on the rules of trade requires reconciling even a greater diversity of interests than exists among supplier nations. Involvement in the more general North-South controversy over the future shape of the international economic system and over the transfer of technology from industrialized to

developing countries could not easily be avoided.[29] More specifically, the
nonnuclear weapon supplier nations could not be expected, in the interest
of nonproliferation, to accept constraints voluntarily that appeared to
hamper their efforts to solve their energy problems. Some of the nonsupplier nations would also oppose rules that might foreclose their ability to
develop nuclear weapons, if they decided to do so for reasons of national
security.

Developing a broad consensus on the rules of trade requires much
more than continuing to involve the nonsupplier nations in the consultations on international nuclear energy problems, although that would be a
necessary condition. The international environment must be favorable to
agreement on large, cooperative ventures. At a minimum, the international order must not appear to be deteriorating, and North-South differences must not seem beyond solution.

Given an acceptable international environment, a consensus on the
rules of trade would still not be something to be negotiated directly in the
near future. To think of the problem in terms of getting more countries to
accept something like the London nuclear suppliers' guidelines is surely
wrong. What is required is the evolution of a set of mutually reinforcing
incentives and constraints that will channel the nuclear energy policies of
all nations, both suppliers and nonsuppliers, in converging directions.

Conclusions

Prospects for achieving substantial improvements in the present international regime for nuclear energy are fair at best.

In terms of geographical coverage, the present regime may be ap-
proaching its high-water mark. Few additional countries with significant
nuclear energy potential are likely to become parties to the nonproliferation treaty. On the contrary, defections from the NPT are possible, either
as a result of worsening security conditions in some regions or as a result
of growing resentment over the NPT's inherent discrimination between
nuclear and nonnuclear weapon states. The one region in which sub-

29. See Munir Ahmad Khan, *Nuclear Energy and International Cooperation: A
Third World Perception of the Erosion of Confidence* (New York: Rockefeller
Foundation; London: Royal Institute of International Affairs, 1979), especially pp.
31–32.

stantial progress in extending the coverage of the present regime might be achieved is Latin America. Bringing the Treaty of Tlatelolco into effect for all Latin American republics except Cuba appears to be a realistic goal.

A few more nonnuclear weapon countries that have chosen not to adhere to the NPT or the Treaty of Tlatelolco might be induced to accept safeguards on all of their nuclear facilities. Prospects for gains in this direction would be greatly improved if all major nuclear suppliers would make full-scope safeguards a condition of exports of nuclear materials, equipment, and technology. The failure of the London nuclear suppliers' group to include such a requirement in the 1978 guidelines indicates that this development is not likely in the near future. The 1978 guidelines may in fact represent close to the maximum feasible achievement in efforts to supplement the NPT by coordinating the policies of nuclear exporters. Converting the guidelines into a formal, binding agreement appears to be neither feasible nor desirable. Arriving at a consensus among both suppliers and importers on the rules of trade in nuclear materials, equipment, and technology would, however, be quite useful.

Such a consensus probably could not be achieved through direct negotiations at this time. It is more likely to be the by-product of successful international efforts to deal with the problems of the nuclear energy industry in ways that serve both energy and nonproliferation goals.

CHAPTER THREE

Assurance of Nuclear Fuel Supplies

A HIGH DEGREE of confidence concerning the future supply of nuclear fuel is essential to the continued development of civil nuclear energy. Nuclear power plants are relatively expensive per unit of installed capacity, and their life expectancy is about thirty years. A typical plant with a light water reactor (LWR) and a capacity of 1,000 megawatts, electric (MWe) coming into service in 1980 will have cost in the neighborhood of $800 million. And the cost is rapidly rising: a 1,000-MWe plant begun in 1980 could eventually cost $2 billion.

Neither governments nor private investors are going to make these large, long-term commitments of capital if they have serious doubts concerning the future availability of nuclear fuel at acceptable prices. Suppliers of nuclear power equipment also have an obvious interest in an assured supply of nuclear fuel because the marketability of their products depends on it. Until recently some firms selling power reactors also undertook to supply uranium for those reactors for a period of years.

One way in which countries interested in the development of nuclear energy can hope to decrease uncertainty concerning fuel supply is by acquiring reprocessing or enrichment facilities. The former would enable them to stretch the uranium supplies that they were able to obtain, and the latter would relieve them of dependence on other countries for enrichment services. But not every country possesses the technological skills required to build reprocessing or enrichment plants. Moreover, from a

41

strictly economic point of view, such facilities on a commercial scale can be justified only as part of a substantial nuclear power program. Some countries nevertheless are willing to pay a premium for increasing the security of their energy supply. Others may see an advantage in moving a large step closer to a nuclear-weapon capability. Several nonnuclear weapon states with still-modest nuclear power programs have in fact shown an interest in reprocessing or enrichment, or both.

Countries with reprocessing or enrichment facilities can produce the essential explosive component of nuclear weapons and could, if they wished, develop such weapons fairly quickly. The fuel assurance problem, however, involves more than reducing incentives to acquire reprocessing and enrichment facilities. It has become a political issue between fuel suppliers and importers, and its solution is important to achieving the degree of international cooperation needed to deal with the problems of civil nuclear energy in the years ahead.

Insecurity concerning nuclear fuel supplies is of two general kinds: fear of fuel supply interruptions because of specific contingencies affecting individual fuel-importing countries, and concern over developments that could adversely affect all fuel-importing countries. These two kinds of insecurity call for different countermeasures and will be discussed separately.

Contingencies Adversely Affecting Individual Fuel Importers

Countries that import natural uranium or that depend on other countries for enrichment services face four contingencies that might threaten their nuclear fuel supplies:

—Politically inspired interruptions of supplies unrelated to nonproliferation policy.

—Interruptions resulting from changes in the nonproliferation policies of supplier nations.

—Accidents and sabotage.

—Commercial risks, including the cancellation of existing contracts or the temporary unavailability of new, long-term contracts.

Some interruptions of fuel supplies already have occurred. For example, in 1977 Canada imposed an embargo on sales of natural uranium to the European Community and Japan while new agreements incorporating stricter nonproliferation provisions were being negotiated. And the United States delayed approval of the export of enriched uranium to India because of differences over nonproliferation policy.

Recent shifts in the nonproliferation policies of several fuel-exporting nations have in fact been a major source of concern for the fuel-importing countries. Those countries also have not been reassured by the behavior of some supplier nations in other fields. Transfers of arms have been influenced by political considerations such as the record of recipients in the observance of human rights, and supplier governments have intervened in other export transactions for a variety of political or economic reasons. The Arab oil embargo in 1973–74 is one prominent example of this kind of behavior. The U.S. suspension of soybean exports in 1973 is another.

The insecurity of fuel importers is undoubtedly increased by the small number of suppliers of either natural uranium or enrichment services. Most of the natural uranium produced in non-Communist countries today is mined in Canada, the United States, and South Africa. Australia has the potential of becoming a major source in the future (see table 1-4). The virtual monopoly of enrichment services that the United States enjoyed for many years is being eroded by others, but by the mid-1980s there will still be only four major suppliers of these services (see table 1-7). Under these circumstances, an importing country that suddenly finds its normal supply of nuclear fuel cut off has few alternatives.

Fortunately, the nuclear fuel cycle is quite resilient.[1] For several reasons, an interruption of fuel supplies would not cause a nuclear power plant to close down for some time, and the loss of generating capacity would be gradual rather than abrupt.

First, the nuclear fuel pipeline is quite long. It typically takes one and one-half to two years for uranium to move from a mill to a light water reactor through the stages of conversion, enrichment, and fabrication. At any time at least one reload for each reactor will be in process between the stages of milling and enrichment and another will be in process after the enrichment stage. An interruption at an early stage would therefore not affect the operation of reactors for some time.

1. The discussion of resiliency draws heavily on Henry D. Jacoby, Thomas L. Neff, and others, "Nuclear Fuel Assurance," Working Paper 1 (Massachusetts Institute of Technology Energy Laboratory with the Center for International Studies, December 1977), especially pp. 15–22.

Second, substantial stockpiles of fuel often exist at fabrication plants and reactors.[2] Many utility companies overestimated their fuel requirements when entering into fixed-commitment contracts for enrichment services. Plans for the construction of new reactors have slipped and plants have operated at lower percentages of capacity than were assumed in calculating fuel requirements.

And third, the fuel in a reactor is used up over a period of years. If a reactor were suddenly to be cut off from all supplies of new fuel—a most unlikely event because at least some of the fuel in the pipeline and in stockpiles probably would be under the physical and legal control of the utility that owned the reactor—no loss of generating capacity would result until the next annual refueling date. The reactor could even continue to operate at a reduced level of power output for several months after that date.

The resiliency of the nuclear fuel cycle must to some extent moderate fears concerning short-term interruptions of fuel supplies. It also eases the development of countermeasures.

Adverse Developments Affecting All Fuel Importers

In addition to the specific contingencies discussed above, the fuel-importing countries have reason to be concerned about two more general developments that might raise the cost of fuel or make it more difficult to obtain. On the one hand, suppliers of natural uranium or enrichment services might collude in ways adversely affecting the interests of the fuel importers. And on the other, imperfections in the markets for natural uranium and enrichment services might prevent the timely expansion of uranium mining and enriching capacities.

Collusion among Suppliers

Because there are so few suppliers of both natural uranium and enrichment services, fuel importers cannot exclude the possibility that several major suppliers will act in concert to gain some economic or political objective.

2. These are in addition to stockpiles some countries—most notably Japan and West Germany—have purchased for political reasons.

There is in fact evidence that in the early 1970s the governments of several uranium-producing countries participated in a short-lived uranium cartel.[3] At the time the international market for uranium was depressed and the United States had in effect excluded other producers from its domestic market by refusing to enrich foreign uranium for use by U.S. utilities. The governments participating in the cartel were therefore seeking both to protect their own economic interests in a time of weak demand for uranium and to counter the effects of U.S. uranium policy.

The cartel apparently ceased functioning in 1974 when external events, including the sharp rise in oil prices, brought about a revival in the market for uranium. The possibility remains that if the price of uranium again becomes depressed, mining companies and some governments directly concerned will be tempted to act jointly to restrict the production and raise the price of uranium.

It is also conceivable that several major suppliers might band together to enforce strict nonproliferation controls over exports of natural uranium or over the provision of enrichment services. To nonmembers, the secret deliberations of the London nuclear suppliers' group in the mid-1970s must have seemed to hold the threat of precisely such a nonproliferation cartel (see chapter 2). The nonproliferation policies of several major producers of natural uranium are closer together, however, than are the policies of the major enrichers. A nonproliferation cartel is therefore more likely to affect the supply of natural uranium than the supply of enrichment services.

Market Imperfections

The fact that some optimism is warranted concerning the adequacy of uranium resources and enrichment capacity (see chapter 1) is not enough to eliminate uncertainty. Imperfections in the present structure of the markets for both natural uranium and enrichment services give rise to reasonable doubts about the reliability of fuel supplies.

NATURAL URANIUM. Public discussion of uranium often focuses on the question of when the supply of this natural resource will run out. The answer is, not for a very long time, if ever, because the earth's crust and

3. See Eleanor B. Steinberg, "The Structure of the International Uranium Market" (U.S. Department of State, April 1978), pp. 6–9. See also *Wall Street Journal,* July 7, 1976 and *Washington Post,* May 8, 1977.

the oceans contain enormous amounts of uranium. The real problem is not an impending shortage of uranium, but its future price.

The price problem has two aspects. First, as the more accessible and richer deposits of uranium are exhausted, mining costs will rise and so will the market price.[4] Second, imperfections in the market may cause price fluctuations that could interfere with the orderly development of nuclear power as a source of energy. Not much can be done about the first aspect of the price problem, except to try to create conditions favoring more exploration for accessible, high-grade uranium deposits. Foremost among these conditions is an efficiently functioning market, the lack of which is the second aspect of the problem.

If private investors and governments are to continue committing resources to the civil nuclear energy industry, they must have a reasonable degree of confidence in the predictability of the price of uranium. In particular, they must not see a high risk of extreme, unexpected changes in price. A sudden drop in the price of uranium could force the closing of some existing mines, the abandonment of plans to open new mines, and the curtailment of exploration activities. An unexpected, large increase in the price of uranium could weaken the economic justification for investing in nuclear, rather than conventional thermal, power plants. It could also stimulate the recycling of plutonium in the present generation of reactors and speed up the construction of fast breeder reactors.

The fact that sharp price changes give opposite signals to investors in uranium mines and power plants could make instability to some extent self-perpetuating. Thus the dampening effect of a drop in the price of uranium on investors in uranium mining could set the stage for a shortage of uranium and a sharp increase in prices several years later. On the other hand, the reduction in future fuel requirements caused by a rise in the price of uranium could in time lead to a glut of uranium on the market and a collapse in the price.

These hazards would be greatly reduced in a market that functioned with classic economic efficiency. In such a market there would be no large discontinuities in demand or supply, and both would be fairly elastic. Buyers and sellers would have easy access to reliable information on current transactions, trading in fixed-price contracts for future delivery would

4. The exploitation of low-grade uranium resources involves large-scale disturbance of the land. Requiring mining companies to restore the land to its original condition—which would be appropriate environmental policy—would add to the cost of the uranium extracted.

facilitate hedging against unexpected price changes, and the market price would move smoothly up or down in response to finely graduated changes in offers to buy or sell.

The market for uranium is young and poorly developed.[5] It possesses none of the attributes of an ideal market. Some information on spot sales is available, but information concerning the longer-term contracts, under which most uranium is marketed, is sketchy at best. Trading in uranium futures has not yet developed. Perhaps most important are the discontinuities in both demand and supply, and demand is quite unresponsive, in at least the short run, to both price increases and decreases.[6] The inelasticity of demand, of course, means that changes in supply can cause disproportionate movements in price.

Discontinuities in supply result from several circumstances. Large investments and long lead times are required to bring new uranium mines and mills into production. Creating the mining and milling capacity needed to produce one ton of uranium metal per year requires on the average an investment of roughly $170,000 (1977 dollars), including exploration costs.[7] It takes from eight to fifteen years to find an economic uranium deposit and put it into production.[8] Investors may not make timely decisions to commit large sums of money to new capacity because of inadequate information concerning market trends and uncertainty concerning the policies of governments. Entry of new firms into the industry is probably relatively difficult, which further increases the possibility that supplies of yellowcake will not increase smoothly as requirements rise.[9]

The demand for yellowcake depends fundamentally on nuclear generat-

5. For more on the nature of the uranium market, see Steinberg, "The Structure of the International Uranium Market."

6. Supply may also be somewhat inelastic. High fixed costs would tend to cause mining firms to maintain output in the face of a price decrease, and the time required to open new mines would make it difficult to raise output quickly in response to a price increase.

7. U.S. Central Intelligence Agency, *Nuclear Energy,* ER-77-10468 (August 1977), p. 33.

8. Uranium Resource Group, National Research Council, *Problems of U.S. Uranium Resources and Supplies to the Year 2010: Study of Nuclear and Alternative Energy Systems,* Supporting Paper 1 (Washington, D.C.: National Academy of Sciences, 1978), p. 51.

9. Inhibiting formation of new firms are high investment requirements, long lead times, and the small number of both producing countries and firms. Many of the larger firms, moreover, appear to be linked. (See the complaint of Westinghouse Electric Corp. v. Rio Algom Ltd. and others, filed in the U.S. District Court for the Northern District of Illinois, Eastern Division, October 15, 1976.)

ing capacity—existing, under construction, and to some extent planned.[10] Nuclear power plants are typically very large and costly per unit of installed capacity. But once a plant has been completed, it will be put into operation almost irrespective of the price of fuel. The level of operation will also depend on technical factors rather than on the price of fuel. The plant is simply too expensive not to be used, and in any case, increased fuel costs can in large part be passed on to consumers whose demand for electricity is also quite inelastic.

The fact that building a nuclear power plant, including locating a site and obtaining governmental approval, can take about as long as bringing yellowcake capacity into operation should make for stability in the uranium market. Lead times are between eight and twelve years in the United States, Canada, Japan, and West Germany.[11] There should be enough time after plans for new nuclear generating capacity have been announced for mining companies to increase their production of yellowcake to meet the increased fuel requirements.

This favorable circumstance—long lead times on the demand and supply sides of the market—has not, however, been sufficient to ensure stability. Three other circumstances affecting demand work strongly in the opposite direction. First, estimated future requirements for yellowcake change by substantial increments because today's nuclear power plants are quite large. For example, a 1,000-MWe plant operating at 70 percent of capacity and using 3 percent enriched uranium from an enrichment plant operating at 0.25 tails assay of U^{235} would require about 5,000 tons of yellowcake during its lifetime. Second, in recent years uncertainty concerning economic prospects and governmental policies have caused the construction of some planned nuclear power plants to be delayed or canceled. And third, the growing tendency of electric utility companies to enter into joint ventures with uranium mining companies has taken some future supplies of yellowcake out of the general market. Such arrange-

10. Demand is also influenced by the inventory policies of firms at various stages of the fuel cycle (conversion, enrichment, fabrication, and electrical generation), by the policies of enrichment plants with respect to tails assay, and by the percentage of installed capacity actually used by nuclear power plants.

11. A lead time is the time elapsed between issuance of a construction permit and the beginning of full commercial operation. Richard K. Lester, *Nuclear Power Plant Lead-Times,* International Consultative Group on Nuclear Energy, Working Paper (New York: Rockefeller Foundation; London: Royal Institute of International Affairs, 1978), p. 11.

ments increase the security of fuel supplies for the utilities concerned, but they make it more difficult for other utilities to ensure the future availability of their fuel supplies at reasonably predictable prices.

The actions of major supplier governments have sometimes added to uncertainty concerning the behavior of the price of natural uranium. For example, the U.S. ban (1968–77) on imports of foreign uranium for enrichment and use by domestic utilities divided the market into two parts and depressed the price obtainable by non-U.S. producers. In 1977, as was noted above, Canada suspended uranium exports to Western Europe and Japan pending the conclusion of new agreements imposing stricter nonproliferation conditions on purchasers of Canadian uranium. And for a number of years political controversy over a complex of interrelated issues (nonproliferation and environmental concerns, and aboriginal land rights) has delayed Australia's reentry into the uranium market as a major producer.[12]

The civil nuclear energy industry may be entering a period in which the susceptibility of the uranium market to large price swings could be especially troublesome. The marked slowdown in the construction of new nuclear generating capacity in the late 1970s may well cause a recession in uranium mining, marked by a sharp fall in the price of natural uranium. Exploration and investment in new mining capacity would as a consequence be discouraged. If the construction of nuclear power plants were to pick up in the mid-1980s, supplies of natural uranium could become extremely tight, causing a steep rise in price.[13]

ENRICHMENT SERVICES. The market for enrichment services is undergoing a fundamental change.[14] The supply of enrichment services was long a U.S. monopoly. However the United States must now increasingly share the market with three other large suppliers (France, the Soviet Union, and the British-Dutch-West German firm, Urenco). By the late

12. Steinberg, "The Structure of the International Uranium Market," pp. 11, 21–24.

13. This hypothesis is developed in Dagobert L. Brito, J. David Richardson, and Gordon W. Smith, "Investigation of Possibilities for a Commodity Agreement in Natural Uranium" (Tulane University; University of Wisconsin; Rice University, November 1979), especially pp. 37–39. The spot price of uranium in fact fell sharply in 1979 and early 1980. See *New York Times,* March 20, 1980.

14. The discussion of the enrichment services market draws heavily on "Uranium Enrichment Present Position," paper prepared by the United States of America for Working Group 3–Supply Assurances, International Nuclear Fuel Cycle Evaluation Program, March 24, 1978.

1980s, Japan, Brazil, and South Africa may also have enrichment facilities (see table 1-7).

One attribute of the present market is not, however, likely to change for the foreseeable future: governmental control of the supply of enrichment services. The U.S. government through the Department of Energy owns all existing and planned enrichment facilities in the United States. The French government owns what amounts to a controlling interest in both Eurodif, whose facilities began operations in 1979 and will reach full capacity in 1982, and in Coredif, which was originally scheduled to enter the enrichment market in 1986 and to reach full capacity in 1990.[15] Ownership of Urenco is divided equally among British, Dutch, and West German interests. The government of the United Kingdom holds all of the British share, and the government of the Netherlands owns more than half of the Dutch share. The German share is entirely in the hands of private firms, although the German government has a strong voice in policy matters.[16] Soviet enrichment facilities are totally government owned, as are the existing or planned facilities of the smaller suppliers of enrichment services.

Governmental control of the supply of enrichment services means that uncertainty concerning whether such services will be available, and on what terms, is in large part political. Countries that rely on others for en-

15. Ownership of Eurodif (Société Européenne d'Usine de Diffusion Gazeuse) is divided among the French government (27.8 percent), the Italian government (25.0 percent), Spanish interests (11.1 percent, of which 60 percent is estimated to be governmental and 40 percent private), Belgian interests (11.1 percent, of which half is governmental and half private), and Sofidif (Société Franco-Iranienne pour l'Enrichissement de l'Uranium par Diffusion Gazeuse) 25 percent, which is in turn owned 60 percent by the French government and 40 percent by the Iranian government. France's share in the ownership of Eurodif therefore comes to 42.8 percent, but through its control of Sofidif, France's effective share of voting rights is 52.8 percent.

Coredif (Compagnie de Réalisation d'Usine de Diffusion Gazeuse) is owned 51 percent by Eurodif, 29 percent by the French government, and 20 percent by the Iranian government. Since France controls Eurodif, it also controls Coredif. It appears unlikely that the new government in Iran will maintain the shah's commitment to Coredif. (Ibid., table 2, pp. 6–7.)

16. Urenco was formed pursuant to the Treaty of Almelo among the three countries concerned. The treaty established a joint committee to deal with sensitive political issues. See C. Allday, "Some Experiences in Formation and Operation of Multinational Uranium-Enrichment and Fuel-Reprocessing Organizations," in Abram Chayes and W. Bennett Lewis, eds., *International Arrangements for Nuclear Fuel Reprocessing* (Ballinger, 1977), pp. 178–81 and 185–87.

richment services must ask what political conditions, especially those of a nonproliferation nature, will be imposed by suppliers.

Despite the relative prominence of political concerns, the evolving system for providing enrichment services can be viewed as a market for purposes of this analysis. There are, of course, buyers and sellers as in any other market, and both are motivated by economic as well as political considerations. The motivation of buyers is in fact predominantly economic, and only their fears are largely political. The governments that invest public funds in the construction of commercial enrichment facilities may be moved by considerations of national power, prestige, or independence. But they must also be able to provide significant justification for their investment in economic terms.

The structure of the enrichment market of the 1980s and 1990s is only now beginning to emerge. On one side are the suppliers, four major and three minor. Among the latter only South Africa may enter the export market, although on a small scale. Japan and Brazil will presumably provide enrichment services largely, perhaps exclusively, to domestic utilities. The export market for enrichment services will therefore probably be shared by the United States, France, Urenco, and the Soviet Union. It is also possible that Australia will enter the market in partnership with one or more other countries.[17]

The ultimate purchasers of enrichment services are the electric utility companies, both publicly and privately owned, that operate or plan to build nuclear power plants. In many cases these utility companies deal directly with suppliers in contracting for enrichment services. The utilities then contract separately with mining and milling firms for yellowcake and with other firms to convert the yellowcake into uranium hexafluoride, which is delivered to the enrichers as feedstock.

In some cases the utility companies deal with intermediaries of one kind or another. Until recently some firms selling nuclear reactors also contracted to supply uranium for the reactors for a number of years. This practice appears to have been suspended at least temporarily as the result of Westinghouse's default on a number of commitments after the sharp rise in uranium's price in the mid-1970s.

17. On January 23, 1979 the deputy prime minister of Australia issued a statement on uranium enrichment which said that the government of Australia "has been actively studying the question of uranium enrichment and it will now press ahead with feasibility studies with potential collaborators including the URENCO Consortium, Japan, France, and other interested governments."

Enrichment services are bought by utilities or intermediaries from enrichers under long-term contracts. No futures market exists for enrichment services, or for lightly enriched uranium, but there is a contract transfer market and the beginnings of a spot market. Contracts with the U.S. Department of Energy run for as long as thirty years. Those with Eurodif, Coredif, and Urenco are for ten years. The commitment period is not specified in contracts with Techsnabexport, the Soviet supplier of enrichment services. The details of enrichment contracts are quite complicated and vary from supplier to supplier.[18]

The key provisions of enrichment contracts are price and quantity. The U.S. Department of Energy adjusts its price periodically in an effort to ensure that its costs will be recovered within a reasonable time, as is required by U.S. law. Techsnabexport charges the U.S. price, or a little less. The prices of the other major suppliers appear to be somewhat higher than those of DOE and Techsnabexport.[19] For many years, DOE's predecessor, the Atomic Energy Commission (AEC), entered into requirements contracts that permitted customers to buy the enrichment services they needed on 180 days' notice. In 1973 the AEC shifted to long-term, fixed-commitment contracts that bound customers to purchase specified amounts of enrichment services, and to deliver the feedstock in advance, for a ten-year period beginning at least eight years after signing. All of the other major suppliers permit some adjustments in the quantities that customers must take. As a consequence of the more liberal policies of its competitors, DOE is offering adjustable, fixed-commitment contracts, under which quantities are fixed for the first three years and subject to 10 percent adjustments (plus or minus) in the fourth year and 30 percent in the fifth year.

How much competition will develop in the market for enrichment services is uncertain. A compilation of contracts that had been entered into by early 1978 to supply reactors scheduled to be in operation in non-Communist countries by 1990 shows DOE in a strong position.[20] No other enricher held enrichment contracts with U.S. utilities, which accounted for almost half of the total nuclear generating capacity covered

18. See "Uranium Enrichment Present Position," table 3, pp. 20–22.
19. In early 1978, the DOE price was $74.85 per SWU and that of Urenco was $120. In January 1977, the Coredif price was 520 French francs, or about $104. Ibid., p. 21.
20. Ibid., table 4, pp. 23–29.

in the survey. At the moment DOE also virtually monopolizes the important Japanese market. And DOE will continue to supply enrichment services to utilities in Western Europe, although a large part of that market will clearly be taken over by Urenco, Eurodif, and possibly later, Coredif. Techsnabexport has made contracts to supply enrichment services to a number of utilities in several Western European countries; it is the sole supplier to Finland.

On the basis of existing contracts, about half of the customers outside the United States have more than one supplier of enrichment services. It is too early, however, to conclude that a trend exists toward multiple sources of supply. An alternate possibility is that Urenco, Eurodif, and Coredif will dominate the market in the countries from which their capital came, DOE will continue to supply the U.S. market, and all of the major suppliers (including Techsnabexport) will compete for the market in the rest of the world. The fact that the countries investing in Eurodif and Coredif have rights to the outputs of those two French-controlled enterprises in proportion to their investments favors this arrangement.

Competition for enrichment contracts is not likely to be conducted in purely economic terms. Political considerations can be expected to give Techsnabexport an unbreakable grip on the Finnish market and DOE an advantageous position in several East Asian countries. Differences in nonproliferation conditions will also play a part. For example, the United States resists reprocessing, but the Western European enrichers do not, making them potentially more attractive to some customers. Even so, the possibility of price competition cannot be ruled out.

A surplus of enrichment capacity is probable in the 1980s. Its size depends on how rapidly requirements in the form of nuclear generating capacity grow and on the extent to which plans for expanding enrichment capacity are carried out (see chapter 1). How excess capacity will be distributed among suppliers of enrichment services during the 1980s cannot easily be determined. It is possible that some suppliers—most likely the new Western European ones—will find themselves operating at a loss. One or more of them might then be tempted to seize a larger share of the market by cutting prices. Other suppliers might well retaliate, setting off a declining spiral of prices and producing a situation in which few, if any, suppliers were covering their full costs.

In theory, this situation would be remedied in time by the elimination of the weaker firms, permitting the survivors to make a profit. This adjustment might, however, be delayed. Prices could fall quite far before any supplier found it economically advantageous to cease operations. (So long as revenues covered variable or out-of-pocket costs, which are presumably a smaller part of total costs than in many industries, it would be better for a firm to stay in business than to quit.) And the governments controlling the enrichment facilities might be willing for political reasons to absorb larger losses over a longer period than would private investors.

Unprofitable conditions in the enrichment industry could be worsened and prolonged—possibly even precipitated—by the prospective buildup of inventories of enriched uranium in the hands of utilities and, to a lesser extent, intermediary agents. This buildup, if it occurs, will result from commitments by customers (utilities and agents) to purchase enrichment services exceeding the current fuel requirements of power reactors for the period from the present until the mid-1980s. Some excess productive capacity will be used and converted into unwanted inventories in the hands of customers. Some customers may be unable or unwilling to cover the carrying charges on these inventories. They may therefore cancel contracts with enrichers, sell fuel at distress prices, or both.

The economic problems of the enrichment industry during the 1980s may be substantially moderated by slowdowns in the construction of new capacity and by decisions to operate existing plants at lower tails assays. Most of the enrichment capacity anticipated for 1985 either is operational or is far advanced in construction, but deferral of plans for Coredif and Urenco could make a substantial difference in prospects for 1990.

The balance between enrichment capacity and requirements in the 1980s and beyond is uncertain. Deferral of new capacity and continued operation at reduced tails assays could hold excess capacity to tolerable levels. But it is also possible that the prospective gap between capacity and requirements will be widened by the construction of new enrichment capacity, an increase in Soviet sales of enrichment services, a further slowdown in the building of nuclear power plants, and the introduction of more fuel-efficient reactors.

The possibility that the uranium enrichment industry will encounter economic difficulties during the 1980s is great enough to be taken seriously. If the industry does run into a period of unprofitable operations, the security of the nuclear fuel supply would not be affected immediately. But the governments that must decide whether to commit resources to enlarging enrichment capacity to meet the needs of the 1990s might delay doing so because of losses experienced in the 1980s. If so, utility companies could for a time encounter difficulty in obtaining new long-term contracts to enrich uranium for new nuclear reactors.

The effect of such a development on the continued growth of the nuclear power industry need not, however, be serious or prolonged. Normal stocks of enriched fuel at various stages of the fuel cycle, plus any excess inventories carried over from the 1980s, would provide a temporary cushion. Moreover, new centrifuge enrichment capacity can be built in only three to four years (excluding time for licensing). A real problem with the supply of enrichment services would be likely only if the decision-making processes of the key governments were paralyzed by policy disputes or by uncertainty over the economic impact of new enrichment technology, such as the laser method under development in several countries.

Possible Countermeasures

The preceding analysis points to several possible sources of insecurity concerning nuclear fuel supplies:

—Specific contingencies interrupting the normal fuel supplies of individual fuel-importing countries.

—Suppliers of natural uranium acting together to hold the price above the competitive level or to enforce strict nonproliferation conditions.

—Market imperfections, sometimes aggravated by governmental policies, causing large and unpredictable fluctuations in the price of natural uranium.

—Because of excess capacity, some enrichment plants operating at a loss during the 1980s, causing the governments concerned to delay building the additional capacity needed to meet the increased requirements of the 1990s.

A variety of countermeasures might be considered to deal with each of these sources of insecurity.

Responding to Interruptions of Fuel Supplies

Because of the resiliency of the nuclear fuel cycle, a country whose normal source of fuel has been interrupted may be able to find an alternate source before it suffers any actual loss of electric output. But the markets for natural uranium and enrichment services are both imperfect and subject to political influence. Success in a search for an alternate source of supply is by no means assured. Some new arrangement to which fuel importers can turn as a last resort may therefore be needed.

The concern of importers over contingencies threatening their fuel supplies might be reduced in three general ways: by concluding international agreements guaranteeing fuel supplies, by creating national fuel stockpiles dedicated to the meeting of specific emergencies, and by establishing an international institution that would supply fuel to an importer whose normal source of supply had been interrupted.

INTERNATIONAL AGREEMENTS. The simplest expedient would be for groups of fuel-importing countries to agree to help one another in an emergency.[21] The effectiveness of this arrangement would be limited by the size of the natural or enriched uranium stocks available to the cooperating countries.

A potentially more effective approach would be for several suppliers of natural uranium or enrichment services to guarantee each other's supply contracts. That is, the suppliers would agree among themselves, and with participating importers, that when in specified circumstances one supplier is unwilling or unable to continue providing fuel to one or more importers, the other suppliers will make up the deficiency.

Cross-guarantees could cover the supply of natural uranium, enrichment services, or both. To be credible, the suppliers entering into the agreement would have to be able to increase their exports to meet any likely contingency. If the interruption of normal fuel supplies was of limited duration, as in the event of accident, sabotage, or a commercial dispute, national stockpiles in supplier countries could provide adequate protection. In the event of more extended interruptions, the guaranteeing suppliers might have to expand their output of natural uranium or enrichment services. This would be no problem if there were excess capacity, but expanding mining or enrichment capacity would be both time-consuming and costly.

21. Some cooperation in meeting nuclear fuel needs already occurs among utility companies. Utilities with surpluses of fuel materials sometimes make loans-in-kind to utilities in short supply. Expansion on this system of swaps has been advocated as a major means of increasing the assurance of nuclear fuel supplies. See Uranium Institute, *The Nuclear Fuel Bank Issue as Seen by Uranium Producers and Consumers* (London: Uranium Institute, 1979), especially p. 9.

In countries in which uranium mining is in private hands, special legislation would probably be required to enable governments to honor their guarantees. A different kind of complication would arise if several governments owned an enrichment facility jointly, but not all of them had entered into the international agreement guaranteeing fuel supplies.

From the purely physical point of view, the workability of an international agreement guaranteeing fuel supplies would depend on who participated. The participating suppliers minus one—any one—must be able to meet any likely contingency covered by the agreement. Physical feasibility is not the only question that must be answered, however. The major fuel suppliers are unlikely to be willing to extend unconditional guarantees. Whether they would agree to guarantees that would be broad enough to deal adequately with the problem—as that problem is seen by the importers—is in fact an open question.

The suppliers would almost certainly not guarantee the fuel supply of a country that had violated the Treaty on the Non-Proliferation of Nuclear Weapons or that had committed a major breach of the safeguards administered by the International Atomic Energy Agency. These restrictions would probably be acceptable in principle to the fuel-importing countries, although they might well ask who was to determine whether a violation of the NPT had actually occurred. Presumably the word of the IAEA would be accepted in the event of breaches of safeguards.

If—as is quite possible—some major suppliers also required adherence to the NPT, acceptance of full-scope safeguards, or renunciation of reprocessing, some importers would decide that the guarantee was not worth the price and refuse to adhere to the international agreement. If many importers reacted in this way, the conditions would have been self-defeating. By trying for too much, an international alternative to undesirable development of national reprocessing and enrichment facilities would have been rendered unworkable.

The policies of the United States as set forth in the Nuclear Non-Proliferation Act of 1978 pose particularly difficult problems.[22] The NNPA establishes strict conditions that must be met before any export of nuclear materials can be approved, and these would clearly apply to any export pursuant to a cross-guarantee. Those consumers who now obtain nuclear fuel (natural uranium or enrichment services) from other suppliers under

22. See app. A for a discussion of the provisions of the NNPA.

somewhat less strict conditions might not find a U.S. guarantee particularly attractive.

If a set of conditions acceptable to both suppliers and importers were found, questions would be certain to arise concerning their application. The fuel-importing countries would not be willing to allow the fuel-exporting countries to decide unilaterally whether the agreed conditions had been observed in specific cases. Nor would the fuel-exporting countries be likely to accept the word of the importing countries. An international arrangement to mediate or arbitrate disputes over the application of the agreement would be necessary. Means of settling disputes among suppliers concerning how to share the responsibility for honoring fuel guarantees would also be desirable. Even more important would be the creation of a mechanism to deal with the problem that caused an interruption of normal fuel supplies in the first place.

These functions could be performed by the IAEA or by another international body established especially for the purpose. Having the IAEA oversee an international agreement guaranteeing fuel supplies has two obvious advantages: the IAEA already exists and its staff possesses much of the required expertise. On the other hand, it would be sheer luck if the complex arrangements for governing the IAEA represented an adequate compromise among the interests involved in negotiating such an agreement. Moreover, the IAEA is already burdened with other functions, and some governments might regard its governing bodies as too politicized to qualify for an impartial mediating role.

STOCKPILES. National stockpiles of nuclear fuel in the hands of suppliers would make a system of cross-guarantees of fuel supplies more workable and therefore more credible to fuel importers. Stockpiles could be even more reassuring if they were specifically dedicated to meeting obligations under the international agreement guaranteeing fuel supplies. Dedicated stockpiles might be controlled and administered by individual suppliers, by individual importers, by regional associations of suppliers and importers, or by an international agency. Dedicated stockpiles in the hands of individual suppliers would have the advantage of administrative simplicity. They would, however, be less reassuring to importers than stockpiles under the importers' own control or under some form of international control.

Location would contribute to the reassuring effect of stockpiles. A stockpile owned by a fuel-importing country, but located in a fuel-exporting country, would clearly not be as reassuring to the importing country as would the same stockpile in its own territory. On the other hand, stockpiles located in the fuel-importing countries might come to be regarded as dedicated to meeting fuel-supply interruptions affecting only those specific countries. In that event the system of guarantees would lose flexibility, and larger stocks of fuel would be required to achieve any given level of assurance than if all stocks were perceived as available to meet contingencies in any participating fuel-importing country.

Establishing dedicated stockpiles also raises difficult financial questions. If ownership were transferred to individual fuel-importing countries—as would appear logical if the stockpiles were located in those countries—the suppliers might expect to be paid the full value of the fuel. If the suppliers retained ownership, they would no doubt desire reimbursement for warehousing and other carrying charges such as interest on the capital tied up in the stockpiles. To make good such a claim, the suppliers would have to assert that the dedicated stockpiles were larger than their normal needs and were maintained solely in support of the international fuel-supply agreement.

How serious these financial problems would be depends principally on the size and composition (natural uranium or enriched uranium) of the dedicated stockpiles. This in turn depends on what the parties to the international fuel-supply agreement thought was necessary and what means of finance were available. If substantial excess uranium mining and enrichment capacity existed, and if suppliers held large stocks (even though not dedicated), small dedicated stocks, established solely for their psychological effect, would suffice.

If large dedicated stockpiles were believed needed, vesting their ownership in importing countries might have to be ruled out because the financial burden would be too great. The carrying charges of the suppliers would be a smaller problem for stockpiles of any given size, and could be covered through a combination of voluntary contributions by suppliers and assessments on importers based on their installed nuclear generating capacity.

Some idea of the cost of fuel stockpiles may be obtained from the following illustrative calculations. Total world requirements for uranium in 1980 (excluding the Soviet Union, China, and Eastern Europe) are in the neighborhood of 30,000 metric tons.[23] If the participants in a fuel-supply agreement decided that a dedicated stockpile of 10 percent of this amount was required, 3,900 short tons of yellowcake (concentrated U_3O_8) would be needed. At $40 a pound, the stockpile would cost $312 million. A warehouse for the stockpile, including handling equipment, might add another $10 million. At 10 percent, interest forgone then comes to $32.2 million a year. Operating costs—principally staff salaries—add perhaps a few hundred thousand dollars, bringing the total annual cost to about $32.5 million.

Maintaining a stockpile of enriched uranium would be more expensive. If world requirements for enrichment services in 1980 are assumed to be about 20 million separative work units (SWUs),[24] a stockpile covering 10 percent would cost about $500 million. Of that amount, $200 million represents charges for enrichment services and $300 million the cost of uranium feedstock.[25] The cost of a warehouse and handling equipment might bring the total investment to $510 million. With interest forgone annually at $51 million, and with $1 million allowed for operating expenses, including security guards, the annual cost of the enriched uranium stockpile would be $52 million.

INTERNATIONAL INSTITUTION. No sharp line separates an effort to increase the assurance of nuclear fuel supplies through an international agreement backed by dedicated stockpiles from one that concentrates on the establishment of a new international institution. An agreement with some kind of international surveillance to settle disputes and with dedicated, nationally owned stockpiles can in fact be viewed as an embryonic form of international institution. And it could be converted into a more formal or elaborate institution if the parties to the agreement so wished.

Most of the recent discussion of a possible international institution to deal with short-term interruptions of nuclear fuel supplies has referred to the institution as a "bank." This term is not the happiest choice, since

23. Nuclear Energy Agency, Organisation for Economic Co-operation and Development and International Atomic Energy Agency, *Uranium: Resources, Production and Demand* (Paris: OECD, 1979), p. 36.

24. OECD Nuclear Energy Agency, *Nuclear Fuel Cycle Requirements and Supply Considerations, through the Long-Term* (Paris: OECD, 1978), p. 29.

25. Two million SWUs can produce 464 kilograms of low-enriched uranium (3 percent U^{235}) at a tails assay of 0.2 percent U^{235}. To get this much LEU, 2.54 million kilograms of natural uranium feedstock (in the form of UF_6) must be used. In January 1980, feedstock cost $117 a kilogram.

an institution reasonably well equipped to perform the proposed functions would bear little resemblance to a bank. Nevertheless, to avoid an undesirable proliferation of different labels for the same thing, the institution under discussion here will be referred to as a fuel bank.

If an international nuclear fuel bank is to be created, a number of practical issues must be resolved. What assets should the bank hold and in what form? How should the bank be financed? What should be its operating principles? Where should it be located? These questions are considered below. Several important institutional and legal questions are reserved for chapter 5, including the bank's organizational structure, decision-making processes, legal status, and relationship with the International Atomic Energy Agency.

The fuel assurances that the bank would provide would be credible to importers only if it were clearly able to supply needed fuel when specified contingencies occurred. The bank would therefore have to hold appropriate physical assets, or claims to such assets. What assets should be held and in what form is not, however, self-evident.

The bank might well find it necessary to hold both natural and low-enriched uranium, since uncertainties have from time to time existed concerning the supplies of both commodities. In the case of natural uranium, the bank could conceivably own mining properties or stocks of unprocessed ore. It would be much more convenient, however, for the bank to hold concentrated U_3O_8 (yellowcake). The low-enriched uranium (LEU) used by light water reactors could probably be held most conveniently in the form of uranium hexafluoride (UF_6). Since different reactors require fuel of different degrees of enrichment, the bank would find it desirable to have stocks of LEU with different percentages of U^{235}. Some supplies of unenriched uranium dioxide powder (UO_2) might also be needed to meet needs of the minority of power reactors that use natural uranium. Holding fully fabricated fuel rods containing either natural or enriched uranium would be inefficient. The design of fuel rods, as well as the pellets that they contain, varies with the type of reactor.

The work of the bank would be greatly simplified if its assets were entirely in the form of claims on fuel held by (or to be produced by) other governmental or private entities. The bank would then not have to manage—and guard—physical inventories of nuclear materials. On the other hand, a purely "paper" operation would probably not provide the degree of psychological reassurance that is needed. Some of the bank's assets should therefore be physical stocks of natural and enriched uranium. No rigid guidelines should be laid down, however, concerning the composition of the bank's assets or the form in which they should be held. The bank's management should be given broad authority to adjust its assets to changing political and economic conditions.

The bank's paper assets, it might be noted, could take more than one form. Some of these assets might in effect be warehouse receipts for fuel owned by the bank, but stored by some other entity. Other assets might be options to buy specified amounts of fuel. These options would be the functional equivalents of the cross-guarantees discussed earlier in this chapter. Their psychological value would be enhanced by the fact that they could be treated as part of the bank's assets. In order to spread the risk that options might not be honored, they would have to be obtained from a number of suppliers.

By holding options to buy fuel, the bank could greatly reduce both its investment in physical stocks and the carrying charges on such stocks. Options would not be free, but they probably could be purchased for a small fraction of the cost of the fuel in question if fuel suppliers anticipated either holding large inventories or possessing substantial excess capacity over the period covered by the options. Excess capacity would be a relevant consideration, because the resilience of the nuclear fuel cycle would permit the writing of options that called for the delivery of fuel on, say, a year's notice in the case of natural uranium and six months' notice in the case of enriched uranium.

An alternative means of gaining access to fuel beyond the amount in the bank's stockpile would be to enter into long-term contracts with suppliers for the periodic delivery of specified amounts of fuel. The bank would accept delivery only if the fuel were needed to meet the needs of customers. Otherwise, the bank would resell the fuel on the spot market. Under this scheme, the bank would stand to gain or lose the difference between the contract price and the spot price.

In one way or another, the bank would have to finance: the initial acquisition and the later replenishment or increase of its basic assets (fuel, claims to fuel, and warehouses); carrying charges on those assets; and operating expenses.

Developing even an illustrative budget for the bank is unavoidably speculative. It is possible, however, on the basis of some arbitrary but not unreasonable assumptions, to get some idea of the rough orders of magnitude involved. The bank might be established with fuel assets sufficient to cover roughly 10 percent of estimated fuel requirements in 1980 (as was done in the case of the illustrative stockpile discussed in the previous section). One-fifth of these assets might be held in the form of actual stocks of natural and enriched uranium. The remainder could be options to buy fuel.

If the same assumptions concerning prices and the cost of warehouses were used as in the case of the illustrative stockpile, and if options were arbitrarily assumed to cost 5 percent of the value of the fuel they represent, the bank's initial investment would total $215 million, broken down as follows:

Assets	Cost (millions of dollars)
Natural uranium	62
Natural uranium options	13
Enriched uranium	100
Enriched uranium options	20
Warehouse	20
Total	215

At 10 percent, interest forgone on this investment would be $21.5 million a year. Other expenses should be quite modest, since the bank would not require a large staff. The annual cost of operating the bank on the stated assumptions would be around $23 million. The bank would not have to budget funds to exercise fuel options; financing for this purpose could be made the responsibility of the country (or in some cases, the utility company) whose normal supply of fuel had been interrupted.

The initial acquisition of basic assets could be financed by the capital subscriptions of participating governments (and perhaps also private firms), and by contributions in cash or in kind from governments. In the beginning, carrying charges and operating expenses might have to be met largely from government subsidies. As the bank got into full operation and began to receive revenue, these subsidies could be reduced and perhaps eventually eliminated.

Two major sources of revenue would be available to the bank. One would be from charges on potential customers for the right to turn to the bank for fuel in specified contingencies. These charges would bear some similarity to insurance premiums; a group of firms subject to the same risk (interruption of fuel supply) would share the cost of maintaining a facility that would help unlucky members of the group. The total of such charges might be set at an arbitrary fraction of the carrying charges on the bank's fuel assets. They might be prorated among customers on the basis of installed nuclear generating capacity.

The other source of revenue would be profits from the sale of fuel. Selling fuel above replacement cost would be justified both because of the need to cover the bank's expenses and because fuel would be especially valuable to buyers who had lost their normal source of supply. It is possible that the bank would sometimes lend fuel and accept repayment in kind. In such cases, the bank could earn revenue by charging interest on the value of the fuel.

If the bank succeeded in becoming self-supporting, it would have the means of replenishing its initial assets. If the bank also established its ability to earn profits, it would be in a position to expand its operations by borrowing the money needed to increase its holdings of fuel and claims to fuel. The bank might borrow from governments or from international financial institutions. Borrowing on capital markets would also be possible, but in that event the bank's indebtedness would have to be guaranteed by participating governments.

Both members (participating firms and governments) and nonmembers should be permitted to make withdrawals of fuel. To make membership a condition of access to the bank's facilities would unnecessarily constrict its ability to provide assurance of fuel supplies. But in order to make participation more attractive, members might be given special discounts or priority in the event of heavy demands on the bank's fuel supplies. Or they might be permitted unconditional withdrawals of fuel within established quotas. The size of these quotas could vary with the amounts of capital subscribed by each member, the annual charge or premium paid for access to the bank's facilities, or both. The quotas should not be so large, however, as to expose the bank to a run that would seriously deplete its assets.

The difficulty arises in determining the conditions that should be met for above-quota withdrawals by members and all withdrawals by nonmembers. Requiring the safeguarding of both fuel provided by the bank and facilities in which such fuel was used would not be unreasonable. Suspending withdrawal rights for violation of the nonproliferation treaty or IAEA safeguards would also seem appropriate. Requiring acceptance of full-scope safeguards might also be feasible. But applying more strict conditions, such as joining the NPT or, even more severe, promising never to engage in reprocessing or enrichment, might be counterproductive and cause some potential participants to go their own way—precisely the kind of behavior that the bank would be designed to discourage.

In this connection, the Nuclear Non-Proliferation Act creates a difficult problem. Section 104 of the NNPA authorizes the president to seek international agreement to establish an international nuclear fuel authority (INFA) with functions similar to, but somewhat broader than, the nuclear fuel bank discussed in this chapter. The same section of the NNPA also directs the president to submit a proposal for the creation of an interim stockpile of enriched uranium. Access of nonnuclear weapon states to both the INFA and the stockpile is limited, however, to those states that "accept IAEA safeguards on all their peaceful nuclear activities, do not manufacture or otherwise acquire any nuclear explosive device, do not establish any new enrichment or reprocessing facilities under their de facto or de jure control, and place any such existing facilities under effective international auspices and inspection."

The requirement of full-scope safeguards and the ban on nuclear explosive devices in the NNPA would not be regarded as unreasonable by many countries, although the exceptions include such key countries as India and Brazil. But some nations consider unacceptable the prohibition of new enrichment and reprocessing facilities or the requirement that any such existing facilities be internationalized. As long as the latter requirements remain U.S. policy, it is difficult to see how an effective system of dedicated stockpiles or an effective nuclear fuel bank could be organized. If the United States participates in either scheme, it would presumably have to insist on conditions that a number of other important countries probably could not accept. And if the United States does not participate—indeed, if it does not take the lead in seeking solutions to the fuel assurance problem—neither a stockpile system nor a bank would be likely to be organized.

One way to meet this problem would be to tailor the bank to the NNPA by limiting access to it to nonnuclear weapon states that do not have, and do not plan to build, national enrichment or reprocessing facilities. This approach would almost certainly rule out a number of important countries, including Japan and West Germany.

Another approach would be to assume that the U.S. Congress would amend the NNPA if presented with good reasons for doing so. Participation in the bank might then be possible for all countries adhering to agreed international arrangements for controlling sensitive fuel cycle facilities. In particular, the bank might be used to promote adherence to a plutonium management system (see chapter 4).

The organizers of the bank would also face the question of whether the bank should be essentially a fuel supplier or a fuel broker. If it is a supplier, it would presumably have to extend the warranties concerning fuel performance that are normally included in fuel sales contracts. Brokers, who merely bring buyers and sellers together, do not have to commit themselves in this way.

Obviously, it would be better for the bank to try to be a broker. The bank could achieve this goal in the case of fuel provided under an option agreement by assigning the agreement to the country whose normal source of fuel had been interrupted. In the case of fuel provided from its own inventory, the bank would have to obtain transferable warranties from the original suppliers.

The choice of a host country for the bank involves political, legal, and security considerations.

The host country should not only be neutral in the usual sense of nonalignment and relative impartiality in East-West and North-South controversies. It should also not be too closely identified with any particular interest in the field of nuclear energy. It definitely should not be a major supplier of uranium or enrichment services.

The host country should be willing to enter into a headquarters agreement with the bank that would adequately insulate the bank and its personnel from executive or judicial interference. Extraterritoriality may in fact be required for the bank's offices and fuel storage areas. The host country should also provide adequate security for the bank and its stocks of nuclear fuel, and it should be generally regarded as both politically stable and unlikely to become involved in an international conflict.

These criteria do not point clearly toward the best location for the bank. They do, however, rule out large categories of countries, including members of NATO or the Warsaw Pact; most, if not all, Middle Eastern countries, and paired adversaries, such as India and Pakistan, North and South Korea, and China and Vietnam. Countries that meet all criteria are not numerous. A few that come to mind are Austria, Sweden, and Switzerland in Europe; Singapore in Asia; and Colombia and Mexico in Latin America.

Preventing Collusion among Suppliers

The possibility that suppliers—more likely suppliers of natural uranium than of enrichment services—will band together to push up prices or to impose strict nonproliferation conditions is in fact the reflection of larger problems: imperfections in the market for uranium and the lack of an international consensus on nonproliferation policy.

All that would seem to be required to prevent the rise of an economic cartel is that the governments of the major uranium-producing countries adopt a firm policy against combinations in restraint of trade. Obtaining agreement on such a policy, however, calls for more than rallying support for the abstract principle of free trade. As was pointed out earlier, governments were involved in the uranium cartel that apparently existed in the early 1970s.

The emergence of a uranium cartel could conceivably be blocked by the United States acting alone. Legal action could be taken under the U.S. antitrust laws against private firms participating in the cartel, if they conducted business or held assets in the United States. Diplomatic pressure could be applied against participating governments. The United States might also consider economic countermeasures, including selling off part of the large DOE stockpiles of natural and enriched uranium[26] at reduced prices and refusing to enrich uranium bought from participants in the cartel. The effectiveness of all of these actions would, however, be uncertain.

Some firms participating in the cartel would be beyond the reach of U.S. antitrust laws, and prosecution of those that were not would be costly and time-consuming, and might be frustrated if the sponsors of the cartel had taken care to give it the form of an intergovernmental agreement. Diplomatic pressure is rarely effective unless it is backed by at least the implicit threat of effective sanctions.

Cut-rate sales of either natural or enriched uranium could hurt the cartel by depressing the price of natural uranium in the spot market. The impact of such sales on new long-term contracts would be less predictable. On the one hand, the cartel might be somewhat inhibited by the sales

---

26. In 1978 the U.S. government had an inventory "equivalent to 67,000 tons of U_3O_8." ("The Nature of the World Uranium Market," draft report submitted by U.S. delegation to INFCE Working Group 3, November 30, 1978, p. 41.) The United States also held stocks of enriched uranium in early 1979 representing 29 million SWUs.

from raising prices. But on the other, utility companies might not be greatly influenced by the availability of cheap fuel on the spot market because they would be reluctant to shift from long-term sources of supply to ones that might prove transitory.

Discriminating against the cartel in the provision of enrichment services would damage innocent utility companies, as well as participating mining firms. Moreover, DOE would expose itself to suits for breach of contract if it discriminated against existing contracts. It would also divert business to other enrichers and could lead to a division of the uranium market, with one part dominated by the cartel and the other by the United States.

Apart from its questionable effectiveness, a unilateral U.S. effort to destroy a uranium cartel could seriously disrupt international cooperation in the field of nuclear energy. It could also add to, rather than reduce, uncertainty concerning the reliability of nuclear fuel supplies. Clearly, it would be better to try to weaken the incentives to form a cartel than to try to destroy one after it had emerged. Foremost among these incentives are the market imperfections that make it difficult for uranium producers to anticipate future market conditions. By reducing the risk of cartel formation, stabilizing the market for natural uranium would contribute indirectly as well as directly to increasing the confidence of consumers in the security of nuclear fuel supplies.

The fear of an enrichment cartel is also unlikely to be dissipated quickly by any simple remedies. Measures to deal with short-term interruptions of nuclear fuel supplies, such as those discussed earlier in this chapter, would help, but a fundamental cure depends on successful efforts to bring about a convergence of the nuclear energy policies of differently situated states. Merely stating this prescription is sufficient to underline the difficulty of applying it.

Progress could be made, however, by instituting a system of regular consultations among governments of supplier countries and those of consuming countries. These consultations should focus on the international rules of trade in sensitive nuclear materials, equipment, and technology. They could become a substitute for the deliberations of the London nuclear suppliers' group, which included no developing countries. Whether the London nuclear suppliers' group should eventually be dissolved would depend on whether the political and psychological benefits from that action appeared to outweigh the possible loss in the effectiveness of the January 1978 guidelines.

Stabilizing the Uranium Market

The problem of stabilizing the uranium market could be approached in a number of ways: a formal commodity agreement might be negotiated, an international institution might be created to exert a major influence on the market, or a system of consultations among governments might be established with a view to concerting policies when necessary. Whatever approach is adopted, the objective would be to make it more likely that mining and milling capacity would keep pace with the requirements of the civil nuclear energy industry.

COMMODITY AGREEMENT. To be politically acceptable (and to conform to UN standards), a commodity agreement would have to include consuming as well as producing countries. To be economically workable, it would have to include all major exporters of natural uranium. A major exporter that remained outside the agreement could disrupt the stabilization policies of participants by pursuing its own commercial advantage.

A commodity agreement could deal with the total yellowcake market in participating countries, or only with the part of the market involving shipments from one country to another. The more comprehensive approach would be desirable from the economic point of view, and in the following discussion it is assumed that it would be adopted. It is further assumed that participants would not impose special economic restraints on the international trade in yellowcake, but would give full support to international stabilization efforts under a commodity agreement.

This assumption, it must be recognized, may not be entirely realistic, but to discuss a commodity agreement that could at any time be undermined by the unilateral actions of participants would be an exercise in futility. It will therefore be assumed that embargoes on imports, such as the one administered by the United States for a number of years, would be prohibited, and that export controls, such as those currently applied by Canada, would be modified to deal solely with nonproliferation conditions.[27]

The central provision in a commodity agreement would establish procedures for determining and periodically revising the range within which the price of uranium (presumably in the form of yellowcake) would be

27. All Canadian exports of natural uranium require governmental approval, which is denied if the price is below that offered domestic buyers. Canada also requires exporters to ensure that adequate fuel will be available for the lifetimes of all reactors existing or to be in operation in Canada within the next ten years.

permitted to move. The agreement might set forth certain principles to be followed in determining the price, such as adequate supplies for consumers and fair returns for investors. As a practical matter, however, price decisions would be negotiated among the governments concerned and formalized by their votes in a continuing body created to administer the agreement. Votes might have to be weighted to reflect the relative importance of participants as suppliers or consumers of natural uranium.

Suppliers and consumers would presumably vote in separate constituencies.[28] Some means of breaking a deadlock between the two groups would probably be needed. Dealing with the potentially dominant role of the United States would be a problem for other participants. In 1977 the United States accounted for nearly 40 percent of the uranium produced in non-Communist areas and had about 55 percent of the total nuclear generating capacity in those areas.

Setting a price range for the spot market would be a fairly straightforward matter although it does not follow that agreement on the range would come easily. Decisions made pursuant to a commodity agreement could not affect prices paid under previously existing long-term contracts that specified either a fixed price or a fixed price with an escalation clause to cover increases in production costs.[29] Prices paid under contracts specifying payments linked in some way to the "market price" could, however, be influenced by way of the spot price. Some contracts call for a price based on (but not necessarily equal to) the spot price, or for the negotiation of prices on a regular schedule (which would presumably be influenced by the spot price).

In 1978, if spot market transactions are excluded, 83 percent of all deliveries of uranium in the United States were estimated to have been made under contracts specifying the price (with or without an escalation clause), and 13 percent under contracts calling for payments linked to the market (or spot) price. Most of the remaining 4 percent represented captive production in which utilities were involved in uranium production. The current trend, however, is running strongly in favor of contracts using the market price approach. Also, ties between utilities and uranium

28. A decision would be needed on whether countries such as the United States and France that both produce and consume uranium could claim votes in both capacities and whether they could vote in both constituencies.

29. Information on the price provisions in uranium contracts is drawn from "The Nature of the World Uranium Market," pp. 17–21.

mining enterprises are increasing. By 1985 only 36 percent of U.S. uranium procurement is expected to be of the contract price variety and 29 percent will be market price. Most of the other 35 percent will be tied purchases.[30]

Comparable estimates for the rest of the world are not available, but on the basis of the above estimates for the United States it appears that a commodity agreement could exert an increasing, if indirect, influence on prices under existing long-term contracts. In principle the participants in a commodity agreement could agree upon a pricing formula for all new contracts, and also might agree to convert old contracts to the new formula. One obvious option would be to set the price at the spot price that prevailed a certain time before delivery. This approach would of course greatly increase the importance of the decision on the range within which the spot price would be permitted to move. Only about 10 percent of all uranium purchases today are in the spot market.

Whatever the pricing formula adopted for new long-term contracts, the prospective growth of tied procurement could pose a problem, since it is not easy to ascertain the price paid in deliveries between affiliated firms. Differences in contract terms other than price, such as nonproliferation conditions, could also make it difficult to administer a single-price system.

But the greatest difficulty of all would be keeping the price within the desired range. As was noted earlier, both the demand and the supply of uranium are probably quite inelastic in the short run. Shifts in either would therefore tend to cause disproportionate changes in price. Also the secular rise in price, as higher-cost deposits of ore were exploited, would force periodic adjustments in the desired range.

It is quite unlikely that the price could be kept within the desired range simply by enforcing market discipline among buyers and sellers, although a certain amount of discipline might help limit price reactions to small changes in supply or demand. If more uranium is being offered than the market will take at the lower end of the desired range, some sellers can be expected to try to maintain sales volume by cutting their prices in violation of the agreement. Similarly if buyers want more uranium than is being offered at the top of the range, some will probably pay more, despite the agreement.

30. Ibid., p. 20.

Fortunately the uranium market possesses two built-in shock absorbers that could cushion the effects on price of changes in supply or demand: the willingness of utilities to hold somewhat larger inventories of both natural and enriched uranium than would be strictly necessary for their operations, and the lack of a close link to the spot price in some long-term contracts.

If the price moved above the desired range—and if this situation were viewed as temporary—utilities would tend to withdraw from the spot market and delay procurements under long-term market price contracts to the extent that they could legally do so. Fuel requirements would for a time be met from inventories. If the price fell below the desired range—and again if this situation were viewed as temporary—utilities would have an incentive to build up uranium inventories.

In both cases it would of course be essential that the movement of the price outside the desired range not be seen as only the beginning of a larger swing. In that event the inventory policies of utilities would tend to accentuate, rather than moderate, the price fluctuation. In other words inventory policies could be relied upon to help stabilize prices only if some other circumstance gave utilities grounds for believing that departures from the desired range would be temporary.

Long-term contracts that specify the price, or use an escalator not related to the spot price, contribute to the stability of the average price under which uranium is procured, although they also limit the ability of a commodity agreement to influence long-term prices by way of the spot market. Contracts that base the price on the spot price are of course more susceptible to influence, but for that reason exert little or no drag on price fluctuations. As was noted earlier, this kind of contract is becoming dominant.

It should be possible to write a contract whose price provisions would strike a balance between susceptibility to influence and vulnerability to sharp changes. (For example, the link to the spot price could be lagged, or limits could be set on the percentage of price change permitted in a given period of time.) Reaching agreement on standard contract provisions would, however, not be easy, and efforts to impose such provisions on buyers and sellers would encounter political and legal obstacles.

Even under the best of circumstances, the attributes of the uranium market that retard sharp reactions to changes in supply and demand could not ensure price stability. They would only make it somewhat more likely that active stabilization measures would succeed. The participants in a commodity agreement would in theory have two such measures at their disposal: manipulation of the flow of natural uranium feedstock to enrichment plants, and creation of a buffer stock that would permit direct intervention in the spot market.

Enrichers—who are all instrumentalities of government—could, if they wished, artificially increase the demand for natural uranium by building up stocks of enriched uranium (that is, they could operate above the level needed to meet the current requirements of their customers). And they could artificially decrease the demand for natural uranium by drawing down their stocks of enriched uranium. (That is, they could stop requiring their customers to deliver uranium hexafluoride to be enriched and sell them enriched uranium from inventories.) Enrichers could also influence the demand for natural uranium by varying their tails assays. The tails assay could be reduced to lower demand and increased to raise demand.

An enricher manipulating the flow of feedstock to enrichment plants would, however, encounter both economic and political problems. Under the conditions of excess capacity expected to exist during the 1980s, enrichers would be reluctant to incur the costs of creating and holding larger inventories simply to increase the demand for natural uranium. Nor would they have much interest in operating at still lower percentages of capacity in order to reduce the demand for uranium. Even if these economic problems did not exist, it is unlikely that the enrichers would agree to turn over decisions on their operating and inventory policies to the participants in a uranium commodity agreement. The alternative— enrichers joining in a buyers' cartel to stabilize the price of natural uranium—would be even less attractive to the uranium producers.

The creation of a buffer stock, which is the classic device for regulating commodity prices under international agreements, would raise a different set of problems. The managers of the buffer stock, operating under general guidelines provided by the participants in the agreement, would buy yellowcake when the spot price fell below the desired price range and sell yellowcake when the price rose above the desired range. To succeed, this kind of operation requires an adequate amount of working capital in two forms: an inventory of yellowcake for checking unwanted price increases, and cash assets for checking unwanted price decreases. This working capital would have to be provided by participants, probably through a system of variable assessments based on the relative magnitudes of their sales and purchases of yellowcake in some past period.

How much working capital would be required depends in large part on how well the desired range fits market conditions.[31] If the spot price came under strong downward pressure, the managers of the buffer stock could spend large sums to bring the price back up to the desired range. Similarly in the face of strong upward pressures, large sales of yellowcake could be made to push the spot price down to the desired range. In both situations, participants would have to decide whether to adjust the desired price range or to provide the managers of the buffer stock with more working capital in the form of cash or yellowcake. Whether they would be willing to put up more working capital cannot be predicted in the abstract, but some limit would certainly exist on the willingness of governments to commit public funds to stabilizing the price of uranium. And, of course, there is also a limit to the amount of yellowcake available for purchase.

The danger would be that neither an appropriate adjustment in the desired price range nor an increase in the working capital of the buffer stock would be made in time. Efforts by managers to contain price fluctuations would lose credibility, and traders in natural uranium would begin to gamble on an impending collapse of the commodity agreement. The situation could then get out of control, and a uranium agreement would join the list of commodity agreements that have failed.[32]

On the other hand, it is just possible that clever buffer stock managers could learn to make the right sales or purchases at the right time and in the right sector of the still-undeveloped uranium market. Their ability to exert the desired influence on the spot price might be increased somewhat by giving them authority to trade in uranium futures. Some buying or selling pressures in the spot market might then be diverted into the purchase or sale of fixed-price contracts for future delivery.

The skill of management could not, however, compensate for the fail-

31. In theory, market conditions could be artificially manipulated on the supply side by establishing production or marketing quotas. Reaching agreement on such quotas would, however, be quite difficult. For example, OPEC has never been able to agree on market shares.

32. For a review of the difficulties in negotiating and carrying out commodity agreements, see L. N. Rangarajan, *Commodity Conflict: The Political Economy of International Commodity Negotiations* (Ithaca, N.Y.: Cornell University Press, 1978), pp. 34–52.

ure of the governments concerned to take timely action to provide additional working capital or to adjust the desired price range. Given the different interests of the participants in a uranium commodity agreement, optimism on either score would not be justified.

INTERNATIONAL INSTITUTION. A commodity agreement would try to stabilize the uranium market largely by intervening directly in the spot portion of the market to achieve specific price objectives. An alternative approach to market stabilization would be to create an international institution with broad authority to promote the favorable evolution of the market over the long run. Such an institution would maintain up-to-date projections of supply and demand, try to foresee gluts and shortages that could cause large price fluctuations, and organize appropriate remedial actions.

These actions could cover a wide range: in some instances, merely informing suppliers, consumers, and interested governments of impending disruptions could have a beneficial effect. In others, the institution might intervene more actively. If exploration for uranium deposits, or exploitation of known deposits appeared to be insufficient to meet anticipated requirements, the institution could try to organize the needed investment, using some of its own funds as a catalyst. Or if new consumers were crowding into the spot market and pushing up the price to an undesirable level because of their inability to obtain long-term contracts, the institution could assume the same intermediary role as was once played by some sellers of reactors.

The institution would also be authorized to operate in the spot market and to deal in uranium futures. It would not, however, be required to achieve any short-term price goals. Its mission would be to try to maintain a long-run balance between uranium production and consumption at prices that would change only gradually. Whether such a mission could be fully effective may be questioned. In any event it would be prudent to begin on a modest scale, learn by experience what is possible, and expand as appeared appropriate and feasible.

In form the institution might be a corporation chartered by governments interested in the long-run stability of the uranium market. The sponsoring governments could supply the institution's initial capital. Additional capital could be raised by borrowing in the financial markets on the basis of guarantees provided by the sponsoring governments.

In order to be credit-worthy, the institution would have to be self-supporting—its revenues would have to cover its expenses plus a return on capital. There is no reason in principle why, given a broad mandate, good management, and adequate initial financing, this could not be achieved. None of the prerequisites of a self-supporting operation can, however, be taken for granted.

Uranium is a highly political commodity. Producing countries commonly regulate the exploration and exploitation of uranium resources and restrict the participation of foreigners. It is by no means certain that all producing countries would welcome the participation of an international institution in their uranium mining industry. If formed at all, the institution might well be subjected to restrictions and exclusions that would interfere with its ability both to carry out its basic mandate and to become self-supporting. The same national sentiments that could limit the institution's mandate could also lead to policy controls that would make good management difficult, and to limits on capitalization that would keep the institution from becoming a major factor in the long-term evolution of the uranium market.

CONSULTATIVE SYSTEM. A less ambitious, and therefore more feasible, approach to the problem of stabilizing the uranium market over the long run would be to establish a consultative system among the principally interested governments, both producers and consumers. This system might consist of a council of governmental representatives that would meet periodically to consider trends and prospects in the uranium market, and a secretariat that would collect data and carry out analyses on behalf of the council.

In a number of countries, private firms are important as buyers or sellers of uranium, or both. In such countries, it would be desirable to bring the private sector into the consultative process. This might be done by setting up industry committees to advise the governments concerned.

Establishment of the consultative system would require a minimum of formality. The interested governments would simply agree to consult from time to time on problems affecting the orderly supply of natural uranium for use in civil nuclear energy industries, and to establish a secretariat that would facilitate their consultations. No formal voting procedures would be needed; the council would take very few collective actions, other than setting work priorities for the secretariat, and those actions could be based on the general consensus of members. An agreement would, however, be required on how the expenses of the consultative system would be shared and how the secretariat would be constituted and recruited.

Precisely what the consultative system would do would be determined by its members. At a minimum, the secretariat could collect information on market transactions and make long-term projections of demand and supply to assist the council in its deliberations. The council might decide to publish both the market information and projections as a means of improving the functioning of the uranium market. The council might also direct the secretariat to conduct in-depth analyses of problems affecting future supply and demand and publish the results of those studies. The quality of the secretariat's information and analysis would obviously depend upon the cooperation of participating governments in collecting and releasing data, some of which have been regarded in the past as sensitive or proprietary.

The principal function of the council would be to discuss solutions to problems identified by the secretariat or raised by one or more of the participating governments. For example, if it appeared that the efficient functioning of the uranium market might be hampered by national controls over exports, imports, or investment, the advisability of removing or moderating these controls would be discussed. If a consensus in favor of certain actions emerged, the governments directly concerned would be under some political pressure to comply, but they would face no sanctions if they decided not to do so.

An issue that would probably be before the council continuously is the adequacy of exploration efforts and plans to invest in new uranium mines. If more exploration and investment were found to be necessary to meet future requirements, the council would consider what might be done. Participating governments would be asked to submit revised national plans with indications of what action, if any, by other governments was needed to ensure their successful execution. Alternatively, if the analysis of investment plans revealed the prospect of a uranium glut, the council would consider how a reduction in the rate of increase in uranium production might be shared.

Both a prospective shortage and a prospective glut could be expected to bring out the diverging interests of producing and consuming countries. Producers would—from the point of view of consumers—be all too ready to solve a shortage by allowing the price to rise and to deal with a surplus in a manner suspiciously like that of a cartel. Consumers, on the other hand, would be seen by producers as anxious to avoid the cost of preventing a shortage and eager to take advantage of a surplus. Hope that a consensus could be reached in dealing with prospective imbalances of supply and demand would rest on the common interest of suppliers and consumers in avoiding sharp fluctuations in the price of uranium.

A consultative system has been outlined above as if it would be an entirely new enterprise. The question naturally arises whether the International Atomic Energy Agency or the OECD Nuclear Energy Agency (NEA) could provide both a forum for consultation among governments and the required secretariat. There can be no doubt on the latter score; both the IAEA and the NEA possess substantial technical resources that should be drawn on by any new consultative system.[33] The IAEA with its wide international membership would be a more suitable consultative forum than the NEA because the Organisation for Economic Co-operation and Development, of which the NEA is a part, consists entirely of non-Communist industrialized states.

The IAEA could conceivably launch the kind of consultative system described above if the governments principally concerned decided it would be desirable. The IAEA might also provide logistic support and, with the NEA, technical services to the consultative system on a reimbursable basis. That system should, however, not be managed by the IAEA, although it could be formally linked to the IAEA.

Ensuring the Supply of Enrichment Services

At first sight, the problem of dealing with a shortage of enrichment services bears some resemblance to that of stabilizing the market for natural uranium. The markets for natural uranium and enrichment services are quite different, however, and a measure that might work in one case could be unsuitable in the other.

Thus a commodity agreement could in theory prevent sharp fluctuations in the price of natural uranium, although there would be serious practical difficulties. It is difficult, however, to see how even a theoretically workable commodity agreement could be formulated for enrichment services. In a sense the enrichment market is already stabilized by reason

33. The staffs of these two agencies are accustomed to working together. The authoritative reports, *Uranium: Resources, Production and Demand,* are their joint product.

of its peculiar structure. Prices are dictated by the sellers and are often adjusted to reflect costs. Uniformity of prices has not developed because of the special relationships between some sellers and buyers, and because price is only one of the numerous and complex provisions in enrichment contracts. Also of considerable importance in judging the relevance of a commodity agreement is the lack of an easily determined spot price that might be manipulated by the operation of a buffer stock.

Giving an international institution responsibility for preventing a shortage of enrichment services could have considerable merit from a nonproliferation standpoint. If the governments principally concerned— those that now have enrichment plants or a serious interest in building them—could agree to an international institution with the exclusive right to construct new enrichment facilities, one path to the acquisition of nuclear weapons would be made more difficult. If there could be further agreement that the new facilities would be located only in nuclear weapon states, the nonproliferation gains would be even more substantial.

Agreement to internationalize all new enrichment facilities would be difficult to achieve at present, and obtaining agreement to limit them to nuclear weapon states would be virtually impossible. Yet the case for an international institution without these nonproliferation advantages is not strong. The problem of ensuring fuel availability, it must be remembered, is ensuring a timely decision by one or more of a small group of governments to build additional enrichment capacity. The same governments would have to provide major support for any internationally sponsored enrichment project. There is no reason to believe that they would be more likely to commit funds to an international enrichment plant than they would to a national one.

If a commodity agreement would be inappropriate and an institutional approach at best premature, a remaining possibility would be to include enrichment services in the consultative system discussed earlier for the natural uranium market. These consultations could then be addressed more broadly to assuring nuclear fuel supplies. In the case of enrichment services, the consultations would provide interested parties with more re- fined projections of supply and demand. If, as now appears likely, a short- age were foreseen in the late 1990s, efforts could be made to stimulate the timely construction of new capacity.

The existence of a consultative system would facilitate both cross- investments by one country in enrichment projects in another, and the formation of consortia to undertake such projects jointly. Such arrangements would not only make it easier to mobilize needed capital, but would also tend to increase the confidence of participants in their future nuclear fuel supplies.

Conclusions

The various measures discussed in this chapter must be judged in terms of both feasibility and effectiveness. Feasibility is primarily a political question, although financial cost must also be weighed. Effectiveness has two aspects: facilitation of the development of civil nuclear energy and discouragement of national actions that would increase the risk of the spread of nuclear weapons.

Interruptions of Fuel Supplies

Three measures to deal with short-term interruptions of nuclear fuel supplies were considered above: cross-guarantees, cross-guarantees backed by dedicated stockpiles, and an international nuclear fuel bank. These measures represent a continuum of decreasing feasibility and increasing effectiveness.

The decreasing feasibility is in part a matter of cost. In a simple system of cross-guarantees, costs are not likely to be significant. Adding dedicated stockpiles involves carrying charges that could be substantial. A fuel bank would also have to have a stockpile and would incur other costs as well.

Decreasing feasibility also reflects greater complexity when moving from guarantees to stockpiles to a bank. Greater complexity means more difficulty in getting governments to agree. It also probably means more problems in adjusting to, or bringing about changes in, existing national policies.

On grounds of feasibility, then, the creation of a system of simple cross-guarantees would appear to deserve priority. Such a system would lack the credibility of guarantees backed by dedicated stockpiles and also the credibility of a fuel bank in which suppliers and consumers would share control. A system of cross-guarantees therefore could be viewed as a useful first step, pending emergence of a clear need to move on first to a system of guarantees backed by dedicated stockpiles and possibly later to an international nuclear fuel bank.

The need for measures more elaborate than cross-guarantees might in fact never arise. Experience may demonstrate that because of the resiliency of the nuclear fuel cycle, ad hoc expedients can deal with nonpolitical interruptions of fuel supplies. The most likely cause of political interruptions—disputes over nonproliferation policy—could be virtually eliminated if a broad international consensus were achieved on the rules of trade in sensitive nuclear materials, equipment, and technology.

Collusion among Suppliers

The danger of an economic cartel in natural uranium was seen to be a manifestation of market imperfections that could cause large, unpredictable price fluctuations. And the fear of a nonproliferation cartel in uranium was seen as a reflection of the lack of an international consensus on how to develop nuclear power without making the spread of nuclear weapons more likely.

Measures addressed specifically to preventing an economic cartel (as opposed to measures designed to stabilize the market) were ruled out as ineffective or counterproductive. It was concluded that a nonproliferation cartel could be made less likely by bringing consumers, as well as suppliers, into consultations on the rules of trade in sensitive nuclear materials, equipment, and technology.

Natural Uranium Market

Three approaches toward stabilizing the market for natural uranium were considered: a commodity agreement, an international institution, and a system of intergovernmental consultations. Whether the countries principally interested in the uranium market as producers, consumers, or both are ready for the first two of these measures is questionable. In any case serious grounds exist for doubting the effectiveness of either.

A commodity agreement would have little chance of success unless it established a buffer stock that could be built up or drawn down to counter undesired price fluctuations. Such an operation would have to be financed by participating governments, and the cost would increase if the target price range lagged too far behind changing market conditions. There is little reason to hope that governments with different interests would permit the managers of the buffer stock to make timely changes in the target price range, or provide the money needed for the prolonged defense of a price range that was under heavy market pressure.

An international institution created to promote the favorable evolution of the uranium market over the long run could succeed only if it had a broad mandate, good management, and adequate initial financing. Sponsoring governments are unlikely to provide these prerequisites of success at this time.

The only feasible approach to the problem of stabilizing the uranium market appears to be the establishment of a system of intergovernmental consultations. At periodic meetings governmental representatives could discuss projections of supply and demand and special studies prepared by a small secretariat. Solutions to impending problems could be discussed, but the meetings would have no authority to direct particular remedial measures.

Whether so informal an approach would be sufficient is uncertain. If experience showed that it was not, the international climate might become conducive to a more structured effort. Of the two such efforts discussed in this chapter, an international institution appears much more promising than a commodity agreement.

Supply of Enrichment Services

The major problem with respect to the supply of enrichment services is the danger of an enrichment capacity shortage in the 1990s. A commodity agreement would not even be theoretically applicable to the enrichment market. Giving an international institution responsibility for building needed new enrichment capacity, to the exclusion of further national efforts, could have attractions from the nonproliferation point of view. It is doubtful, however, whether the few governments that are now in the enrichment business would agree at this time to internationalize future enrichment facilities.

The most feasible approach in the enrichment market, as in the market for natural uranium, is to rely on intergovernmental consultations. The system of consultations might well embrace all aspects of the nuclear fuel supply, including assuring the construction of adequate enrichment capacity.

CHAPTER FOUR

The Back End of the
Fuel Cycle

THE BACK END of the nuclear fuel cycle includes the various actions that might be taken with respect to spent nuclear fuel.[1] Spent nuclear fuel bears little resemblance to the residues left by other fuels. It is highly radioactive, and some of its components will remain so for thousands of years. It contains residual uranium[2] and plutonium[3] that could be extracted by chemical reprocessing and recycled as nuclear fuel. The plutonium could also be used in nuclear weapons.

Because of these characteristics, the management of spent nuclear fuel involves difficult environmental, economic, and security problems, some of which require international solutions. This study is primarily concerned with the security aspects of the management of spent fuel, but environmental and economic aspects also deserve attention. For ease of

1. After nuclear fuel has been subjected to neutron radiation in a reactor for a period of time, its main fissionable component (U^{235} in current reactors, both light water and heavy water) becomes depleted, and it loses its ability to contribute effectively to a sustained nuclear reaction. This spent fuel must be removed from the reactor and replaced by fresh fuel.

2. The percentage of U^{235} in residual uranium from a heavy water reactor (HWR) is too low to make its recycling in current reactors attractive. Residual uranium from a light water reactor (LWR), however, contains a somewhat higher percentage of U^{235} than does uranium in its natural state (0.8 percent as opposed to 0.7 percent). It may therefore be economic under some circumstances to recycle residual uranium from an LWR after re-enriching it to 3–4 percent U^{235}.

3. The plutonium is created in the reactor by the irradiation of U^{238}.

presentation, the following discussion refers to spent fuel from today's dominant light water reactors (LWRs), unless otherwise indicated.

Alternatives for Managing Spent Fuel

The end point in the management of spent nuclear fuel is a final disposal that removes the fuel or its dangerous radioactive components from the biosphere permanently. At present the question of the best means of final disposal has not been resolved and is the subject of intense public controversy in a number of countries. But it is not necessary to take sides in this controversy in order to examine the problems arising before final disposal.

Spent fuel can follow two general paths after discharge and a period of storage in a pool at a reactor. It can be reprocessed to extract the plutonium and residual uranium, with the remaining waste products consigned to final disposal. Or it can be held in retrievable storage for varying periods of time, pending a decision on reprocessing or disposal without reprocessing.

Opinions vary concerning the need to reprocess spent fuel. Proponents argue that reprocessing makes final disposal easier by separating different categories of waste products.[4] They also argue that the plutonium and residual uranium in spent fuel must be recaptured to stretch the limited supplies of natural uranium.[5] Opponents of reprocessing emphasize the security dangers involved in creating inventories of separated plutonium. They argue that final disposal of spent fuel without reprocessing is quite feasible, and that uranium resources are adequate to meet needs for at least the remainder of the century. They further contend that the cost of

4. This is the position of the governments of a number of industrialized countries. For example, at the Eleventh Annual Conference of the Japan Atomic Industrial Forum, held in Tokyo in March 1978, André Y. Giraud, chairman, French Atomic Energy Commission, stated that "ecological considerations alone would make reprocessing necessary." At the same conference, Manfred Popp of the West German Ministry for Research and Technology declared that "reprocessing is being considered a prerequisite for sufficiently safe waste management."

5. Recycling plutonium and residual uranium in LWRs reduces requirements for natural uranium by up to 30 percent and for enrichment services by up to 20 percent. Nuclear Energy Agency, Organisation for Economic Co-operation and Development, *Objectives, Concepts and Strategies for the Management of Radioactive Waste Arising from Nuclear Power Programmes* (Paris: OECD, 1977), p. 36.

reprocessing may well exceed the savings achieved by recycling pluto-nium and residual uranium in the present generation of reactors.[6]

Proponents of reprocessing either claim that recycling is economic to-day or shift the argument to other grounds. They state that increased se-curity of fuel supply has a value that cannot be fully reflected in calcula-tions of the commercial cost and benefit of recycling. They further argue that reprocessing is necessary to gain the technical knowledge and ac-cumulate the supplies of plutonium that will be needed when fast breeder reactors come into use.[7] Opponents of reprocessing contend that ques-tions remain concerning the safety and economic feasibility of breeders and that in any case the decision to reprocess can be deferred.

Early emergence of a clear international consensus for or against re-processing is not likely. The misgivings of the United States, the principal proponent of deferring the reprocessing decision, will probably persist. And the commitments of several other industrialized nations to energy policies involving reprocessing will not easily be shaken. The United States has considerable leverage on the issue because of its legal right to approve or disapprove the reprocessing of a large part of spent fuel of U.S. origin,[8] and because it is still the major supplier of enrichment ser-

6. See *Report to the President by the Interagency Review Group on Nuclear Waste Management* (Department of Energy, 1979), p. 73. The report finds that "re-processing is not required to assure safe disposal of commercial spent fuel in appro-priately chosen geological environments." The International Nuclear Fuel Cycle Evaluation came to much the same conclusion by finding that radioactive wastes from any of the fuel cycle studies (including once-through cycles that do not re-process spent fuel) "can be managed and disposed of with a high degree of safety and without undue risk to man or the environment." INFCE, *Waste Management and Disposal: Report of Working Group 7*, INFCE/PC/2/7 (Vienna: International Atomic Energy Agency, 1980), p. 13.

See Nuclear Energy Policy Study Group, *Nuclear Power Issues and Choices* (Ballinger, 1977), pp. 92–94; and Ted Greenwood, "Why Reprocess?" in Abram Chayes and W. Bennett Lewis, eds., *International Arrangements for Nuclear Fuel Reprocessing* (Ballinger, 1977), p. 17, for more on opposition to reprocessing.

7. Fast breeder reactors, which are being developed in several industrialized countries, may be able to generate up to 1.4 times as much fissionable fuel as they consume (*Nuclear Power Issues and Choices*, p. 337). In the form of breeder given most attention, this generated fuel is plutonium, which can be obtained for recycling only by reprocessing. The initial fuel load of breeders can be either plutonium or enriched uranium, or a mixture of the two. The argument is complicated by the fact that some countries may start operating advanced thermal reactors before the breeders. These reactors are designed to use a mixture of plutonium and uranium.

8. Most U.S. agreements for cooperation with other countries in the field of nuclear energy give the United States this right. The notable exception is the U.S. agreement with the European Atomic Energy Community (Euratom).

vices to non-Communist countries. The United States could not, however, stop all reprocessing, even if it were prepared to exert very heavy pressure.

Part of the spent fuel arising from the operation of commercial reactors clearly will be reprocessed. Some already has been.[9] And some spent fuel will be placed in retrievable storage to await either reprocessing or final disposal. Retrievable storage of a considerable proportion of the spent fuel that will arise in the next decade or so is in fact inevitable. Spent fuel arisings will exceed reprocessing capacity for many years,[10] and officially approved means of final disposal of spent fuel do not yet exist in any non-Communist country. This discussion therefore explores the problems involved in both options for managing spent nuclear fuel: retrievable storage and reprocessing.

Retrievable Storage

Virtually all spent fuel that has arisen thus far in the nuclear age is stored under water in pools at the reactors from which it was removed.[11] These pools were originally designed to hold 1⅓ to 1⅔ fuel cores, or the amount of spent fuel generated over about five years. In a number of countries, the capacity of the pools is being expanded to accommodate spent fuel from ten to fifteen years of reactor operations.

Additional pools could in theory be built near reactors, but this is not always possible owing to lack of space or the opposition of local residents. Also, if the fuel rods deteriorate, removing them from the pools could be a problem.

As more spent fuel accumulates at reactors, pressure to move it elsewhere will increase. If final disposal is ruled out, and if reprocessing capacity is not immediately available, some form of retrievable storage away from reactors will have to be provided. One possibility is centralized storage in the country in which the spent fuel was generated. Other possibilities are storage in the country that originally supplied the fuel, by re-

9. See Greenwood, "Why Reprocess?" pp. 18–24.
10. OECD Nuclear Energy Agency, *Nuclear Fuel Cycle Requirements and Supply Considerations, through the Long-Term* (Paris: OECD, 1978), pp. 33–37.
11. For a survey of storage facilities at and away from reactors, see INFCE, *Spent Fuel Management: Report of Working Group 6,* INFCE/PC/2/6 (Vienna: IAEA, 1980), pp. 33–38.

processors, or in regional facilities established under multinational auspices.

STORAGE BY CONSUMING COUNTRIES. If there is no alternative, countries with nuclear power plants can be expected to develop national storage facilities for spent fuel. From an economic point of view, this would not in every case be the best solution to the problem caused by the accumulation of spent fuel at reactors. There are probably significant economies of scale in the retrievable storage of spent fuel, and countries with only a few power reactors would be unable to take full advantage of those economies.[12]

National storage of spent fuel by individual consuming countries would also not be the best arrangement from a nonproliferation point of view. Although most national spent fuel depositories would presumably be placed under international safeguards, the inventories of unseparated plutonium under national control would grow with the passage of time, and more and more of it would become less radioactive and easier to reprocess.

Some governments of nonnuclear weapon states might find the construction of small national reprocessing plants increasingly attractive. Although the immediate gain thus sought might well be only an increase in energy security, a large step toward a nuclear weapon capability would also have been taken.

This development might in theory be prevented or retarded by establishing international criteria for reprocessing spent fuel held in national depositories. The governments concerned would, however, have little incentive to limit their own freedom of action. And even if they agreed to do so, the reality of their physical control over the spent fuel depositories would not be changed.

STORAGE BY SUPPLYING COUNTRIES. The countries providing enrichment services could also store spent fuel for their customers. They could require the return of spent fuel, as the Soviet Union does with its customers in Eastern Europe.[13] Or they could offer to accept voluntary deposits

12. See the economic analysis of spent fuel storage costs by Boyce Greer and Mark Dalzell in "Nuclear Nonproliferation and the International Management of Spent Reactor Fuel," report of the Nuclear Nonproliferation Study Group (Harvard University, 1979).

13. Gloria Duffy, *Soviet Nuclear Exports*, P-6044 (Santa Monica, Calif.: Rand Corp., 1977), p. 6.

of spent fuel, as the United States has said it might do to a limited extent.[14]

The obligatory return of spent fuel to supplying countries (other than the current, long-standing arrangements between the Soviet Union and the Communist nations of Eastern Europe) is probably not negotiable. If one major enricher tried to impose this rule on its customers, some of them might take their business elsewhere. The near-monopoly of the United States in the provision of enrichment services is a thing of the past, and a surplus of enrichment capacity is anticipated in the 1980s.

The major enrichers—the United States, France (through its control of Eurodif), and Urenco (controlled jointly by the United Kingdom, the Netherlands, and West Germany)—could conceivably agree to require the return of spent fuel, but this is not likely to happen. For such a scheme to work, participants would have to agree on terms to be granted depositors of spent fuel, including the conditions under which withdrawals would be permitted. (Lacking such agreement, a particular enricher could gain a competitive advantage.) Given the different views on nonproliferation issues of the countries concerned, particularly on the question of reprocessing spent fuel, developing a common set of terms would be difficult. If initial agreement were achieved, the enrichers would still face the continuing problem of maintaining a united front in the face of the opposition of many fuel-importing countries.

Some fuel importers would regard an agreement by major enrichers to require the return of spent fuel as an effort to keep them in a permanent state of dependence and as a threat to their ability to provide for their own energy needs. To the best of their abilities, some of them would try to get out from under the power of the enrichers by seeking other sources of enriched uranium, building heavy water reactors that use natural uranium, and developing their own enrichment facilities. In time, the nonproliferation advantages of a system requiring return of spent fuel would at least in part be counterbalanced by increases in the independent nuclear capabilities of the fuel-importing countries.

14. At the opening session of the International Nuclear Fuel Cycle Evaluation, President Jimmy Carter declared, "We are also eager to help solve the problem of the disposal of spent nuclear fuel itself. We cannot provide storage for the major portion of the world's spent fuel, but we are willing to cooperate. And when a nation demonstrates to us your need for spent nuclear fuel storage, we hope to be prepared to accept that responsibility, working closely with you." "INFCE: Remarks at the First Plenary Session of the Organizing Conference, October 19, 1977," *Public Papers of the Presidents: Jimmy Carter,* vol. 2 (Government Printing Office, 1978), pp. 1812–14.

The voluntary return of spent fuel to the supplying countries would probably be feasible under some circumstances, but no precedent exists for this arrangement. The limited U.S. offer to store spent fuel from other countries has not yet been put into effect.[15]

A fuel-importing country would presumably be willing to return spent fuel to the country of origin if it were economically advantageous. If finding a suitable storage site within its own borders happened to be difficult, the fuel importer might even be willing to pay a modest premium to store its spent fuel elsewhere.

In the simplest case, the country returning the spent fuel would retain ownership over it and would be permitted to withdraw it at any time for any purpose. The fuel importer would compare the cost of moving spent fuel to a new facility within its own borders and storing it there, with the cost of shipping it to the supplying country and paying storage charges. The key economic question would be whether the economies of scale in the supplying country's storage facility exceeded any savings in transportation cost realized by keeping the spent fuel at home. If the supplying country gave its customers the full advantage of the economies of scale, it appears reasonable to assume that in some cases storage there would be cheaper than in the fuel-importing country.

The calculations of the fuel-importing country would be more complicated if the fuel supplier sought to control the withdrawal of spent fuel returned to it for storage. The importer would have to consider the probability of its wanting to reprocess the spent fuel at some future time and whether the supplying country would agree to the withdrawal of fuel. Criteria governing withdrawals might be agreed on, but uncertainties would remain that would make the return of spent fuel to the supplying country much less attractive from the point of view of the fuel-importing country.

It might be easier therefore to negotiate a straightforward transfer of ownership of the spent fuel from the importing to the supplying country. If this were done, the supplier might still request payment for relieving the importer of its waste-disposal problem. It is much more likely, how-

15. The Nuclear Non-Proliferation Act of 1978 (22 U.S.C. 3201) does, however, specify the procedures to be followed by the U.S. government in entering into agreements to accept spent fuel from other countries. The act added section 131 to the Atomic Energy Act of 1954. Section 131(f) deals with the storage or other disposition of foreign spent fuel in the United States. With limited exceptions, Congress is given sixty days in which it can disapprove any arrangement to accept foreign spent fuel.

ever, that the supplying country would have to pay for title to the spent fuel.

The supplying country would presumably place a nonproliferation value on recovering the spent fuel from the control of the fuel-importing country. Otherwise, it would not be willing to accept the spent fuel at all.[16] The fuel-importing country would be aware of the nonproliferation motivation of the supplying country, and might argue that it was entitled to compensation for the plutonium and residual uranium in the spent fuel.

The price paid for the spent fuel might in fact purport to be the value of the plutonium and uranium in it. This value is in principle the present discounted value of the fresh fuel that it would replace in a power reactor, minus the present discounted value of various costs, including transportation, storage, reprocessing, re-enrichment of the residual uranium, fuel fabrication, and waste disposal.[17] Estimating the value of spent fuel therefore requires assumptions concerning the time of recycling, the price of uranium at that time, the costs to be covered, and the appropriate discount rate.

Opinions may differ on all of these variables. The methodology used to estimate the value of the contained plutonium and residual uranium might structure negotiations over a buy-back of spent fuel by the supplying country. But this methodology cannot determine the outcome. Any price agreed upon would reflect political considerations, as much as economic ones.

An alternative to paying in money for spent fuel would be for the supplying country to reimburse the importing country in enriched uranium equivalent in fuel value to the plutonium and residual uranium in the spent fuel. This would respond directly to the interest of the fuel-importing country in security of energy supply. Whether such an arrangement would be a fair exchange in a commercial sense is at best uncertain.[18]

16. But if the anticipated surplus of enrichment capacity occurs, enrichers might then become willing to buy back spent fuel to gain a competitive advantage, quite apart from any nonproliferation considerations.

17. For a thorough exploration of the methodology of estimating the value of spent fuel, see Kenneth A. Solomon, *Nuclear Reactor Spent Fuel Valuation: Procedure, Applications, and Analysis,* R-2239-DOE, prepared for the Department of Energy (Santa Monica, Calif.: Rand Corp., 1978).

18. The difficulty of estimating the value of the plutonium and residual uranium in spent fuel has already been noted. It would be only a coincidence if that value per ton of spent fuel equaled the current cost of the amount of fresh enriched uranium yielding the same energy in a power reactor.

From the nonproliferation point of view, the voluntary return of spent fuel to the fuel-supplying country would clearly have advantages. Moving spent fuel from fuel-importing, nonnuclear weapon states to the countries that originally supplied the fuel would reduce incentives to build national reprocessing plants as a means of facilitating the disposal of nuclear waste. No new proliferation risk would be created, because the suppliers of LWR fuel, with which we are concerned here, necessarily possess enrichment plants and already have (or could readily acquire) the means of making the explosive component of nuclear weapons. The largest enrichment plants are in fact in the United States, the Soviet Union, and France, which already have nuclear weapons.

Whether the return of spent fuel to the supplying countries is politically feasible at this time, however, is questionable. The leaders of supplying countries must cope with public opposition to accepting what has been called other people's nuclear garbage. They must be able to argue convincingly that security advantages of taking back spent fuel from their customers outweigh the environmental risks. A simple bailment with no restrictions on withdrawals might not be good enough for a skeptical public. A repurchase of spent fuel would be more defensible in terms of nonproliferation goals, but resistance to paying more than a nominal price is likely.[19] Because of these obstacles, it cannot be assumed that other suppliers will follow the U.S. offer to accept limited deposits of spent fuel, or even that action will be taken on that offer.

STORAGE BY REPROCESSORS. Spent fuel deposited in storage facilities at reprocessing plants is obviously intended for reprocessing. It is therefore in a different category from spent fuel placed in storage pending a decision on reprocessing or final disposal. Storage of spent fuel by reprocessors does, however, relieve fuel consumers of the need to develop other away-from-reactor storage facilities. It must therefore be taken into account in dealing with the overall problem of storing spent fuel.

Interim storage of spent fuel by reprocessors will probably become increasingly important during the next few years. The two major reprocessors, British Nuclear Fuels, Ltd. (BNFL) and Compagnie Générale des Matières Nucléaires (Cogema) have between them only enough storage capacity to hold 40 years of spent fuel arisings from one 1,000-MWe

19. As long as the U.S. government continues to advocate the deferral of reprocessing, it will have an especially hard time convincing the public that it should pay the full value of spent fuel purchased from other countries.

LWR. By 1985, however, their storage capacity will have increased sevenfold.[20] They appear to be accepting spent fuel that they will not be able to reprocess for some time.

How far this process will go is not clear. As the major reprocessors reach currently planned reprocessing capacity, they could adjust their stocks of spent fuel to the minimum level needed to ensure smooth operation of their plants. Or they could in effect go into the storage business by accepting larger deposits of spent fuel. They might even continuously expand their storage facilities to accommodate their customers. Since the reprocessors would benefit from experience and the economies of scale, they could probably provide storage space more cheaply than some fuel-importing countries could build for themselves.

The commercial calculations of reprocessors and fuel-importing countries will not, however, be the only determinants of how much spent fuel is stored at reprocessing plants. Much of the spent fuel that will arise in the next decade or so is of U.S. origin, and under existing agreements with other countries (except the European Community), that fuel can be reprocessed only with U.S. approval.[21] Whether reprocessors would be willing to store fuel that may not be reprocessed is at least questionable.

If storing spent fuel at reprocessing plants means committing it to the reprocessing path, the United States and possibly other suppliers of natural uranium or enrichment services can be expected to have serious misgivings. Quite apart from their legal rights over spent fuel, the fuel-supplying nations have substantial influence over the nuclear energy policies of many fuel importers. The supplying countries might well use their influence to try to block or retard the growth of stocks of spent fuel at reprocessing plants.[22]

STORAGE IN REGIONAL FACILITIES. The problem of storing spent fuel could be approached regionally. Several countries in the same part of the

20. In 1979 BNFL's storage capacity at Windscale was 1,000 metric tons. By 1985 capacity will be increased to 4,400 tons with plans eventually to reach 5,400 tons. Cogema's storage capacity at La Hague is 250 tons and will be increased to 4,250 tons by 1985.

21. Section 404(a) of the NNPA directs the president to renegotiate agreements that do not now give the United States this power.

22. Opposition to the accumulation of large stocks of spent fuel at reprocessing plants would of course disappear if agreement could be reached on reprocessing as part of the new international plutonium management and storage system discussed later in this chapter.

world could jointly build and operate a storage facility. Such a facility would have financial advantages for countries with small nuclear power programs. It would also be attractive to countries that, because of geology, population density, or public resistance, might have difficulty finding suitable sites for national storage facilities.

From a nonproliferation standpoint, the storage of spent fuel in regional facilities would also be preferable to a continued build-up of spent fuel inventories under purely national control. This would be so even if withdrawals of spent fuel could be made without restriction, since any withdrawals would attract attention and their purpose could be questioned. Imposing restrictions on withdrawals would probably be counterproductive by discouraging participation in regional storage arrangements.

Several practical problems would have to be solved to achieve the theoretical benefits of regional storage of spent fuel. Assuming that several countries were interested in regional storage (which cannot of course be taken for granted), agreement would have to be reached on: the organization of the entity that would build and operate the facility; the means of financing construction; the allocation of operating expenses; and the choice of a site. (These and other issues are discussed in chapter 5.)

The resolution of these questions—if agreement on them is ever achieved—would be strongly influenced by the participants' assumptions about the eventual disposition of their spent fuel. For example, if they believed permanent disposal without reprocessing was most likely, sites suitable for such disposal, as well as for retrievable storage, would be sought. If (as appears more likely) they believed reprocessing would be desirable, sites suitable for a reprocessing plant would be given priority.

These practical problems could presumably be solved if potential participants saw clear advantages in the regional storage of spent fuel. In some parts of the world (South Asia and possibly also South America), the political incompatibility of potential participants may rule out regional storage arrangements. The European Atomic Energy Community (Euratom), however, provides a legal framework for regional storage in Western Europe, and the United States has shown interest in promoting the establishment of a multinational spent fuel storage facility on a Pacific island. This project was discussed inconclusively by U.S. and Japanese officials on two occasions during 1979, and in early 1980, Japan agreed to share with the United States the cost of a feasibility study of the project.[23]

In all areas, the cost of regional, as opposed to national, storage would be an especially important consideration. If regional storage required transportation of spent fuel over long distances and heavy expenditures on infrastructure (such as port facilities, utilities, and roads), it could cost considerably more than national storage, despite the economies of scale provided for some participants. Regional storage would not necessarily be precluded, however, simply because it was more expensive than national storage. Difficulties in locating a suitable site on their own territories might make some countries willing to accept the higher cost of regional storage. The suppliers of nuclear fuel could also make regional storage more attractive to importers if it were presented as part of a larger plan for international cooperation in nuclear energy.

Reprocessing

In considering reprocessing as a means of managing spent fuel, several simplifying assumptions have been made.

First, it is assumed that the plutonium and the residual uranium extracted from spent fuel by reprocessing will be retained for eventual use as reactor fuel and will not be discarded as waste.

Second, the plutonium emerging from a reprocessing plant is in a form that could easily be diverted to military use. A number of "technical fixes" have been proposed that would make plutonium less accessible for military purposes: diluting the plutonium (that is, never separating it from the uranium); creating or maintaining a radiation barrier (spiking the plutonium with radioactive material or never separating it from all radioactive fission products); and reducing access to plutonium by designing side-by-side reprocessing and fuel fabrication plants. These expedients may be useful supplements to other safeguards, but they would not seriously inhibit diversion by a national government, nor would they have much effect on the relative merits of the various largely institutional arrangements being considered in this study.

23. See *Japan Economic Journal* (March 20, 1979), p. 3; *Washington Post,* September 23, 1979; and *Nuclear Engineering International,* vol. 25 (March 1980), p. 5.

Third, as was the case in the discussion of retrievable storage, the following will be concerned solely with spent fuel from light water reactors unless otherwise indicated.

A decision to reprocess raises three fundamental questions:
—Where should reprocessing take place?
—Should ownership and management of reprocessing plants be national or multinational?
—How can diversion of plutonium, at reprocessing plants or later in the fuel cycle, be prevented?

LOCATION OF REPROCESSING. If nonproliferation were the only consideration, reprocessing plants should be restricted to nuclear weapon states. But this arrangement would never be accepted by the nonnuclear weapon states. Moreover, as has been pointed out, a number of such states already have small reprocessing plants, and some of them may be major reprocessors before the end of the century.

An alternative, which is somewhat more consistent with present trends, favors limiting reprocessing plants to nuclear weapon and "fuel cycle states."[24] A fuel cycle state is a country whose civil nuclear energy program is, or will be, large enough to support a reprocessing plant of economic size.[25] Another formulation, amounting to much the same thing, advocates the construction only of large plants.[26] Such plants would presumably be built in countries with large nuclear energy programs—again, the nuclear weapon and fuel cycle states.

Under either of these formulations, the existing or planned large reprocessing plants in France, West Germany, Italy, Japan, and the United

24. See Ryukichi Imai, "A Japanese Proposal to Resolve INFCE Impasse: Narrow Down the Issues and Focus on the Workable," *Atoms in Japan,* vol. 22 (September 1978).

25. Conventional wisdom says the economic capacity is at least 1,500 tons annually. Such a plant could reprocess spent fuel arising from fifty 1,000-MWe reactors. There is some reason to believe that the unit reprocessing costs of a 1,500-ton plant would be a third less than those of a plant half that size. On the other hand, the economies of scale probably do not end at 1,500 tons.

26. See Mason Willrich, "A Workable International Nuclear Energy Regime," *Washington Quarterly,* vol. 2 (Spring 1979), pp. 13–30. Another related formulation is that of Joseph S. Nye, Jr., who called for avoidance of "sensitive facilities that involve weapons-usable materials unless they can be shown to be economically necessary." Address before the Uranium Institute, London, July 12, 1978, reprinted in *U.S. Department of State Bulletin,* vol. 78 (October 1978), p. 42.

Kingdom would qualify. The small plants in Belgium and India would not.[27] Presumably, these could be grandfathered in, or approved under an exemption for existing pilot plants. Any additional small plants built in the future would be regarded as unjustified and therefore illegitimate.

A regime of large plants only (or one limiting new plants to nuclear weapon and fuel cycle states) would have the effect at least temporarily of confining most reprocessing activity to countries that are commonly regarded as relatively safe from the nonproliferation point of view. Such a policy would not, however, prevent the eventual construction of plants in countries that are not so safe. Nor could it keep today's safe countries from becoming less so in the future.

In any event, a large plant policy would be seen by the developing countries as discriminatory and as a threat to their ability to increase the security of their energy supply over the long run. Whether the industrialized countries could agree on this policy and then put together a combination of incentives, controls, and sanctions that would induce the developing countries to accept this policy is at best uncertain.

Certainly, controls on the transfer of reprocessing technology to unapproved locations would not be enough to ensure conformity to a large plant policy. A number of developing countries already know something about reprocessing and could in time build plants of their own. In some situations, one or more industrialized country might be able to block the construction of a small (or, in their eyes, unjustified) reprocessing plant by threatening economic or other sanctions.[28] Fuel suppliers with contractual rights to veto the reprocessing of fuel they had originally supplied would be in an especially good position to discourage the building of new reprocessing facilities.

A policy based entirely on controls and sanctions would, however, involve heavy political costs for the industrialized nations. Whether they could maintain a common front in the face of the opposition of the devel-

27. It might require some stretching to call Italy a fuel cycle state, and West Germany might also fall short of the mark if its nuclear power program continues to encounter strong public opposition. But these countries and Belgium could be included by regarding the entire European Community as a fuel cycle state.

28. Such sanctions may have been at least implicit in the pressure the United States reportedly put on South Korea to drop its plans to buy a reprocessing plant from a French firm. The termination of U.S. aid to Pakistan was precipitated by evidence that Pakistan was seeking an enrichment capability, but it was taken in the context of Pakistan's continued efforts to build a reprocessing plant.

oping countries is also questionable. In any event, an effort to impose restrictions on the developing countries would scarcely be the way to obtain their cooperation in measures to keep the growth of civil nuclear energy from contributing to the spread of nuclear weapons.

Controls and the implicit threat of sanctions could have a useful influence in limiting the number of reprocessing plants, but incentives would also have to be offered to gain the concurrence of countries not now owning such plants. These incentives might include access to international storage facilities for spent fuel and the opportunity to become partners in multinational reprocessing plants.

OWNERSHIP AND MANAGEMENT OF PLANTS. With one minor exception, all existing reprocessing plants have been nationally owned.[29] Under present plans, all reprocessing plants that will come on line between now and 1990 will also be nationally owned. (National ownership implies national management.)

In recent years some observers, particularly in the United States, have come to regard multinational ownership of reprocessing plants as better than national ownership.[30] The owners of different nationalities, it is assumed, would not conspire to divert plutonium to nonpeaceful use, but would act to prevent such diversion by any of their number. It is often assumed that participation in a multinational plant would be regarded by many countries as an attractive alternative to building their own plants. But the validity of these assumptions cannot be tested in the abstract, and will vary with the composition, organization, and economic prospects of specific multinational reprocessing ventures.

One can imagine multinational groupings that would be as prone to abuse a reprocessing capability as any single nation. Such groupings are not likely, however. Combinations of countries that might form a multi-

29. The exception is Eurochemic, which was formed in 1959 by thirteen of the countries belonging to the European Nuclear Energy Agency. Eurochemic operated a pilot reprocessing plant at Mol, Belgium, from 1966 until 1974. United Reprocessors, Ltd., is a multinational corporation, but it does not own or invest in reprocessing plants. It was formed by British, French, and German reprocessing interests to coordinate development of the industry and to share technology. See Chayes and Lewis, *International Arrangements for Nuclear Fuel Reprocessing*, especially pp. 23, 85, and 182–85.

30. A variant of this position is incorporated in the U.S. NNPA. For example, the fuel assurances authorized by the act are explicitly denied nations that fail to place existing reprocessing facilities "under effective international auspices and inspection" (sec. 104[d]).

national reprocessing enterprise include one or more countries committed to opposing the further spread of nuclear weapons. This is the case because any feasible combination must include at least one country that possesses the technology for commercial reprocessing of power reactor fuel. The number of such countries today is small, and all of them appear to be firmly on the side of nonproliferation. These countries would, moreover, probably be deeply involved in the management and operation of a multinational reprocessing plant and could block any effort by other partners to use the plant for military purposes.

This advantage of multinational reprocessing must, however, be weighed against a possible disadvantage: by participating in a multinational reprocessing enterprise, some countries might gain access to technology and working experience that they do not now possess. They might as a consequence be enabled to circumvent supplier controls on the transmission of such technology and decide to build reprocessing plants of their own.

It is difficult to judge how serious this problem would be. On the one hand, denying some partners access to the technology by excluding them from managerial and sensitive operating positions would constitute discrimination and could well cause them to refuse to take part in the enterprise. On the other, knowledge gained through participation might not make much difference. Quite a bit of information on reprocessing can be found in the public literature, and international controls on the transmission of reprocessing technology are by no means airtight. Moreover, building a small plant to reprocess spent fuel that has been irradiated in a reactor for only a short time—and that is the best source of weapons-grade plutonium[31]—is relatively easy. Knowing how to carry out the much more difficult task of reprocessing spent fuel that has been in a commercial reactor for a year or more would be quite unnecessary.[32]

In any event, the main potential advantage of multinational reprocess-

31. Because it has been irradiated longer, spent fuel from commercial power plants contains larger amounts of an isotope of plutonium that reduces the reliability of nuclear weapons.

32. Dean Acheson took the title of his memoirs, *Present at the Creation* (Norton, 1969), from the following statement attributed to Alfonso X, "the Learned," King of Spain from 1252 to 1284: "Had I been present at the creation I would have given some useful hints for better ordering of the universe." One such hint (which could scarcely have occurred to King Alfonso) would have been to reverse the relative difficulties of reprocessing for military and civilian energy purposes.

ing from the nonproliferation standpoint is its limiting effect on the number of national reprocessing plants. To serve this purpose, multinational reprocessing must be relatively attractive.

The fuel-supplying countries could of course tip the scale heavily in favor of multinational reprocessing by vetoing or placing onerous restrictions on national reprocessing. But quite apart from this possibility, joining a multinational venture could be advantageous for countries with modest civil nuclear energy programs. Multinational plants would serve several countries, so they could be quite large and might achieve significant economies of scale. Many participants in multinational reprocessing ventures might therefore be able to extract the plutonium and residual uranium from their spent fuel more cheaply than they could if they built their own plants.[33]

Multinational reprocessing could therefore be seen by participants as an economical contribution to the long-term security of their energy supply. Many participants would also see reprocessing as a means of making it easier to dispose of the nuclear wastes in their spent fuel. But these advantages could be canceled if the rules on access to plutonium were more restrictive at multinational facilities than at national reprocessing plants. Discrimination against developing countries in access to plutonium could in fact be fatal to any effort to make multinational reprocessing the preferred, or at least the accepted, alternative to national reprocessing. Encouragement of multinational reprocessing could help to limit it to large plants. It could not be used to apply especially strict nonproliferation criteria to developing countries.

Multinational reprocessing enterprises could be organized to take over existing national plants or, more likely, to build new plants. In the latter case, plant location would be a major problem. Ideally, the plants should be built in nuclear weapon states or in countries with stable governments and little incentive to acquire nuclear weapons. These criteria would rule out the building of multinational reprocessing plants in many developing countries, and would reinforce the need to avoid discrimination against such countries in the structure of multinational enterprises.

33. INFCE supported the view that there are substantial economies of scale in reprocessing, but noted that one large developing country (apparently India) reported that in its particular circumstances multiple smaller reprocessing plants may be economic. INFCE, *Reprocessing, Plutonium Handling, Recycle: Report of Working Group 4*, INFCE/PC/2/4 (Vienna: 1980), pp. 10 and 103.

The organizers of a multinational reprocessing enterprise would have to resolve a number of difficult structural problems. The basic issues considered in designing a new international institution—control over policy, finance, legal status, and relationship with existing international organizations—will be examined in chapter 5.

A multinational reprocessing enterprise must also find a way to achieve an acceptable level of industrial efficiency. This could be difficult if the enterprise were staffed at all levels by a mixture of personnel from all participating countries. Differences of language, training, experience, and national outlook would greatly complicate the tasks of management.

From a managerial point of view, it would probably be best to entrust the operation of the plant to an executive agent who would rely on a staff drawn largely from a single participating country. This approach, however, might be regarded by other participants as discriminatory and even as an attempt to prevent them from acquiring reprocessing technology. Moreover, by making the enterprise less multinational (except at the policymaking level) this approach would reduce somewhat the protection against misuse of the reprocessing plant. Some compromise between multinational and single-nationality staffing would therefore be sought.

PREVENTING DIVERSION OF PLUTONIUM. Preventing the diversion of separated plutonium to nonpeaceful uses is one of the most serious problems facing the civil nuclear energy industry. Separated plutonium could be diverted at the reprocessing plant, at the fuel fabrication plant, at the reactors into which it is recycled, or while in transit between any of these points. In addition, substantial inventories of separated plutonium will almost certainly be built up in the future.[34]

Preventing the diversion of plutonium at various points in the fuel cycle is partly a matter of technical safeguards (detecting unauthorized movements of plutonium) and partly one of international policy (determining what movements are to be authorized).

The question of safeguards lies largely outside the scope of this study. It might be noted here, however, that the IAEA, which administers the international safeguard system, has had very little experience in the safe-

34. Nonmilitary stocks of separated plutonium in non-Communist countries in 1977 have been estimated to exceed 36 metric tons. For the remainder of the century, plutonium is likely to be separated from civil reactor spent fuel more rapidly than it is recycled and used as fuel. If no plutonium is recycled, stocks could exceed 160 tons in 1990 and 450 tons by the year 2000. Ibid., p. 35.

guarding of reprocessing plants. New techniques—probably involving greater emphasis on continuous containment and surveillance of plant perimeters, as well as modifications of the materials accountancy approach now stressed in safeguarding reactors—are being developed and refined. Changes in plant design may also facilitate the application of safeguards.

But the best place for exercising policy controls is probably at the plutonium storage depot. Policy can then be expressed in terms of how and where plutonium is to be stored, and the conditions under which it can be withdrawn from storage.

Plutonium could be stored under national control in the countries owning it (usually the countries generating the spent fuel from which it had been extracted). National storage facilities could be safeguarded, and withdrawals monitored to check on compliance with any agreed international rules. Nevertheless, national storage involves substantial risks. Stocks of plutonium, probably growing in size, would be dispersed widely throughout the world. Each stock would be under the effective physical control of a national government and subject to diversion to military use with little or no warning.

The establishment of international depositories for plutonium has been studied by the IAEA secretariat and others.[35] A legal basis for international plutonium depositories already exists, although it may not be entirely adequate to meet today's problems. Article XII.A.5 of the statute of the International Atomic Energy Agency authorizes the agency, as an adjunct to its administration of safeguards, to require the deposit with it of any plutonium not needed for research or use in reactors. The agency is required to return deposited plutonium promptly for these two peaceful uses, subject to international safeguards.[36] Article XII.A.5 has never been

35. IAEA Secretariat, "International Management and Storage of Plutonium and Spent Fuel" (Vienna: IAEA, July 1978). See also Russell W. Fox and Mason Willrich, *International Custody of Plutonium Stocks: A First Step Toward an International Regime for Sensitive Nuclear Energy Activities,* International Consultative Group on Nuclear Energy Working Paper (New York: Rockefeller Foundation; London: Royal Institute of International Affairs, 1978). In December 1978 the IAEA convened an expert group to prepare detailed plans for an international plutonium storage system. This group was still at work in mid-1980.

36. Article XII of the statute of the IAEA reads in part:
A. With respect to any Agency project, or other arrangement where the Agency is requested by the parties concerned to apply safeguards, the Agency shall have the

invoked, but the possible wisdom of doing so has been given increased attention recently.[37] Another possibility would be to base a system of plutonium depositories on the more general provisions of article III.A.1 of the statute, which authorizes the IAEA to "perform any operation or service useful in research on, or development or practical application of, atomic energy for peaceful purposes." The IAEA staff is currently reported to be favoring the use of article XII.A.5 over III.A.1.

Certainly, sequestering existing and future stocks of plutonium in internationally controlled depositories has attractions. The number of such depositories could be kept small. And giving an international agency, such as the IAEA, legal custody over the plutonium in the depositories would inhibit action by any government to seize the plutonium and divert it to nonpeaceful use.[38]

A number of issues would have to be resolved if a system of international plutonium depositories is to be created, whether under the authority of the IAEA statute or on some other basis.[39] Two fundamental questions are what plutonium should be deposited and under what conditions should it be released. Other important questions concern the location of depositories, means of financing their construction and operation, and the organization of the institution that would build and manage them.

The rules on deposit and withdrawal could be based on the same principle: no separated plutonium (other than military plutonium in nuclear

---

following rights and responsibilities to the extent relevant to the project or arrangement:

5. . . . to require that special fissionable materials recovered or produced as a by-product [of reprocessing] be used for peaceful purposes under continuing Agency safeguards for research or in reactors, existing or under construction . . . and to require deposit with the Agency of any excess of special fissionable materials . . . over what is needed for the above-stated uses in order to prevent stockpiling of these materials, provided that thereafter at the request of the member or members concerned special fissionable materials so deposited with the Agency shall be returned promptly to the member or members concerned for use under the same provisions as stated above. . . .

37. Action to apply article XII.A.5 would have to be taken by the IAEA board of governors.

38. The international agency might be given surveillance responsibilities, rather than legal custody, thus reducing the administrative and financial burdens of the agency. But this arrangement would probably provide a less effective barrier against diversion of plutonium to nonpeaceful use.

39. IAEA Secretariat, "International Management and Storage of Plutonium and Spent Fuel," explores in some detail the problems involved in establishing an international plutonium management system under authority of the IAEA statute.

weapon states) that is not to be used for peaceful research or as fuel in power reactors within a reasonable period of time should exist outside the international depositories. Applying this principle would clearly be difficult, even within the group of states that would be willing to join in the establishment of international plutonium depositories.

One problem would be the treatment of existing stocks of civil plutonium. Transfer of these stocks to international depositories might be resisted by some of the governments concerned. Some of these stocks might have to be left in national hands, at least for a transitional period, in order to obtain agreement to the international storage of plutonium separated in the future. National stocks should, however, be subjected to the same withdrawal rules as plutonium in international depositories.

Another problem would be determining what is a reasonable time, or more precisely, how much plutonium should be in the pipeline between an international depository and a specific reactor or research project? In the case of a reactor, the answer would be the amount required for the efficient, uninterrupted production of electric power. But formulating a general rule applicable to all research projects would be more difficult. The dimensions of the problem could be reduced by encouraging multinational cooperation in peaceful research involving the use of plutonium.

In the case of withdrawals, a decision would be required on the chemical form in which plutonium would be permitted to move from an international depository to a reactor or a research project. Shipments of plutonium metal, which can be used directly in efficient nuclear weapons, would be particularly hazardous from the nonproliferation point of view. Plutonium oxide is much less attractive militarily, although it can be used in crude weapons. Mixed oxide fuel (uranium and plutonium oxide) would be safer. Some research projects may require plutonium metal or plutonium oxide, but as a general rule, it would be best to limit shipments to mixed oxide fuel. Applying this rule would require locating the plutonium depositories and fuel fabrication plants together.

A difficult question is whether withdrawals should be permitted for recycle in light water and other thermal reactors. To do so would negate much of the advantage of establishing international plutonium depositories.[40] If many countries opted for thermal recycle, plutonium would

40. The depositories would have some nonproliferation value if the only conditions of withdrawal were advance notice and declaration of the reason for withdrawal.

exist at large numbers of reactors and in transit along many transportation routes. Except for the reduced size of plutonium stocks in national hands, the situation would be little better than one in which all plutonium was stored under safeguards in the countries owning it.[41]

A formal exclusion of thermal recycle might not be negotiable. If not, much the same result could be achieved by informal ancillary understandings deferring decisions on thermal recycle for a specified period. Such understandings could be obtained in return for commitments by fuel suppliers not to exercise their legal rights over deposited plutonium for the same period.

Limiting withdrawals to use in research projects and recycle in breeder reactors would at first drastically restrict the amount of plutonium that could be held outside international depositories. The amount would of course increase as breeders come into use in future decades. For many years, however, stocks of plutonium would exist at reactors in only a few countries. Exposure of plutonium in transit to breeder reactors would also be relatively limited.

If withdrawals are to be so restricted, however, why would any country be willing to turn its plutonium over to international custody? Those few countries that expect to need plutonium as fuel for breeders in the next two decades might be willing to give up thermal recycle. But the majority of countries with civil nuclear energy programs have no definite plans to use breeders. So in depositing plutonium, they would be giving up control over an energy asset with no clear prospect of ever being able to recover it.

This problem might be met by giving depositors the option of selling their plutonium. Payment could be in money or in low-enriched uranium. Countries with breeder programs might provide a ready market for plutonium. If this proved not to be the case, the institution administering the depositories could be the purchaser, if it were provided funds for that purpose. How much money would be required over a period of years would depend on the success of the institution in reselling the plutonium it purchased.

The carrying charges on funds tied up in plutonium would be one of

41. Recycle in LWRs is often opposed on the grounds that it is at best marginally economic. This situation could change if the cost of enriched uranium rose more rapidly than the cost of reprocessing. But even if LWR recycle were clearly advantageous in economic terms, it would still involve risks to nonproliferation efforts.

the operating expenses of a plutonium depository. Other expenses would include carrying charges on funds invested in the storage facility, salaries of administrative and security personnel, and a contribution to the expenses of the central staff of the institution administering the entire system of depositories.

The minimum cost of building a storage depot with a capacity of 50 tons has been estimated at $10 million.[42] At an interest rate of 10 percent, annual carrying charges on this investment would be $1 million. Staff salaries and other operating expenses, including a contribution to central administration might be set arbitrarily at another $1 million a year. If the storage depot were half full, the annual cost of storing a ton of plutonium would then be $80,000.[43] This total would of course be somewhat higher if the depository system owned some of the stored plutonium and if carrying charges on that plutonium were regarded as operating expenses.

A plutonium storage depot could in principle be financed entirely by storage charges. Such charges could cover both the cost of the capital borrowed to pay for construction and day-to-day operating expenses. As a practical matter it would be desirable, however, for the depot—or the larger system of which it is a part—to be launched with a substantial amount of capital subscribed by participating governments or utility companies.

Requirements for storage space would depend on how much separated plutonium accumulated over a period of time. If no plutonium were recycled, and if all separated plutonium were turned over to international custody, the equivalent of three or four 50-ton depots might be needed by 1990. The location of these depots would be an important decision.

In terms of both storage costs and risks of diversion, a few large depots are better than a large number of small ones.[44] Reducing the amount

42. IAEA Secretariat, "International Management and Storage of Plutonium and Spent Fuel," p. 28.

43. This cost does not appear to be excessive because if plutonium is used as reactor fuel, it will clearly be a valuable commodity. A market price for plutonium does not yet exist, but the price in several small plutonium sales contracts recently supervised by the Euratom Supply Agency ranged from $10 to $15 per gram of fissionable material, or $10 million to $14 million per metric ton. *Nuclear News* (August 1979), p. 42.

44. The annual cost per ton of storage in a 10-ton depot could be three to four times as great as in a 50-ton depot. IAEA Secretariat, "International Management and Storage of Plutonium and Spent Fuel," p. 29.

of time plutonium spends in transit should also be given considerable weight in choosing the sites of plutonium depositories. These considerations combine to favor locating the depositories next to commercial-sized reprocessing plants. On the basis of present plans, by 1990 large depots would then be needed at reprocessing plants in France, the United Kingdom, Italy, Japan, and possibly West Germany.

These depots could also receive plutonium from the small pilot plants in Belgium, West Germany, and Japan. Exposure of plutonium in transit would be small, pending the initiation of breeder recycle (and assuming that no other recycle would take place). Even after breeder recycle began, exposure would probably not be large for some time, as the initial operation of breeders is expected to be limited to Western Europe and Japan.

Pilot reprocessing plants in areas distant from Western Europe and Japan pose a problem. Shipping plutonium to the large depots in the latter areas would involve considerable exposure of plutonium in transit. This disadvantage is, however, outweighed by the risk (and possibly also the cost) of establishing a number of small depositories. If reprocessing plants are built in regional nuclear service centers, access to plutonium depots would be required. Whether depots would be needed in the service centers would depend on the distance from other depots.

One of two general approaches might be taken to the establishment of an international plutonium storage system. One would use the legal authority of article XII.A.5 (or possibly article III.A.1) of the IAEA statute. The other would seek a new international agreement on a system of plutonium depositories and then negotiate an appropriate relationship with the IAEA. This might be done on a global or a regional basis. The institutional alternatives in establishing a system of plutonium depositories are considered in detail in chapter 5.

Conclusions

Two developments with respect to spent fuel from civil power reactors pose difficult problems from the nonproliferation point of view:
—Stocks of spent fuel in nonnuclear weapon states are increasing, which means that the amounts of unseparated plutonium are also increasing.

In addition, the storage problem caused by spent fuel arisings creates incentives to build national reprocessing plants.

—Reprocessing capacity is expanding, and actual reprocessing of spent fuel is likely to grow. Stocks of separated plutonium will as a consequence increase.

Assuming that a final disposal of spent fuel is not possible or is not desired, the alternatives to national storage are storage at existing reprocessing plants in other countries, construction of multinational regional storage facilities, and return of spent fuel to the countries that originally supplied it. Even in combination, these alternatives could not be expected to eliminate the need for national storage.

Storage at reprocessing plants can be carried only so far, unless the reprocessors are willing to go into the storage business. It also has the disadvantage of at least seeming to encourage reprocessing on an increased scale.

The economics of multinational storage cannot be judged in the abstract. Moreover, whether agreement could be reached to build multinational facilities in any given region remains to be seen. Prospects in some regions are poor.

Returning spent fuel to the countries of origin is in principle the best alternative. (Insofar as LWRs are concerned, the supplying countries are enrichers that already possess, or can readily acquire, the means of making the explosive component of nuclear weapons.) Making return of spent fuel compulsory is probably not feasible, however, and for many countries voluntary return must be made economically attractive. This might best be done through an offer to repurchase spent fuel. The political feasibility of a buy-back scheme is, however, untested. And, public opinion in the fuel-supplying countries could limit how much spent fuel could be returned.

Viewed realistically, even all of the alternatives to national storage combined cannot be expected to keep the fuel-importing, nonnuclear weapon states from accumulating substantial inventories of unseparated plutonium. Those alternatives can, however, reduce incentives to build national reprocessing plants.

The prospect of reprocessing on a growing scale calls for measures to channel the growth of the industry and to control its output of plutonium.

Limiting reprocessing plants to nuclear weapon states, plus a few other states with large civil nuclear energy programs (fuel cycle states) would be advantageous from the nonproliferation point of view, but probably is not politically feasible. The next best approach is to try to discourage the construction of any but large, economically efficient plants. This would limit the number of such plants, which is itself a desirable goal.

Controls on the transfer of reprocessing technology and the implicit threat of sanctions (denial of nuclear fuel, for example) could help prevent or delay the construction of small reprocessing plants, but incentives would also be needed to obtain the cooperation of the developing countries. The opportunity to become partners in large multinational reprocessing plants could be one such incentive. Another would be the availability of alternatives to the national storage of spent fuel.

All commercial reprocessing plants should be placed under safeguards, but safeguards alone would not reduce the risk of plutonium diversion to an acceptable level. Controls should also be placed on movements of plutonium and on the purposes for which it can be used. A good way to strengthen controls would be to require the deposit of all plutonium in depots administered by the IAEA or a specially constituted international body. Withdrawals would be permitted only in conformity with internationally agreed rules.

Such rules should permit the withdrawal of plutonium for use in a research project or in a breeder reactor within a reasonable time. Recycle of plutonium in today's thermal reactors should, if possible, be avoided (it is in any case only marginally economic, if that) on the ground that it would involve excessive exposure of plutonium in transit and at widely dispersed power plants. Recycle in breeder reactors would be permitted because it is essential to their economic rationale. Countries that do not have definite plans to use breeders would be given an opportunity to sell their plutonium to those that do or to the agency operating the international plutonium depositories.

The international plutonium storage system should be the centerpiece of any international effort to deal with spent fuel. If a choice has to be made, the use of available incentives and sanctions to achieve the establishment of the plutonium storage system should take priority over other goals, such as reducing the stocks of spent fuel in nonnuclear weapon states, limiting the number of reprocessing plants, and placing some of them under multinational ownership.

Getting firm control over movements of plutonium and its uses can make a crucial difference and requires formal international agreement. The other goals are less absolute, and partial success is worthwhile. Moreover, these goals are best approached by continuous, informal efforts, rather than by formal negotiations. Serious consideration should be given to the establishment of a continuing forum in which interested governments can consult on a variety of nuclear energy questions, including cooperation in the management of spent fuel.

CHAPTER FIVE

New Institutional Arrangements

IN CHAPTERS 3 and 4, a number of international measures to deal with the problems of managing spent fuel and increasing the assurance of fuel supplies were considered. All of these measures would bring governments into relationships intended to last for some time. They may therefore be thought of as new institutional arrangements.

These arrangements fall into three broad categories: informal consultative arrangements, formal agreements and institutions, and multinational fuel cycle facilities. This chapter will examine in some detail what would be involved in adopting the more promising institutional arrangements in each category.

Consultative Arrangements

In previous chapters, arrangements for continuing international consultation on three specific subjects were found to be desirable: the uranium market, the supply of enrichment services, and trade in sensitive materials, equipment, and technology. The utility of a general forum in which views could be exchanged on the full range of questions affecting the development of civil nuclear energy was also underlined.

Because by their very nature these consultative arrangements would not be expected to produce substantive decisions, no formal decision-

111

making machinery would be required. Such procedural or administrative problems as did arise could probably be settled by consensus or, if that failed, by simple majority vote. It would be necessary, however, to determine the relationship of each consultative arrangement to the International Atomic Energy Agency (IAEA) and to deal with questions concerning participation.

Some relationship with the IAEA is clearly desirable, both to avoid even the appearance of undermining the prestige of the IAEA and to take advantage of the specialized skills present in the IAEA staff. Consultative arrangements could in fact be initiated by the director general of the IAEA or by the agency's board of governors.

If a consultative arrangement were initially established outside the framework of the IAEA, an appropriate relationship with the agency could probably be negotiated with little or no difficulty. In a resolution or memorandum of understanding, the IAEA would recognize (and by implication endorse) the consultative arrangement and agree to give favorable consideration to requests for specialized staff services. The participants in the consultative arrangement would agree to pay the costs of such services and to file periodic reports with the agency. No provisions for IAEA supervision or control would be needed.

Obtaining adequate participation would be essential to the success of any consultative arrangement. What is adequate, however, depends upon the problems to be considered. In some cases, participation raises difficult political and practical issues.

Consultations on the uranium market should ideally include the major producers (Australia, Canada, South Africa, the Soviet Union, and the United States), the major importers (Japan and the Western European countries, either individually or collectively), and several developing countries. But could this group ever be assembled? And how many smaller, but still significant, producers or importers of uranium should be invited to participate?

It is quite possible that the Soviet Union would decline an invitation to join consultations on the uranium market because it would not want to expose itself to pressure to reveal its uranium resources and production.[1]

1. The Soviet Union did not respond to requests for this information from International Nuclear Fuel Cycle Evaluation working groups. The authoritative analyses of world uranium resources, production, and requirements published periodically by the International Atomic Energy Agency and the Nuclear Energy Agency of the Organisation for Economic Co-operation and Development do not include Soviet data.

Failure to obtain Soviet participation would not be fatal, since the Soviet Union is not now a major factor in the international market for natural uranium. Its imports of natural uranium are from other centrally planned economies in Eastern Europe. It does export enriched uranium, but the uranium it enriches for export is provided by its foreign customers.[2]

A much more serious—and even more likely—contingency would be the refusal of some other participants to sit down with South Africa because of objections to its racial policies, reinforced by fear of offending black African nations. It might be noted that this problem caused the United States to agree to omit South Africa from the list of countries invited to participate in the organizing session of the International Nuclear Fuel Cycle Evaluation. The important role of South Africa in the uranium market could not be ignored, and some means of taking its plans and policies into account would have to be found. One possibility would be for a participant that has diplomatic relations with South Africa to conduct private supplemental consultations with South Africa on behalf of the entire group.

Considerations of efficiency argue for keeping the consultative group on the uranium market small. Political considerations, however, work strongly in the other direction.[3] If the consultative group was formed as the result of an IAEA initiative, it would be difficult to exclude any IAEA member wishing to join. If the initiative was taken by several major producers and importers outside the IAEA framework, membership could be limited to countries whose production or imports constituted some arbitrary share of the market.

The uranium consultative group could also assume responsibility for monitoring the prospective adequacy of enrichment capacity. The markets for natural uranium and enrichment services are interrelated. Demand in both markets depends largely on nuclear generating capacity, and the precise level of requirements for natural uranium is affected by the tails assay policies of enrichers. Therefore the group could watch both enrichment and mining activities.

2. Gloria Duffy, "Soviet Nuclear Exports," *International Security*, vol. 3 (Summer 1978), pp. 104–05.
3. Taiwan poses an exception to the idea that political considerations make for a large consultative group. Efforts to include Taiwan in the uranium consultative group—or any other consultative arrangement—would be opposed on political grounds by many other potential participants. Despite the fact that it has a substantial civil nuclear energy program, Taiwan was not invited to take part in INFCE for fear of offending China (which does not yet have any nuclear power stations).

Some countries, however, have a much stronger interest in one of the two markets than in the other. Thus, useful consultations on the uranium market could scarcely be held without Canada's participation, although Canada is neither a supplier nor a consumer of enrichment services. Similarly, the Netherlands is not an important factor in the uranium market, but because of its one-third ownership of Urenco, it definitely should be involved in consultations on enrichment.

The best solution might be to form a single consultative group on nuclear fuel supply that would include as many as possible of the countries with major interests in either the uranium or enrichment markets or both. Subgroups with overlapping membership could meet from time to time to consider in greater detail those problems relating primarily to one market or the other.

As was brought out in chapter 2, an arrangement for consultation on the rules of trade in sensitive nuclear materials, equipment, and technology already exists, but it is limited to suppliers and has been concerned with nonproliferation constraints and not with assurances of supply. The wider consultations that would be desirable at some future date could be brought about by inviting importing countries to join the London nuclear suppliers' group. An alternative, which appears to be preferable, would be to make a fresh start and organize a new group consisting of both importers and suppliers.

Some importing countries might fear that an expanded London suppliers' group would continue to be dominated by suppliers. But in any event, something would be lost in submerging the group in a larger entity. If it were not formally disbanded, it could more easily be reassembled to deal with new problems. Moreover, the continued (even if inactive) existence of the London nuclear suppliers' group could have an inhibiting effect on suppliers who might be tempted to promote sales by weakening nonproliferation requirements.

A new consultative arrangement including both importers and suppliers would probably function more effectively if it consisted of only the more important countries in each category. But consultations including all interested countries would in principle be more likely to result in a broad international consensus on the rules of trade. In this and other consultative arrangements on specific problem areas, the conflict between the goals of efficiency and broad geographical coverage could be reconciled more easily if there were also a general forum for discussing international nuclear energy problems.

At its June 1980 meeting, the board of governors of the IAEA established a committee open to all members to advise the board on "ways and means in which supplies of nuclear material, equipment and technology, and fuel cycle services can be assured on a more predictable and long-term basis in accordance with mutually acceptable considerations of nonproliferation." [4] It is too early to judge how this new committee will function, but it could become the general forum for discussing nuclear energy problems that is needed in the post-INFCE period.

The new committee may find it desirable to do much of its work through an executive committee and specialized consultative groups. The executive committee and the specialized groups would be smaller and meet more frequently than the full committee.

The full committee would select the members of the executive committee and might also name the members of the specialized groups, although in some cases it would be sufficient merely to recognize the existence of groups formed by the principally interested governments. Formal procedures and lines of authority should be minimized. The full committee could properly determine the major tasks to be undertaken by its executive committee, but it probably should not try to guide the work of the specialized consultative groups.

Formal International Agreements and Institutions

Some of the measures discussed in chapters 3 and 4 involved formal international agreements or the creation of new international institutions. Two of these measures can profitably be examined in greater detail here: the nuclear fuel bank and the international plutonium storage system.

The Nuclear Fuel Bank

Although establishment of a fuel bank does not appear likely in the near future, examining the concept in greater detail is worthwhile. The U.S. government has given the idea considerable currency and remains publicly committed to it. Moreover, a system of cross-guarantees, backed by dedicated stockpiles, is feasible and can be viewed as a way station on

4. Board of Governors, IAEA, "Possible Tasks of the Agency After the conclusion of the International Nuclear Fuel Cycle Evaluation," agenda item 13 (GOV/1997), June 20, 1980.

the road to the fuel bank. If the bank is to be established someday, a number of legal and institutional issues must be solved, in addition to the policy problems considered in chapter 3.

STRUCTURE AND CONTROL. The international agreement creating the bank would have to specify how to provide policy guidance for the bank's operations and how to select officers charged with day-to-day management. These two provisions would determine where control of the bank would be vested, and framing them would involve a complicated balancing of diverse political and economic interests, both public and private.

On the political level, governments, parties, interest groups, and individual leaders vary in their degree of commitment to checking the spread of nuclear weapons and hence in the firmness of their support for an institution proposed with this goal in mind. The economic interests of importers of nuclear fuel, uranium miners, owners of enrichment facilities, and producers of nuclear energy equipment also clearly differ. Each of these groups and their governments will tend to see different opportunities and disadvantages in the proposal to create an international nuclear fuel bank. Some governments of course have more than one of these groups in their constituencies.

The problem of control is further complicated by its inevitable connection with the question of finance and with the wider controversy over the future of the international economic system. The industrialized countries must provide the bulk of the bank's capital, and they can therefore be expected to insist on a major, if not controlling, voice in its policies. The developing countries, however, are certain to resist the creation of an international institution dominated by the industrialized countries. The cleavage between the interests of the industrialized and developing nations is widened by the fact that the major suppliers of both natural uranium and enrichment services are industrialized, while most developing countries must import their fuel.

If agreement on how to control the bank is to be reached, it will probably be through the distribution of power among several differently constituted bodies. Many such arrangements are possible. Only one is presented here for illustrative purposes.

The first body to have influence over the policies of the bank would of course be the conference convened to create it. This conference could—and probably would—establish general guidelines for the bank, as well as deal with the problems of continuing policy guidance and selection of officers. The conference might meet only once, or it might constitute itself a continuing body to meet periodically to review, and if necessary amend, the guidelines. It can be assumed that the conference would operate under the rule of one country, one vote. Any participants whose support was essential to the success of the venture would, however, in effect have a veto, since they, like other participants, could refuse to ratify conference decisions with which they disagreed.

The conference might entrust the governance of the bank to two bodies, which will be called here the governing council and the board of directors. The council would be composed of representatives of participating governments, chosen by those governments. In order to keep the council from being too large, some of its members might represent several governments. The board would represent investors in the bank who would cast votes for directors in proportion to the size of their capital subscriptions. Some of the investors might be private firms, which would have the desirable effect of making the bank more economic and less political.

If each member of both bodies were given a single vote, and if all decisions were made by a majority of members, the council would eventually be dominated by developing countries and the board from the beginning by industrialized countries. This outcome could be moderated in several ways: for purposes of representation on the council, countries could be grouped so as to increase the number of representatives from the industrialized countries. Also in the case of particularly important decisions, the affirmative vote could be required of council members who were both a majority on the council and who represented countries with a specified percentage of nuclear generating capacity. The representation of developing countries on the board of directors could be increased by assigning some seats on a regional basis. The dominance of the industrialized nations on the board could be further reduced by requiring more than a majority vote for some decisions.

A key question would be which decisions would be made by the council, by the board, or would require the concurrence of both bodies. Given the differences in their constituencies, it would appear logical to assign predominantly political decisions to the council and decisions that are largely economic to the board. Particularly important matters, whether political or economic, would come before both bodies.

For example, the council would pass on the applications of additional governments desiring to participate in the bank. The board might, among other functions, pass on proposals by management with respect to pricing policy and the composition of the bank's fuel assets. Both the council and the board might review the bank's annual budget, vote for senior officers and approve borrowings above a specified amount.

One important issue, disputes over denial of fuel by the bank's management, probably could not be handled by either the council or the board, given their differing representation of supplier and consumer interests. Some special machinery, such as a panel of impartial experts, might be required to mediate such disputes.

LEGAL STATUS. The bank should in effect be an international corporation. That is, it should be a legal person, with the ability to own real and personal property, enter into contracts, incur debts, and sue and be sued in the courts of participating countries.

At the same time, the bank should enjoy some privileges and immunities not possessed by ordinary corporations. The bank, its officers, and assets should be exempt from national taxes, and its assets should not be subject to seizure to satisfy judgments of national courts. It should also be permitted to stand in the place of clients to whom it has supplied fuel and seek to enforce the contractual rights of those clients to fuel from their normal sources of supply.

Fuel shipments by the bank should move freely across national borders, subject only to routine customs inspection and national safety regulations. Shipments should not be subject to customs duties or other taxes.

The bank might be a UN specialized agency or it might be established outside the UN system. The course followed could depend on the sponsorship of the conference called to create the bank.

RELATIONSHIP WITH THE INTERNATIONAL ATOMIC ENERGY AGENCY. The bank's stock of nuclear fuel should be subject to IAEA safeguards both while it is in the bank's custody and after it has been withdrawn to meet specified contingencies. And, as has been previously mentioned, the facilities using fuel from the bank should also be safeguarded by the IAEA.

Other relationships between the bank and the IAEA are also conceivable. The bank could be created as a department within the IAEA.[5] Or it might be an autonomous agency with its own management, but subject to the policy guidance of the general conference and board of governors of the IAEA. It would be surprising, however, if the balance of interests

5. Article IX.A of the IAEA statute already authorizes the agency to accept and store fissionable material made available to it by members.

represented in the IAEA's governing bodies would also be a workable compromise among the somewhat different interests involved in a nuclear fuel bank. The absence of a specific role for private interests in the direction of the IAEA is particularly notable. A more workable arrangement would be for the IAEA to approve the bank's charter, provide secretariat services on a reimbursable basis, and receive an annual report, but not exercise any control over the functioning of the bank. Whatever the eventual relationship, the IAEA might be called on to help the bank get started. The bank could in fact be organized within the IAEA and only later be made a separate, autonomous body.

PARTICIPATION. Economic and nonproliferation considerations combine to make a large nuclear fuel bank better than a small one.

The bank needs suppliers of natural uranium and enrichment services as members because they can provide the bank with its basic assets, either as contributions or as investments in kind. The bank could in theory obtain all of its capital in monetary form and buy natural and enriched uranium from suppliers, but it would be more likely to avoid onerous nonproliferation conditions on the use of these assets if the suppliers belonged to the bank. Moreover, the suppliers include several wealthy countries that are among the most promising sources of capital, whether in money or in kind.

The bank needs members with large nuclear generating capacities in order to keep annual charges for access to the bank low.[6] This argues in favor of including countries such as Japan as members, even though their plans to build national reprocessing or enrichment plants make them ineligible to receive U.S.-origin fuel from the bank under existing U.S. law. And finally, if the bank is to make the maximum contribution toward reducing incentives to build national reprocessing or enrichment plants, it must be joined by as many nonnuclear weapon countries as possible.

Although the case for a large bank is quite strong, a beginning could be made on a more modest basis, provided that sufficient capital could be raised and basic assets could be obtained without restrictions that would severely restrict later expansion.

Plutonium Storage System

In chapter 4, two general approaches to the establishment of an international plutonium storage system (IPS) were identified: using the au-

6. It is assumed that all or a major share of the bank's operating expenses would be prorated among members on the basis of their generating capacities.

thority of article XII.A.5 (or possibly article III.A.1) of the IAEA statute or seeking an entirely new international agreement.[7] In the latter case, an appropriate relationship between the IPS and the IAEA would have to be negotiated separately.

It will be assumed here that under either approach, establishing an IPS would require a single step. A gradual approach is also conceivable, however. The basis for an IPS might be created by obtaining agreement successively on approved uses and management practices with respect to plutonium; the publication of end-use statements for plutonium by the governments concerned; and procedures to verify end use.[8]

STRUCTURE AND CONTROL. If an IPS were established under the authority of the IAEA statute, the IAEA board of governors would have to create a special unit to administer the system and provide the unit with guidelines for the deposit and withdrawal of plutonium, the means of finance, and operating procedures. These guidelines could not, however, cover all questions that would arise, including the choice of sites for depositories and the resolution of disputes over proposed withdrawals.

The board could attempt to handle questions not settled by the guidelines, but this would be quite cumbersome for a body not in continuous session and some of whose members are from countries without nuclear power programs. If the board found it necessary to create a special policy body to oversee the unit charged with administering the IPS, the geographical composition of this body would clearly be controversial. The dispute might have to be referred to the general conference of IAEA, in which each member of the agency has one vote.

7. Three papers are particularly useful in exploring the institutional problems involved in establishing an international plutonium storage system: IAEA Secretariat, "International Management and Storage of Plutonium and Spent Fuel" (Vienna: IAEA, July 1978); IAEA Expert Group on International Plutonium Storage, "An International Plutonium Storage Regime," IAEA-IPS/EG/33 paper by the U.S. Expert, May 7, 1979; and Russell W. Fox and Mason Willrich, *International Custody of Plutonium Stocks: A First Step Toward an International Regime for Sensitive Nuclear Energy Activities,* International Consultative Group on Nuclear Energy Working Paper (New York: Rockefeller Foundation; London: Royal Institute of International Affairs, 1978).

8. This gradual approach is described by Johan Lind of the Swedish Foreign Ministry in "Institutional Solutions to the Proliferation Risks of Plutonium," paper prepared for the Stockholm International Peace Research Institute Symposium on Internationalization of the Nuclear Fuel Cycle, October 31–November 2, 1978, Stockholm, Sweden.

The IAEA would also find it difficult to establish an organizational structure and a system of policy guidance that would be acceptable to all or most of the potential participants in an IPS. Certainly, the distribution of voting power in IAEA's governing bodies bears no relation to the distribution of economic interests among potential participants. This disparity between policy control and economic interest could to some extent be reduced by giving countries with large nuclear power programs a strong voice in the special policy body established to oversee the administration of the IPS. The ultimate policy authority would, however, remain in the board of governors and the general conference.

Making a fresh start outside the IAEA would also have disadvantages. It would not be easy to negotiate a statement of general principle as good as article XII.A.5—as lacking in precision as that article undoubtedly is. Also, while the distribution of voting power in the IAEA is scarcely ideal for the operation of an IPS, reaching agreement on a better distribution would be difficult. Moreover, giving the IAEA—rather than some new international body—custody over deposited plutonium avoids a wasteful duplication of effort. The depositories would in any case be subject to IAEA safeguards, and if the IAEA had custody over the plutonium, the staff at each depot could also serve as safeguard inspectors.

LEGAL PROBLEMS. The relationship between the body administering the IPS and participating governments would be spelled out in the agreement creating the system or in guidelines issued by the IAEA board of governors pursuant to the IAEA statute. Special legal understandings would also be required to define the rights and obligations of countries in which plutonium depositories would be located, countries across whose territory plutonium would pass on its way to or from depositories, and countries that had supplied the fuel or source material from which plutonium subject to the rules of the IPS had been generated.

At a minimum, host governments should be asked to grant diplomatic status to the international personnel responsible for plutonium in depots on their territory. At a maximum, the depots themselves could be treated as international enclaves. If this were not done, a key question would be whether the host governments or the IAEA (or another international agency) would actually operate the depots.

If the host governments assumed this function, they might also take custody of plutonium in the depots. The international agency would then be limited to ruling on requests for withdrawal of plutonium and detecting unauthorized withdrawals. If the international agency both operated the depots and took custody of the plutonium, the lines of responsibility would be somewhat clearer, but the administrative burden on the agency would be greater.

Under either arrangement, decisions would be required on the allocation of costs. A clear understanding would also be needed on the authority of the international staff over plutonium in transit within the territory of the host countries. The desirability of special arrangements for reprocessing plants and fuel fabrication plants located with plutonium depositories would also have to be considered. Normal safeguards for such facilities might be sufficient, but greater security could be provided if the international staff controlling (or operating) the plutonium depositories also had surveillance authority over adjacent reprocessing or fuel fabrication plants.

In the case of countries over which plutonium would be transported, agreement would be needed on the rights of IPS personnel to accompany plutonium shipments and on the immunity of such shipments from seizure. The safety and security rules to be observed in moving plutonium would have to be specified, and an understanding reached on responsibility for physical security. The security of plutonium depots would presumably be the responsibility of the host country.

One of the most difficult questions would be the rights of fuel suppliers over plutonium subject to the IPS. If the suppliers did not waive their rights, each request for withdrawal of plutonium would have to be approved by both the IPS and the supplier (or suppliers) of the fuel from which the plutonium had been generated. This would be regarded as quite onerous by the owners of the plutonium and could make them unwilling to participate in the IPS. Some suppliers would be reluctant to waive their rights and would demand in return that the IPS establish strict rules concerning permissible uses of plutonium and its physical security.[9]

DISPUTES AND VIOLATIONS. Disputes would be likely to arise between the entity administering the IPS and both participating and cooperating governments.[10] Occasions for disagreement are not hard to imagine:

9. In the case of the United States, the Nuclear Non-Proliferation Act of 1978 might have to be amended to permit the executive branch to waive its rights over plutonium of United States origin controlled by the IPS.

10. A government could of course fall into both the participating and co-

denial by the IPS administration of a request to withdraw plutonium, diversion of plutonium to an unauthorized use by a participating government, or failure of IPS personnel to observe safety regulations in shipping plutonium across the territory of a cooperating government. Some means of resolving these and other disputes would be needed.

Disagreements between the IPS administration and participating governments could be resolved within the system. Appeals to the body responsible for policy guidance (the IAEA board of governors or a specially constituted unit) might be permitted. If the volume of appeals became too heavy, the policy body might establish a panel to hear them. Appeals involving alleged major violations of IPS rules and, potentially, the application of sanctions (such as expulsion or forfeit of stored plutonium) would, however, probably have to be decided by the policy body itself.

Disputes between the IPS administration and cooperating governments over matters such as transit rights or the legal status of IPS personnel would have to be handled differently. The governments concerned would not be asserting rights as members of the IPS, but would be making claims as outside parties under agreements with the IPS administration. Appeals to the policy level of the IPS would not be appropriate. The agreements should therefore specify procedures for submitting disputes to mediation or (if the parties agreed) binding arbitration.

PARTICIPATION. Clearly, the participation of all nonnuclear weapon states with civil nuclear energy programs would be desirable. From the narrow, nonproliferation point of view, nuclear weapon states would not have to join the IPS. To allow them to stand aside, however, would compound the discrimination against nonnuclear weapon states already imposed by the NPT. The IPS would place significant burdens on participants, and on grounds of equity the nuclear weapon states should not be made exempt.

Achieving the broad participation that would be desirable may not be possible. Some countries that have declined to adhere to the NPT or to accept full-scope safeguards would also probably not join the IPS. In some such cases, the motive would be to avoid an unwelcome intrusion

---

operating categories: it could be a member of IPS and at the same time enter into an agreement with the IPS administration to permit the establishment of depositories on its territory or the shipment of plutonium across it.

into their domestic nuclear activity. In others, it would be to preserve the nuclear weapon option, or even actively to pursue it.

The Soviet Union has consistently been reluctant to reveal much information about its civil nuclear energy industry. It might therefore decide not to participate in the IPS, but to influence the policies of the IPS through its role in the IAEA. Soviet allies in Eastern Europe with nuclear energy programs might also not join the IPS, but for a different reason. These countries receive their nuclear fuel from the Soviet Union and are required to return spent fuel to the Soviet Union without reprocessing it.[11] They therefore do not have access to separated plutonium.

Even though important gaps in coverage would no doubt remain, a large proportion of countries with civil nuclear energy programs might eventually join the IPS. Some would do so primarily because of their desire to put as much separated plutonium as possible under international controls. Others would be influenced by the belief that through the IPS they would have greater assurance of benefiting from the plutonium in their spent fuel than if they were at the mercy of the changeable policies of their fuel suppliers.[12]

Governments strongly interested in widening participation in the IPS might consider providing special incentives. For example, participants could be given preferred access to national or multinational facilities for the storage of spent fuel. Some suppliers of natural uranium or enrichment services might require their customers to join the IPS. This kind of leverage, however, should be used cautiously, if at all, since it could cause some countries to seek an independent fuel cycle. Moreover, the IPS is most likely to succeed and gain new adherents if participation is essentially voluntary.

Multinational Fuel Cycle Facilities

Multinational control of sensitive fuel cycle facilities has been advocated as a means of reducing the risk that such facilities would be used in nuclear weapon programs. Multinational sponsorship can also help mobilize capital for expensive nuclear projects. In chapter 4, the develop-

11. Duffy, "Soviet Nuclear Exports," p. 87.
12. Depending upon the precise provisions of the IPS (see chapter 4), participants could benefit from the plutonium in their spent fuel by recycling it or by exchanging it for money or enriched uranium.

ment of multinational facilities for the storage of spent fuel was found to be a desirable alternative to the expansion of national storage capacity. And large, multinational reprocessing plants were seen to be preferable to smaller, less efficient, and more numerous national plants.[13]

Storage of Spent Fuel

Much of the discussion of multinational storage of spent fuel has assumed that it would be one of the functions of regional nuclear fuel cycle centers (RNFCC).[14] In their most ambitious version, such centers would include the full nuclear fuel cycle. They have usually been conceived of, however, as being limited to storage, reprocessing, and possibly fabrication of mixed oxide fuel. Construction of a spent fuel storage facility is sometimes seen as a first step in developing an RNFCC, none of which yet exist.[15]

Establishing a spent fuel storage facility in the framework of an RNFCC would require agreement among participating governments on a site for the center and its legal status, and on arrangements to construct and operate the storage facility. The site ideally should be free of serious local or international political problems. It should also be physically suitable for the storage of spent fuel and possibly other fuel cycle functions. That is, it should not be excessively vulnerable to natural disasters and it should be easily provided with key utility and transportation services. The site should, moreover, be secure in two senses: it should not be in an area seriously threatened by hostilities, and the host country (if a

13. Late in this century, multinational efforts may also be needed to create additional enrichment capacity. See Michael Mihalka with Marvin Miller and Kenneth A. Solomon, *International Arrangements for Uranium Enrichment,* R-2427-DOE, prepared for the U.S. Department of Energy (Santa Monica, Calif.: Rand Corp., 1979).

14. The basic study on this subject is IAEA, *Regional Nuclear Fuel Cycle Centres: 1977 Report of the IAEA Study Project,* vols. 1 and 2 (Vienna: IAEA, 1977). This study is summarized in V. Meckoni, R. J. Catlin, and L. L. Bennett, "Regional Nuclear Fuel Cycle Centres: IAEA Study Project," paper prepared for the International Conference on Nuclear Power and Its Fuel Cycle, Salzburg, Austria, May 2–13, 1977. For a concise discussion of what is involved in establishing an RNFCC, see Commission of the European Communities, *Nuclear Science and Technology: A Reference Regional Nuclear Fuel Centre,* EUR-5955 (Luxembourg: CEC, 1978).

15. See *Nuclear Power and Nuclear Weapons Proliferation,* vol. 1: *Report of the Atlantic Council's Nuclear Fuels Policy Working Group* (Washington, D.C.: Atlantic Council of the United States, 1978), pp. 107–08.

nonnuclear weapon state) should be perceived as unlikely to decide to acquire nuclear weapons.[16]

The governments concerned could agree to make the site of the RNFCC an international enclave with its own local administration. But they would be more likely to buy or rent the site from the host government. Title or leasehold rights could be held by a corporation controlled by the participating governments.

A different corporation could be formed to build and operate a spent fuel storage facility on the RNFCC site. The investors and stockholders in this corporation would not be the governments themselves, but the utility companies (both publicly and privately owned) that would use the storage facility. The capital subscriptions, and therefore the voting rights, of the participating utilities might be in proportion to their nuclear generating capacities. The spent fuel storage corporation would function in most respects as a commercial enterprise. Its storage fees should be set at a level that would in time cover its costs, including a normal return on capital.

Despite its largely commercial nature, the spent fuel storage corporation would have to maintain a continuing political relationship with the sponsoring governments. Those governments would be responsible for the observance of IAEA safeguards over the storage facility and for any further development of fuel cycle facilities at the RNFCC. Other questions could arise requiring governmental decisions. For example, if access to the storage facility were to be limited to countries that had joined the plutonium storage system (assuming that one is established), exclusion of ineligible utilities would essentially be up to the sponsoring governments, rather than the spent fuel storage corporation.

The individual governments could no doubt influence the corporation's policies by way of the participating utilities, particularly if they were government owned. A continuing means of consultation among the governments would also be useful. This could be provided by establishing an intergovernmental policy committee.[17] This committee could also consider proposals for further development of the RNFCC.

16. For an effort to weigh these and other factors in solving a site-selection problem, see Guna S. Selvaduray, Mark K. Goldstein, and Robert N. Anderson, "Finding a Site to Store Spent Fuel in the Pacific Basin," *Nuclear Engineering International* (September 1979), p. 44.

17. The joint committee that controls the political aspects of Urenco/Centec functions similarly. See C. Allday, "Some Experiences in Formation and Operation

Two alternatives to the RNFCC approach might be considered. One would be to create a regional spent fuel storage facility with no thought of eventually building other fuel cycle facilities on the same site. The other would be for the IAEA to assume responsibility for operating regional spent fuel storage facilities.

The first of these approaches has been considered for the Pacific Basin.[18] In March 1979, the United States invited Japan to join in establishing a spent fuel storage center on a sparsely inhabited Pacific island. Other possible participants would be South Korea, Taiwan, and the Philippines.[19] Details of the U.S. proposal have not been made public, and Japan has not yet agreed to it.

The second alternative has been studied in some detail by the IAEA secretariat.[20] If the IAEA were to decide to provide a storage service for spent fuel, it would presumably do so under the authority of the IAEA statute. The institutional and legal problems involved would then be similar to those discussed earlier in this chapter in connection with the plutonium storage system. The expert group established by the IAEA to study the question has tentatively decided, however, that an international spent fuel storage system is not needed at this time.

Reprocessing

As was mentioned above, a multinational reprocessing plant could be built as part of an RNFCC.[21] The legal and institutional arrangements would then be similar to those for a spent fuel storage facility at an RNFCC. It is probably more realistic, however, to think of multinational reprocessing enterprises as separate from any plans for regional centers. A multinational enterprise could be formed either to take over an exist-

of Multinational Uranium-Enrichment and Fuel-Reprocessing Organizations," in Abram Chayes and W. Bennett Lewis, eds., *International Arrangements for Nuclear Fuel Reprocessing* (Ballinger, 1977), p. 181.

18. See International Energy Associates, Ltd., *Concept for Developing a Pacific Basin Spent Fuel Storage Consortium: Institutional Factors*, EN-77-C-03-1583, prepared under Department of Energy contract for Boeing Engineering and Construction, April 29, 1978.

19. *Japan Economic Journal*, March 20, 1979, p. 3.

20. IAEA Secretariat, *International Management and Storage of Plutonium and Spent Fuel*, pp. 37–60.

21. See Chayes and Lewis, *International Arrangements for Nuclear Fuel Reprocessing*, for useful discussions of various problems in multinational reprocessing.

ing national reprocessing plant or to build a new plant. To simplify exposition, it will be assumed here that the objective is to build a new plant.

The initiative for forming a multinational reprocessing enterprise could be entirely private, but this is not likely. Heavy involvement by governments would be virtually certain. Fuel cycle facilities everywhere are subject to close governmental regulation, if they are not actually government owned. Reprocessing with its potential for contributing to a nuclear weapons program is properly the subject of special governmental concern. Moreover, national energy policy is as likely to be the reason for joining in a multinational reprocessing venture as is a desire for commercial profits.

The countries joining in a reprocessing enterprise are likely to include one country with previous experience in the required technology. The others would probably have civil nuclear energy programs that are not large enough to justify building a national plant of economic size. A degree of political compatibility among the participating governments would be essential, although they would not all have to be from the same region.

The corporate form would be suitable for a multinational reprocessing enterprise. It could be incorporated under the laws of the country in which its plant would be located, or it could be specially constituted under an international agreement among the participating countries. If those countries were members of a regional compact, such as Euratom, the compact might provide the legal basis for incorporation.[22]

As in the case of the spent fuel storage enterprise discussed above, the stockholders in a multinational reprocessing enterprise could appropriately be the utilities using its services. The sponsoring governments could no doubt influence the policies of the corporation through the utilities. Given the political sensitivity of reprocessing, however, a continuing forum for intergovernmental consultation would be even more necessary than in the case of spent fuel storage.

Construction of the reprocessing plant could be financed at least in part by the capital subscriptions of the participating utilities. It might be

22. Chapter V of the Treaty Establishing the European Atomic Energy Community authorizes the establishment of joint undertakings that are "of fundamental importance to the development of the nuclear industry in the Community. . . ." *Treaties Establishing the European Communities* (Luxembourg: Office for Official Publications of the European Communities, 1973), pp. 543–46.

necessary to raise additional funds, however, by selling bonds guaranteed by the sponsoring governments. There is no reason why the multinational enterprise could not cover its costs from charges for its services. It would presumably not have been built unless additional reprocessing capacity were needed, and its stockholders would provide a reliable clientele.

As was noted in chapter 4, staffing a multinational reprocessing enterprise could be a problem. Reprocessing spent fuel from commercial reactors is a sophisticated technology. Efficient operations might be difficult with multinational staffing throughout the plant. On the other hand, relying largely on personnel from only one of the participating countries might not be acceptable to the others.

The external relations of the multinational reprocessing enterprise would also raise problems. The reprocessing plant would presumably be subject to IAEA safeguards, either because of the legal obligations of the government on whose territory it was located or because of the policies of fuel suppliers with rights over the spent fuel delivered to it. A separate decision would be required, however, on joining any international system that may be established to control separated plutonium. The fuel suppliers might well insist that the plant be brought into such a system. An understanding with the suppliers on this and other issues would in fact be essential.

Conclusions

The various institutional arrangements described in this chapter do not collectively constitute a new international approach to nuclear energy problems. Some are feasible now; the time for others has not yet come. But these arrangements are no more than building blocks. When they are to be put in place, and how they could relate to one another, are crucial questions that will be considered in the next chapter.

CHAPTER SIX

Achieving New Forms
of Cooperation

IN PREVIOUS chapters the need for new cooperative measures to respond to a number of problems in the civil nuclear energy industry was pointed out. These problems, whose solution has recently become more pressing, include the achievement of a consensus on the rules of trade in sensitive nuclear equipment, materials, and technology; establishing better controls over separated plutonium; and increasing the assurance of nuclear fuel supplies.

The new forms of international cooperation in nuclear energy proposed here would not replace the present international regime, but supplement it. The Treaty on the Non-Proliferation of Nuclear Weapons and the safeguards administered by the International Atomic Energy Agency will continue to be important means of checking the spread of nuclear weapons. Expanding the coverage of the NPT and increasing the technical effectiveness of safeguards deserve sustained attention, as does bringing the Treaty of Tlatelolco into effect for more Latin American republics. But improving the present regime will not be enough; new forms of international cooperation are needed.

In a sense, the process of moving toward new forms of international cooperation is already under way. The test explosion of a nuclear device by India in 1974 revived concern over the further spread of nuclear weapons. Concern was increased by indications that other nonnuclear weapon states were interested in acquiring reprocessing facilities, even though in some cases the economic need for such facilities was not apparent.

In 1976 the U.S. government undertook a fundamental review of its nonproliferation policies. This review led to a statement on nuclear policy by President Gerald R. Ford emphasizing the need to control both separated plutonium and reprocessing technology. The president announced that the United States would defer the reprocessing of spent fuel and the recycling of plutonium until there was "sound reason to conclude that the world community can effectively overcome the associated risks of proliferation." He also called on other nations to join in a three-year moratorium on the export of reprocessing technology and facilities.[1]

In April 1977 newly elected President Jimmy Carter issued a brief statement on nuclear power policy, in which he went beyond his predecessor by deferring "indefinitely the commercial reprocessing and recycling of the plutonium produced in the U.S. nuclear power programs."[2] He also announced that he was exploring with other governments the establishment of an international nuclear fuel cycle evaluation program.

Almost a year later, President Carter signed into law the Nuclear Non-Proliferation Act of 1978 (NNPA), which codified an even more restrictive U.S. nonproliferation policy. Among other provisions, this complicated piece of legislation[3] sought in various ways to induce countries importing nuclear fuel from the United States to accept a U.S. veto on the transfer or reprocessing of that fuel (if the United States did not already have that right under existing agreements) and to place all of their civil nuclear facilities under IAEA safeguards.

Few governments reacted favorably to the changes in U.S. nonproliferation policy (Canada and Australia were the major exceptions). Resentment was widespread over what many viewed as a unilateral effort by the United States to impose its views on other countries.

Tensions were eased somewhat when President Carter acted on his ear-

1. "Statement on Nuclear Policy, October 28, 1976," *Public Papers of the Presidents: Gerald R. Ford, 1976–77*, vol. 3 (Government Printing Office, 1979), pp. 2763–78.
2. U.S. Arms Control and Disarmament Agency, "Nuclear Power Policy: Statement by the President on His Decisions Following a Review of U.S. Policy," April 7, 1977.
3. 22 U.S.C. 3201. See app. B for a further description of the NNPA. Immediately after its enactment, the NNPA was referred to in some Washington circles as the 1978 Act for the Relief of the Legal Profession.

lier proposal and invited other interested countries and international organizations to take part in a study of all aspects of the nuclear fuel cycle. This study, which came to be known as the International Nuclear Fuel Cycle Evaluation, was launched at an organizing conference that met in Washington, D.C., from October 19 to 21, 1977. Forty governments and four international organizations were represented at the organizing conference.[4] Eventually sixty-six governments took part in INFCE. The final communiqué of the organizing conference stated that the purpose of INFCE was to explore the best means of advancing two objectives: making nuclear energy widely available to meet the world's energy requirements and minimizing the danger of the proliferation of nuclear weapons. The communiqué made clear, however, that "INFCE was to be a technical and analytical study and not a negotiation" and that "participants would not be committed to INFCE's results."[5]

The work of INFCE was done by eight working groups and a technical coordinating committee consisting of the twenty-two cochairmen of those groups and chaired by Professor Abram Chayes of Harvard Law School, who had also chaired the organizing conference. Two plenary conferences were held in Vienna. The first, to review the progress of work, met from November 27 to 29, 1978. The second and final plenary conference was held from February 25 to 27, 1980. In the course of INFCE, the working groups held sixty-one meetings and produced more than 20,000 pages of documents. The technical coordinating committee met nine times and prepared a fifty-three-page summary and overview of INFCE's work that was submitted to the final plenary conference.[6]

One might ask what was the end result of all of this activity, but that would be the wrong question. The INFCE was not a self-contained activity with clear goals against which success or failure could be judged. It was part of a larger process that may lead to new forms of international cooperation designed to facilitate the continued growth of civil nuclear energy without increasing the risk of a further spread of nuclear weapons. The

---

4. The International Atomic Energy Agency, the Commission of the European Communities, the International Energy Agency, and the Nuclear Energy Agency of the OECD.

5. International Nuclear Fuel Cycle Evaluation, *INFCE Summary Volume*, INFCE/PC/2/9 (Vienna: IAEA, 1980), pp. 54–55.

6. INFCE, "Communiqué of the Final Plenary Conference of INFCE," INFCE/PC/2/12 (Vienna: IAEA, February 27, 1980), p. 2.

INFCE must eventually be judged in terms of its contribution to that process.

The reports produced by INFCE contain an impressive amount of information and analysis that, at least for the next few years, will be useful to governments in developing concrete measures for international cooperation. It would be a mistake, however, to look to INFCE documents for policy guidance. The INFCE was not designed to produce policy recommendations and did not do so.

What INFCE said is not of great or lasting importance. Its massive reports contain at least a little comfort for adherents to a variety of policy positions. What is important is INFCE's apparent success in promoting a common way of looking at nuclear energy problems. After INFCE, the existence of a connection between the civil nuclear energy industry and the problem of nuclear weapons proliferation will be taken for granted. Similarly, after INFCE it will be difficult to consider nonproliferation measures without weighing their consequences for energy supplies. Perhaps most important, INFCE has reinforced the view that the future development of the civil nuclear energy industry is a proper object of international attention.

The Case for an Evolutionary Approach

The INFCE has created significant momentum in the international consideration of nuclear energy problems. It does not follow that a comprehensive approach to those problems would succeed. A consensus on precisely what should be done about each problem does not yet exist. Seeking agreement on a grand design for the civil nuclear energy industry at this time would be an exercise in futility. It is in fact difficult to visualize what an appropriate grand design would be. The future is clouded by major uncertainties, and the basic problems involved in creating a new international regime for nuclear energy cannot be settled quickly. Therefore an evolutionary approach is almost certainly best.

Major Uncertainties

The process of building a new nuclear energy regime will unavoidably be affected by other international developments that cannot be foreseen.

The state of East-West and North-South relations will strongly influence prospects for obtaining a broad geographical participation in new cooperative measures. Of these two major axes of world politics, North-South relations are most important in the present context. An international nuclear regime that did not include most of the developing countries with civil nuclear energy programs would have only limited value. These countries are more likely than industrialized countries to need international help in solving the problems of their emerging nuclear energy industries. A number of them also have security reasons for at least considering the acquisition of nuclear weapons. Their willingness to enter into new cooperative arrangements in the field of nuclear energy can be expected to vary with their perception of the responsiveness of the industrialized countries to their economic concerns.

Prospects for participation of the Soviet Union and its allies in the various cooperative measures proposed here would not be good under the best of circumstances and would be all but nonexistent under conditions of renewed cold war. In a period of East-West confrontation there would be the further danger that some non-Communist developing countries would shy away from cooperation with industrialized Western countries in an effort to preserve their nonaligned status.

Failure of the Communist countries to join in new international cooperative measures for nuclear energy would be inconvenient today, but not fatal. The Soviet Union in effect administers a separate nuclear regime for itself and its allies.[7] This regime, however, is by no means totally isolated from the nuclear energy industries in other areas. The Soviet Union is an important supplier of toll enrichment services to Western Europe, has sold power reactors to Finland and Libya, and has agreements for cooperation in nuclear energy research with several other non-Communist countries. Rumania—often the odd-country-out in the Eastern bloc—has contracted to buy four 600-MWe CANDU reactors from Canada.[8] If the links between the civil nuclear energy industries in Communist and non-Communist areas grow, the cooperation of the Soviet Union and other Communist countries will be increasingly important to the success of any new cooperative arrangements, even if they do not participate in them.

7. See Gloria Duffy, *Soviet Nuclear Energy: Domestic and International Policies,* R-2362-DOE, prepared for the U.S. Department of Energy (Santa Monica, Calif.: Rand Corp., 1979).
8. *Nuclear Engineering International* (June 1979), p. 7.

Quite apart from the unpredictable course of North-South and East-West relations, the uncertain future of the civil nuclear energy industry itself makes it difficult to conceive of a grand design to deal with its problems. Estimates of the future expansion of nuclear generating capacity have already been sharply reduced as a result of lowered expectations of economic growth and political controversy over the safety of nuclear power plants. A further scaling back of projections of future nuclear generating capacity is quite possible. An upsurge of interest in nuclear power is also possible in response to rising oil prices and doubts concerning the reliability of oil imports.

The rate of growth of nuclear generating capacity will be the principal determinant of requirements for uranium, enrichment services, and spent fuel storage capacity. It will also strongly influence policies on reprocessing and the acquisition of national reprocessing and enrichment facilities. With slow growth, the problems considered in this study would be less urgent. Individual countries, however, could encounter difficulties even though the overall supply of uranium and fuel cycle services was sufficient to meet requirements.

A final uncertainty that is relevant to the present discussion is the fate of the existing international regime for nuclear energy. Ideally, the existing regime should provide a firm foundation for new cooperative efforts, but this is by no means assured. Defections from the NPT are quite conceivable, and the acquisition of nuclear weapons by one or more additional countries may even be probable. The threat of either of these contingencies would divert diplomatic energies and political capital from the work of creating new forms of international cooperation.

Basic Problems

Two basic problems must be solved in developing new cooperative arrangements. First, some discrimination among differently situated countries may be unavoidable. If so, how can it be made acceptable? Second, what is the proper balance between restraints and positive inducements in seeking adherence to the new arrangements?

The existing regime discriminates in favor of nuclear weapon states, but attempts—with imperfect success—to make that discrimination tolerable, by imposing certain obligations on those states.[9] New forms of international cooperation would not overturn this division of the world into nuclear weapon haves and have nots. New arrangements might in fact discriminate between nonnuclear weapon states that have large civil nuclear energy programs and all other nonnuclear weapon states. Under this approach, only states with large programs would be regarded as having valid economic grounds for possessing sensitive fuel cycle facilities.

This approach can be defended on grounds of realism; it merely recognizes the true state of affairs. It also appears to be consistent with the goal of nonproliferation in that the states with large programs today are generally regarded as having little incentive to acquire nuclear weapons. Neither of these arguments, however, could be expected to make the discrimination acceptable to those states disadvantaged by it. More concrete considerations, positive or negative, would be required.

As a general rule, positive inducements are greatly to be preferred over sanctions. Sanctions are resented and often conflict with other policy goals of governments applying them. Moreover, sanctions can frequently be circumvented, given enough time. In the field of nuclear energy, the sanctions that are most likely to be applied are denial of access to nuclear technology, services, and materials. Such denial could, however, provide a powerful stimulus for more countries to develop autonomous national fuel cycles.

The new forms of international cooperation should be built on perceptions of mutual advantage. Persuasion and the offering of positive inducements rather than the threat of sanctions should be the dominant diplomatic method. This principle, however, would not preclude supplier countries from trading their legal rights over fuel in return for adherence by others to new cooperative arrangements.

An Illustrative, Phased Approach

If major uncertainties on the international scene and difficult problems argue for a gradual approach, the questions of priorities and the sequence

9. The nonproliferation treaty requires all parties (article IV) "to facilitate . . . the fullest possible exchange of equipment, materials, and scientific and technological information for the peaceful uses of nuclear energy." The treaty also requires

of actions become crucial. The answers do not depend solely on judgments concerning the relative urgency of various possible measures. Feasibility and the possible establishment of useful links between measures must also be taken into account.

Opinions may differ on what should be done and when. Moreover, shifting circumstances may force changes in plans. The phased approach presented here is therefore only illustrative. The institutional arrangements described in chapter 5 are used as building blocks. The numbered phases set forth below need not be sharply separated in time, but would almost certainly overlap.

Phase One

The place to begin is probably with the establishment of a general international consultative forum to consider the problems of the civil nuclear energy industry. The creation of such a forum in the relatively near future could help to preserve the momentum achieved by INFCE.[10] It could also be a constructive way to respond to the criticisms of the present nuclear regime that were made at the second conference to review the operation of the nonproliferation treaty that met in August and September 1980.[11]

Having the forum in place early could facilitate the adoption of other measures later in the phased program. Initial discussion of some of those measures could take place in the forum, and it could be used to create working groups on particular projects. A subordinate consultative group on the uranium market could be created concurrently with the establishment of the general forum. This group, or a parallel one, could later assume responsibility for monitoring the market for enrichment services.

The general forum and any subordinate specialized groups should not be seen as a continuation of INFCE under another name. The forum should be more policy oriented than INFCE. Its purpose should be to

---

(article VI) all parties "to pursue negotiations in good faith on effective measures relating to cessation of the nuclear arms race at an early date and to nuclear disarmament. . . ." Although these provisions bind all parties to the treaty, article IV is clearly directed primarily at the nuclear suppliers (some of which are nuclear weapon states) and article VI at the nuclear weapon states.

10. The committee of the whole created by the IAEA board of governors at its June 1980 meeting could become the needed general forum, although the committee's initial terms of reference focus on the problem of assurance of supply.

11. *New York Times,* September 8, 1980.

stimulate and facilitate constructive actions, not to prepare long studies. By making this clear, the misgivings of any governments that might feel that 20,000 pages of INFCE documentation are enough could be reduced.

Phase Two

At the present stage of development of the civil nuclear energy industry, the most important problem is how to impose adequate international controls over separated plutonium. A case could be made for including establishment of an international plutonium storage system (IPS) in phase one. But despite the amount of work that has been done on the IPS in the IAEA, obtaining agreement on the system is bound to be a complicated, time-consuming task. It is therefore more realistic to seek agreement as part of phase two.

The major suppliers of natural uranium and enrichment services could, if they wished, give a strong impetus to the creation of the IPS by offering to relinquish their unilateral controls over plutonium placed under the system (or alternatively to approve automatically any transfer, storage, or use of plutonium that conformed to the rules of the system).

Since such an offer would carry the implicit threat of disapproval of reprocessing and subsequent transfer, storage, or use of plutonium outside the system, the suppliers would find it desirable also to offer a more positive incentive. For that reason, cross-guarantees of fuel supplies could usefully be included in phase two. One of the conditions of eligibility for the guarantees could be agreement to join the IPS and abide by its rules.

Phase Three

A program to provide additional storage space for spent fuel could begin earlier, but might not produce significant results until phase three. Such a program would have two aspects: the return of some spent fuel to supplying countries, following the Soviet example, and the establishment of multinational storage centers—probably on a regional basis. Conditioning access to either of these storage arrangements on membership in the IPS might be considered. This link should not be imposed, however, if it appeared that it would have the effect of keeping more spent fuel in national storage depots.

If all went well, phase three could also include establishment of the general principle that large reprocessing plants were acceptable, but—with a few unavoidable exceptions for existing facilities—small plants were not. The supplier countries could have attempted to enforce this principle earlier in the program by holding back approval of reprocessing of spent fuel in small, new plants. By phase three, it might be possible to obtain wider agreement on this approach by offering countries that would otherwise want to build small national plants the opportunity to join in large multinational ventures.

Some would argue that at this point, if not sooner, all reprocessing should be placed under multinational auspices.[12] Whether this would be feasible is questionable. In any event, the need for multinational oversight would be reduced if—as is assumed here—the IPS were already in place. Multinational reprocessing need not be adopted as a general rule, but is a useful alternative to small national efforts.

Phase Four

By phase four, if not earlier, it might be possible to achieve a broad international consensus on the rules of trade in sensitive nuclear materials, equipment, and technology. Consultations designed to produce such a consensus should begin soon, but in view of the complexity of the subject, early agreement should not be expected. The United Nations conference on peaceful uses of nuclear energy that the UN General Assembly, acting in response to a Yugoslav initiative, has resolved should be held by 1983 may provide an opportunity to advance this effort.[13]

The consensus on the rules of trade could eventually be committed to writing, much as the guidelines of the London nuclear suppliers' group have been. An attempt to formalize the consensus in a treaty would probably not be worth the effort and might lose the support of countries that would be willing to cooperate, but would not want to be legally bound to do so.

In substance, but not necessarily in form, the consensus would be principally a bargain between the exporters and importers of specified ma-

12. For example, the NNPA enunciates a clear preference for having all reprocessing facilities under "effective international auspices and inspection"; 92 Stat. 123, sec. 104(d), and 92 Stat. 126, sec. 403(b)(1).
13. General Assembly, 34 sess., agenda item 14, A/34/L.10, October 31, 1979.

terials, equipment, and technology. A list of covered sensitive items similar to the trigger list appended to the London nuclear suppliers' guidelines would be required. The exporters would in effect assure the availability of the specified items to importers that voluntarily followed certain rules. Some of these rules might be derived from measures taken in earlier phases of the program. Thus there might be an understanding that, with a few exceptions, any reprocessing would take place in large plants and that all separated plutonium would be handled in conformity to the plutonium storage system. Other rules might apply the large plant principle to the enrichment of imported natural uranium and require importers of specified items to accept safeguards on all of their nuclear facilities. All relevant rules could in addition continue to apply to specified items that were re-exported and to facilities built on the basis of imported technology.

In brief, the consensus on rules of trade would be designed to do two things: to round out and fill gaps in the regime created step-by-step in previous phases of the program, and to shift from a system based on the implicit threat of exporters' sanctions to one resting on an informal compact between exporters and importers.

Continued Evolution of Cooperative Efforts

Just as a grand design for the civil nuclear energy industry is not feasible, it would be wrong to think that the process of dealing with the problems of the industry will someday be completed. Continued evolution and adjustment to changing circumstances will be both likely and desirable. If fast breeder reactors are brought into use on a large scale early in the next century, the problems facing the industry will change. Cooperative international actions may then be required whose nature can be only dimly seen today.

Closer at hand, some of the institutional arrangements that were discussed in this study, but were not included in the illustrative phased approach, may merit more serious consideration. If cross-guarantees prove not to be enough to moderate fears of fuel supply interruptions, they may have to be backed by dedicated stockpiles. Eventually, creation of a fuel bank might be seen as necessary. Similarly, if uncertainties concerning uranium supplies and prices increase, despite the establishment of a system of international consultations, creation of a new institution to deal with the problem could gain support.

From time to time, proposals have been made for an authoritative international body to regulate the civil nuclear energy industry. The Baruch Plan immediately after World War II would have given an international agency exclusive authority to conduct intrinsically dangerous operations in the field of nuclear energy. President Dwight D. Eisenhower's "Atoms for Peace" proposals in 1953 would have established a powerful international institution to take custody of a pool of nuclear materials diverted from military stocks and distribute those materials under appropriate conditions to civil nuclear energy projects throughout the world. More recently, the Nuclear Non-Proliferation Act of 1978 called on the president of the United States to negotiate "the establishment of an international nuclear fuel authority (INFA) with responsibility for providing agreed-upon fuel services and allocating agreed-upon quantities of fuel resources to ensure fuel supply on reasonable terms in accordance with agreements between INFA and supplier and recipient nations."[14]

Nothing of course came of the Baruch Plan. The IAEA, whose creation is traceable to Eisenhower's initiative, bears little resemblance to the powerful institution that he had in mind. And the proposed INFA has aroused little interest or support outside the United States.

Creation of an overall body to administer an international regime for civil nuclear energy would be premature if the arguments made here for a gradual approach are accepted. In any event, negotiation of an agreement to establish such a body is not feasible today. At best, this concept must be regarded as an idea whose time has not yet come.

Conclusions

New international cooperative arrangements for nuclear energy would be built on the foundation of the existing regime. An evolutionary approach would be more likely to succeed than a comprehensive approach that attempted to deal with all problems at once.

A phased cooperative program might begin with the establishment of a general consultative forum in which the problems of the civil nuclear energy industry could be discussed. Specialized subgroups could be formed as needed. Subsequent phases might create a plutonium storage

14. 22 U.S.C. 3223, sec. 104(a)(1).

system, cross-guarantees of fuel supplies, a program to develop additional storage capacity for spent fuel, and—as required—multinational reprocessing facilities. At some point a broad international consensus might be reached on the rules of trade in sensitive materials, equipment, and technology.

Continued evolution of the international cooperative arrangements in response to changing circumstances should be facilitated. Creation of an institution to administer all aspects of an international regime for nuclear energy will probably continue to be neither feasible nor necessary. Coordination among governments in dealing with the problems of civil nuclear energy can be achieved through the consultative forum.

It is appropriate to ask then whether the program proposed here is an adequate response to the near-nuclear weapon problem that is the subject of this study. Certainly, a stricter program could be devised that would seek to impose absolute barriers to the further spread of facilities capable of making the explosive components of nuclear weapons. Such a program would, however, be neither negotiable nor workable.

The program proposed here represents a compromise between nonproliferation and energy goals. Such a program would have a better chance of gaining broad international support than one that focused more narrowly on the problem of checking the spread of nuclear weapons. The value of the program purely from the nonproliferation point of view would nevertheless be substantial. Among other gains, separated plutonium would be placed under international control, incentives to acquire national reprocessing and enrichment plants would be weakened, and a consensus on the trade in sensitive nuclear materials, equipment, and technology would be achieved.

Only time will tell whether the new forms of international cooperation in nuclear energy that this program would create would make a critical difference in preventing the use of civil nuclear energy facilities for nonpeaceful purposes. Such an achievement would be worth the effort, but it is well to remember that it would deal with only part of the nuclear proliferation problem. As long as nations have strong incentives to acquire nuclear weapons, the danger of their further proliferation remains.

The Present International
Nuclear Regime

RALPH T. MABRY, JR.

ALTHOUGH there has been a continuous buildup and refinement of nuclear weapons since the failure of the Baruch Plan in 1946, there have also been a number of significant efforts to achieve a measure of control over the spread of nuclear arms. These efforts are manifested today in a wide variety of policies, arrangements, and institutions designed to promote the widespread and beneficial enjoyment of nuclear energy while at the same time reducing the risk of continued proliferation. Most notable among them have been the creation of the International Atomic Energy Agency (IAEA), the conclusion of the Treaty on the Non-Proliferation of Nuclear Weapons (NPT), and the present international safeguards system.

This appendix traces the development of antiproliferation efforts and describes how the system functions. It then considers some of the problems inherent in the present regime.

The International Atomic Energy Agency

Ever since the first detonation of a nuclear explosive some thirty-four years ago, the United States has been in the forefront of efforts to control the spread of nuclear weaponry. A review of the development of U.S. nuclear policy in the earlier years of the atomic era is an important first

145

step to an understanding of the existing regime for the control of the uses of nuclear energy.

Early Background

The first U.S. response to the risk of nuclear weapon proliferation was to attempt to keep secret all information relating to the use and application of atomic energy. Although it was apparent to some that there would be no indefinite U.S. monopoly of nuclear technology, it was nevertheless considered essential that the United States prohibit the dissemination of sensitive data on the design of atomic weapons and the transfer of fissionable materials abroad.[1] Accordingly, the U.S. Congress enacted the Atomic Energy Act of 1946 which provided, among other things, that until "effective and enforceable international safeguards have been established, there shall be no exchange with other nations with respect to the use of atomic energy for industrial purposes."[2]

On the international front, in November 1945, the president of the United States and the prime ministers of Great Britain and Canada met in Washington, D.C., to develop a common international strategy on atomic power. On the basis of these discussions, an "Agreed Declaration on Atomic Energy" was signed embodying an agreement to make available "detailed information concerning the practical industrial application of atomic energy" only after "effective enforceable safeguards against its use for destructive purposes" had been established.[3] The three governments went on to call for the creation of an international commission within the United Nations to design and implement these safeguards.[4] In December 1945 the Anglo-American-Canadian proposal was effectively ratified by the Soviet Union,[5] and resulted in the creation of a

1. See, for example, the remarks of Senator Brian McMahon upon introducing his bill for the control of atomic energy in September 1945. *Congressional Record,* vol. 91, pt. 6, 79 Cong. 1 sess., pp. 8362–63.

2. Atomic Energy Act of 1946, 60 Stat. 756.

3. Agreed Declaration on Atomic Energy, 1 U.N.T.S. 123, par. 6. See also *Multilateral Agreements,* Legal Series no. 1 (Vienna: International Atomic Energy Agency, 1959), p. 1.

4. 1 U.N.T.S. 123, par. 7.

5. Soviet endorsement of the plan was obtained following American and British cabinet level discussions on the proposal in 1945, which led to the issuance of a joint communiqué. The communiqué is reproduced under the title "The Establishment by the United Nations of a Commission for the Control of Atomic Energy," in U.S. Department of State, *International Control of Atomic Energy: Growth of a Policy* (Government Printing Office, 1946).

United Nations Atomic Energy Commission upon a unanimous vote of the UN General Assembly on January 24, 1946.[6]

The primary task of the UNAEC was to hear and make recommendations on international atomic energy issues, and not to establish controls under its own rather limited authority. The commission was, in other words, to serve as a forum for enlightened debate. In anticipation of this opportunity, U.S. Secretary of State James F. Byrnes appointed a five-member committee in January 1946 to work out a comprehensive American proposal. Under the chairmanship of Dean Acheson, the committee appointed a board of consultants headed by David E. Lilienthal, then chairman of the Tennessee Valley Authority, to undertake an intensive study of the problem. The board's study, *A Report on the International Control of Atomic Energy,* more widely known as the Acheson-Lilienthal Report, was approved by the committee and submitted to the secretary of state in March 1946.[7]

Perhaps the most significant contribution of the Acheson-Lilienthal Report to early views on the containment of nuclear weapons was that it correctly perceived that the production of fissionable materials, and not the design of the weapon itself, was the critical step in achieving nuclear weapon capability. It found that nuclear explosive materials were indistinguishable from certain forms of nuclear fuel required for nonmilitary purposes. The board harbored few illusions about the capacity of nations other than the United States to achieve nuclear weapon status. At the same time, however, it recognized that the need for alternative energy sources would serve as a powerful inducement to the development of national nuclear programs. It concluded therefore that in order to establish peaceful nuclear industries without at the same time furthering military programs, it would be necessary to subject to full, intensive international control all nuclear material (including source materials),[8] all facilities producing such materials, and all reactors using more than minor quantities of fissionable materials. The report further argued that the requisite intensity of control could not be achieved solely through inspections and other forms of external supervision. The report accordingly advocated the establishment of an international authority having full ownership and

6. UNGA/RES/1 (1), January 26, 1946.
7. See U.S. Department of State, *A Report on the International Control of Atomic Energy* (GPO, 1946).
8. Broadly defined to include natural uranium ore.

operating control over all items and activities susceptible to being diverted to nuclear weapon production.

The Acheson-Lilienthal Report became, with some modifications, the basis of the American proposal for nuclear control presented to the United Nations by Bernard Baruch in June 1946.[9] Among other things, the Baruch Plan called for the creation of an International Atomic Development Authority entrusted with: control over any production of fissionable materials; managerial control or ownership of all potentially dangerous activities; the power to control, license, and inspect all other nuclear energy activities; and research and development responsibilities sufficiently sophisticated and broad in scope to maintain the authority in the technical lead and thus enable it to detect more accurately any misuse of atomic energy. The plan would have also committed the United States to cease the manufacture of atomic weapons, dispose of existing bombs, and provide the authority with full information on the production of atomic energy.

The Soviet Union countered with a proposal calling for the international prohibition of both the production and deployment of nuclear weapons.[10] It insisted that priority should be given to prohibition and that any system for controlling atomic production was only of secondary importance. There was also a significant difference of opinion on the role of the proposed authority within the United Nations system. In the Soviet view, great power unanimity was a fundamental feature of the United Nations and since the authority would play a vital role in sharing world security, it should therefore be subject to Security Council oversight. By contrast, the United States reasoned that no control system could be effected if the controls established were subject to a Security Council veto by one of the very powers that might be violating them.

These and other disagreements between the Soviet Union and the United States were never successfully resolved. The ensuing impasse within the UNAEC and the first Soviet nuclear explosion in 1949 ap-

9. The plan was presented to the UNAEC in a series of speeches and memorandums reproduced in Department of State, *International Control of Atomic Energy*, pp. 13–16. The plan was accepted by the majority of the UNAEC and was substantially incorporated in the commission's first report as reproduced in Department of State, *International Control of Atomic Energy: First Report of the United Nations Atomic Energy Commission to the Security Council, December 31, 1946* (GPO, 1947).

10. See Department of State, *International Control of Atomic Energy*, app. 22.

parently convinced many that a total system of international atomic energy control of the type envisioned by the Baruch Plan was no longer feasible, if indeed it ever had been. Not surprisingly, on January 11, 1952, the UNAEC was dissolved.

"Atoms for Peace" and the Establishment of the IAEA

What may be regarded as a significant era in international nuclear policy was inaugurated by President Dwight D. Eisenhower in his famous "Atoms for Peace" address before the UN General Assembly on December 8, 1953.[11] This speech outlined an approach to proliferation which was at once less radical and more pragmatic than that attempted in the UNAEC. Whereas the Baruch Plan had foreseen the ownership of all nuclear materials by an international authority, the more modest Eisenhower proposal called for the establishment of a pool of strategic materials which would be siphoned off military stockpiles and distributed for use in national civilian programs. The proposed agency would control the distribution of nuclear materials, but would not own any significant quantities. After they had been established, the controls would then be reinforced by a system of international antidiversionary inspections.

The inspections provision marked the beginning of a fundamental shift in U.S. foreign policy. By ending the policy of secrecy prescribed by the Atomic Energy Act of 1946, it opened the door to U.S. cooperation in the nuclear field. In 1954 the U.S. Congress amended the Atomic Energy Act to authorize, if not encourage, expanded international cooperation.[12] In 1955 some sixty nations participated in the Geneva Conference on the Peaceful Uses of Atomic Energy which, among other things, led to the declassification by leading nuclear powers of previously sensitive information directly relevant to nuclear power production.

But if there was an abandonment of the so-called secrecy-denial policy of the immediate postwar era, concern over the risk of nuclear weapon proliferation had by no means diminished. U.S. nuclear cooperation was conditioned on express assurances that peaceful nuclear assistance would not be diverted to military uses. The 1954 act, for example, provided for

11. "Atomic Power for Peace," address by President Dwight D. Eisenhower before General Assembly of the United Nations, December 8, 1953, in *Atoms for Peace Manual,* Doc. 84-55, 84 Cong. 2 sess. (GPO, 1955), pp. 5–6.
12. See Atomic Energy Act of 1954, 68 Stat. 919, especially sec. 144.

a number of substantive and procedural conditions to U.S. cooperation in nuclear power development. Although the act authorized the president to enter into international arrangements in support of the concept of an "International Atomic Pool," no cooperative agreement could be executed without a formal "guaranty" by each recipient country that no materials and equipment supplied would be used "for research on or development of nuclear weapons, or for any other military purpose."[13] Furthermore, the act required each agreement to be authorized by the president and submitted to the Joint Committee on Atomic Energy where it would come into effect only after a certain period of time had elapsed, thereby affording congressional oversight, if not formal veto power, over each proposed arrangement.[14]

Pursuant to this authority, the United States executed bilateral agreements for civilian atomic energy cooperation with some twenty-seven countries in 1955, each providing for extensive guarantees against diversion of the equipment and materials supplied to military purposes.[15] Although the concept of on-site inspection by outside authorities had not yet matured, a prototypical safeguards system based on contractual warranties began to take shape. A common feature of all early agreements on international nuclear cooperation was guarantees against the transfer of nuclear materials to third parties, and a pledge by the recipient country to maintain such safeguards as would be necessary to assure their physical security.[16]

After a series of multilateral negotiations which lasted for several years, the Statute of the International Atomic Energy Agency was opened for signature on October 26, 1956. Although the Eisenhower initiative had been an important catalyst in the long and complex negotiations which finally gave birth to the IAEA, in the end the new agency bore only a limited resemblance to the kind of institution that was foreseen in the Atoms for Peace address. The original Eisenhower concept was that the agency would serve as a custodian of a pool of nuclear materials entrusted to it

13. 68 Stat. 940, sec. 123, 124, and 144.
14. 68 Stat. 940, sec. 123(b)–(c).
15. "Bilateral Agreements for Cooperation in the Civil Uses of Atomic Power, May–July 1955," in *Atoms for Peace Manual*, p. 370.
16. See, for example, "Agreement for Cooperation Concerning Civil Uses of Atomic Energy Between the Government of the United States of America and the Government of the Turkish Republic," in *Atoms for Peace Manual*, pp. 433–36, art. VI and VII.

and would be responsible for distributing these materials to civilian nuclear projects around the world. Similarly, under the first U.S. draft of the statute, the agency would act as a banker of the materials in its custody by lending or leasing such amounts as might be required by recipient nations, and thereby retaining title to them. Within the framework of this original scheme, the supplier countries would have been contractually obligated to contribute to the agency's stockpile of materials.

However, by the time the final draft was agreed upon, the notion that the agency should act as a custodian of a pool of demilitarized materials was reduced to the idea that the organization would merely arrange and supervise transactions among its members.[17]

The concept of obligatory contribution was abandoned in favor of an entirely voluntary arrangement related more directly to the needs of the agency and its members than to an effort to demilitarize significant amounts of strategic materials.[18] In the end, all that remained of the bold proposals submitted by President Eisenhower was the more timid and slightly ambiguous language of article IX.A of the IAEA statute which provides that: "[fissionable] materials . . . made available to the Agency may, at the discretion of the member making them available, be stored either by the member concerned or, with the agreement of the Agency, in the Agency's depots."[19]

Attention subsequently focused on the establishment of an antiproliferation regime of less ambitious dimensions than had been envisioned under the Eisenhower plan. In effect, the internal safeguards function implicit in the Eisenhower concept gave way to greater emphasis on an external system under which there would be less reliance on the distributive and supervisory function of the agency, and greater reliance upon its authority to detect diversions from peaceful nuclear activities. The latter safeguard concept had already found expression in U.S. bilateral

17. The decline of support in the United States for a strong IAEA supply function is illustrated in Warren H. Donnelly, *Commercial Nuclear Power in Europe: The Interaction of American Diplomacy with a New Technology,* Committee Print, prepared for the Subcommittee on National Security Policy and Scientific Developments of the House Committee on Foreign Affairs, 92 Cong. 2 sess. (GPO, 1972), pp. 61–62.

18. Paul C. Szasz, *The Law and Practice of the International Atomic Energy Agency,* Legal Series 7 (Vienna: International Atomic Energy Agency, 1970), pp. 381–82.

19. 8 U.S.T. 1094.

agreements, which by 1956 provided for increasing numbers of fuel transfers and consequently more detailed and comprehensive control measures. Typically, these so-called Agreements for Cooperation contained stipulations establishing the right of the United States to "review the design" of reactors using materials supplied by the United States and, more fundamentally, the right to on-site inspection of "all places and data necessary to account for" any nuclear materials provided under the agreement.[20] Not surprisingly, the IAEA safeguard provisions bore a remarkable resemblance to the U.S. bilateral arrangements which were negotiated at that time, although in some respects they were still more comprehensive.

The Safeguard System's Statutory Framework

The international safeguard mechanisms established under the IAEA statute are provided for in a network of statutory provisions.[21] This results partly from the fact that the agency was established to perform two related but distinct control functions: establish controls on nuclear materials held by the agency itself under article IX (that is, internal safeguards), and establish controls on the nuclear items and activities in a state in order to prevent their diversion to any military objective (external safeguards).

The primary purpose of the internal safeguard function is to provide for the physical security of materials within the agency's custody or, more specifically, to protect against their diversion, unauthorized removal, and forcible seizure.[22] However, thus far these particular safeguards have never been applied since the agency has not yet functioned as the custodian of a pool of nuclear materials contributed to it under article IX.[23]

20. David F. Cavers, "International Cooperation in the Peaceful Uses of Atomic Energy," *Vanderbilt Law Review,* vol. 12 (December 1958), pp. 17–49.

21. The relevant provisions include the IAEA statute, articles II, III.A.5, XII, XIV.B.1(b), XIV.C, as well as III.B.1, III.B.2, IX.H, IX.I.2. IAEA, *Statute* (Vienna: IAEA, 1973).

22. See IAEA, *Statute,* articles III.B.2, IX.H, IX.I.2, and XII.B.

23. Ibid. Articles IX.C and IX.F were never interpreted to *require* of member states a contribution of fissionable materials to the IAEA. Any such contribution has been deemed completely voluntary. And although the IAEA secretariat did in fact serve notice on the membership pursuant to article IX.F, no contributions were received within the statutory one-year period and no efforts were undertaken to extend it. As a consequence the agency has never been in possession of article IX materials,

In contrast, the external safeguard function remains the agency's most significant contribution to the development of an antiproliferation regime. Unlike internal safeguards, external safeguards are intended to establish controls over materials in which the agency has no possessory interest. Under the terms of the statute these measures are designed to ensure that nuclear materials, services, equipment, facilities, and information made available by the agency or at its request, or under its supervision and control, are strictly confined to peaceful activities.[24] Many of the details of this safeguard function are specified in the enabling provisions of article XII which, in pertinent part, confers upon the agency the following rights and responsibilities: (1) examine and approve of the design of nuclear facilities; (2) enforce health and safety measures; (3) require the maintenance and production of operating records; (4) approve the means to be used in nuclear fuel reprocessing; and (5) carry out on-site inspections of safeguarded facilities.[25]

---

although there have been several proposals since 1957 to create a fund of special materials and a number of U.S. bilateral supply agreements requiring that materials not required by the recipient nation be offered for sale to the IAEA; see Szasz, *The Law and Practice of the International Atomic Energy Agency,* Agreement for Cooperation between the United States and the European Atomic Energy Community, pp. 386–88. A 1959 U.S.-Euratom agreement thus provides for an excess materials tender to the agency, 10 U.S.T. 75, art. III.E.

24. Note that the IAEA has engaged in a wide variety of activities which directly or indirectly involve the application of safeguards. Most notably, the agency provides technical and materials assistance to petitioning member states for the development of their civilian nuclear programs. Article XI.F.4(b) requires recipient nations to agree to be subject to IAEA safeguards as a condition precedent to this assistance. Similarly, the agency may be called upon to oversee a transfer of fissionable materials from one nation to another under a trilateral safeguards agreement. IAEA, *Statute.*

25. More specifically, article XII (ibid.) provides as follows:

A. With respect to any agency project, or other agreement when the Agency is requested by the parties concerned to apply safeguards, the Agency shall have the following rights and responsibilities to the extent relevant to the project or arrangement:

1. To examine the design of specialized equipment and facilities, including nuclear reactors, and to approve it only from the viewpoint of assuring that it will not further any military purpose, that it complies with applicable health and safety standards, and that it will permit effective application of the safeguards . . .

2. To require the observance of any health and safety measures prescribed by the Agency;

3. To require the maintenance and production of operating records to assist in ensuring accountability for source and special fissionable materials used or produced in the project or arrangement;

As is suggested by these enabling provisions, the statute establishes the foundation for development of an international safeguard system based upon the concept of strict accountancy. The underlying rationale is that the risk of weapons proliferation is diminished by closely monitoring the use and disposition of all sensitive nuclear materials and equipment subject to IAEA supervision.

Under the statute, the scope of the agency's supervisory authority is not confined to materials and equipment made available to members under the agency's technical assistance program. IAEA safeguards are also required to be applied either at the request of the parties to any bilateral or multilateral supply arrangement or at the unilateral request of a state to any of that state's activities in the field of atomic energy.[26]

The statute addresses the question of the enforcement of safeguards by emphasizing the application of limited sanctions against violators. Under article XII.C, inspectors are required to inform the IAEA director general of any diversions for military purposes. The director general is in turn required to submit all such unfavorable reports to the board of governors, which then renders a final determination of the charge on the basis of simple majority vote. Upon finding that a violation has occurred, article XII.C directs the board to call upon the state or states involved to remedy the noncompliance, and report its findings to all IAEA members, as well as to the Security Council and General Assembly of the United Nations. If the breaching state refuses to comply within a reasonable time, the board is authorized to direct that all assistance being provided

---

4. To call for and receive progress reports;

5. To approve the means to be used for the chemical processing of irradiated materials solely to ensure that this chemical processing will not lend itself to diversion of materials for military purposes . . .

6. To send into the territory of the recipient State or States inspectors . . . who shall have access at all times to all places and data . . . as necessary to account for source and special fissionable materials supplied . . . and to determine whether there is compliance with the undertaking against use in furtherance of any military purpose. . . .

26. Ibid., article III.A.5. Careful analysis, therefore, suggests four distinct motives for submission to safeguards: (1) the desire to receive IAEA technical assistance for a nuclear energy program; (2) the desire to receive such assistance from another state or multinational organization that requires submission to IAEA safeguards as an alternative to its own; (3) domestic or external political pressure; and (4) participation in a bilateral, regional, or international arrangement that requires the submission of all, or certain nuclear activities to agency safeguards.

by the agency or its members be curtailed or suspended;[27] call for the return of materials and equipment made available to the state;[28] or as provided in article XIX.B, suspend any noncomplying member from the exercise of the privileges and rights of membership.

It should be emphasized that membership in the IAEA does not carry with it any affirmative obligation either to refrain from military nuclear activities or to submit to agency safeguards. Nor is a member under any duty to refrain from assisting other states in undertaking nuclear activities or to require that any assistance it grants be subject to its own or the agency's control. The agency's safeguards cannot, and were not intended to, achieve any general disarmament objective. Rather, their purpose is the more limited one of detecting proscribed activities and inhibiting proliferation by threatening to expose them. The possibly limited efficacy of statutorily authorized sanctions in aid of this objective,[29] and indeed, the reliability of the safeguard system itself are therefore largely dependent on the political and moral suasion of nuclear weapon states.

The Development of the Non-NPT Safeguard Regime

Although it provides the basis for the agency's safeguards, the IAEA statute was never meant to be more than a framework for the system. Much of the substance of the safeguard system is to be found in the many bilateral and multilateral agreements between the agency and the states concerned.[30] Of course, in principle, the statutory framework alone would be sufficient, as the statute expressly states that safeguards would only be exercised on the basis of an agreement between a state and the agency. However, since the formulation of even minor agreements would have been too lengthy and complicated in the absence of basic guidelines, on

27. It is unclear whether such a sanction would require members to solicit and accept the return of items and materials furnished outside the framework of an agency project or rendered at the request of the agency. The affirmative obligations of member states with respect to safeguards and nonproliferation generally is extremely limited.

28. See also IAEA, *Statute*, article XII.A.7.

29. As a practical matter, the potentially most severe sanction of withdrawing the misused items would require the compliance of the breaching state.

30. See Benjamin Sanders, *Safeguards Against Nuclear Proliferation*, Stockholm International Peace Research Institute Monograph (Cambridge: MIT Press; Stockholm: Almqvist and Wiksell, 1975).

January 31, 1961, the IAEA adopted its first safeguard document, also known as the Agency's Safeguards System (1961).[31]

The 1961 safeguard document was of limited application. It related only to reactors with less than 100-megawatt, thermal output, although it was foreseen that procedures for the application of safeguards to larger facilities would eventually be developed. Accordingly, on February 26, 1954, the board of governors approved an extension of the system to larger reactors.[32] Finally, on February 25, 1965, approval was granted for a slightly revised system commonly known as INFCIRC/66 (for Information Circular 66).

In February 1966 the system was extended to include reprocessing plants, and in 1968 amendments were passed for the inclusion of materials in conversion and fuel fabrication plants. As revised by these two additions, this safeguard system is generally referred to as INFCIRC/66/Rev.2.[33]

The INFCIRC/66/Rev.2 provides the basic guidelines for the negotiation of all safeguard agreements between the agency and countries that are not parties to the NPT. These safeguard agreements constitute the undertaking of the consenting state to submit to the application of IAEA safeguards. There are fundamentally three categories of safeguard agreements: project agreements under which IAEA safeguards are applied to an agency project; unilateral submission agreements under which states voluntarily place part or all of their nuclear activities under agency safeguards; and safeguard transfer agreements under which parties to bilateral cooperation agreements designate the IAEA as agent for the application of safeguards.[34]

It is worth noting that INFCIRC/66/Rev.2 has no independent legal significance inasmuch as it becomes binding only upon the entering into force of a safeguard agreement between the agency and the states concerned. Its provisions are binding only to the extent that they are incorporated by reference in the individual safeguard agreements. In practice, many of the provisions of the guidelines, such as those relating to control

---

31. IAEA, *Principles and Procedures for the Attachment and Application of Safeguards by the Agency*, INFCIRC/26 (Vienna: IAEA 1961).

32. Ibid., INFCIRC/26/Add.1.

33. Reprinted in Sanders, *Safeguards Against Nuclear Proliferation*, app. 4, p. 95.

34. Ibid., INFCIRC/66/Rev.2, par. 19.

procedures and those pertaining to the termination or suspension of safeguards, are routinely incorporated by reference. In some respects therefore safeguard documents serve as the repository of the boilerplate clauses of safeguard agreements. Specific provisions may be fashioned to conform to individual cases. However, many such details are incorporated in so-called subsidiary arrangements.

As discussed in greater detail below, INFCIRC/66/Rev.2 safeguards are facility-specific in that they are applied to individual facilities and are not based on a full, fuel cycle materials flow system. The circular provides for the auditing of nuclear material records maintained by the state, verification of the amount of safeguarded materials by physical inspection, and agency review of the facilities.[35] Design review is undertaken for the purpose of determining whether the facility in question will permit the effective application of safeguards. Agency verification is accomplished by containment and surveillance techniques. Containment methods include the application of locks, seals, and other devices on nuclear storage areas to prevent changes in material content without the agency's knowledge.

Facility-based safeguards are relatively easily applied to lightwater reactors (LWRs).[36] Typically, LWR fuel rods are sealed prior to delivery to the reactor site and remain closed unless reopened for waste treatment or reprocessing. Discrete fuel elements and bundles can also be counted and sealed by agency inspectors. The removal of spent fuel rods during reloading and their storage in cooling ponds adjacent to reactors are monitored by film and television cameras as well as by remote radiometric equipment. To help assure the accuracy of these instruments, tamper-resistant equipment is used. Fiber optic seals to enable field verification of sealed units are now under development.[37]

The first safeguard document took two years to negotiate, and the revised INFCIRC/66 was several more years in preparation. It will be of interest to recall that one of the reasons for the relatively slow development of the IAEA safeguard system was the initial reluctance of many nations to forgo a bilateral approach. Along with a reluctance to provide

35. Ibid. Note particularly INFCIRC/66/Rev.2, pars. 30, 33, 49, 50, and 57.
36. See, generally, Congress of the United States, Office of Technology Assessment, *Nuclear Proliferation and Safeguards* (Praeger, 1977), pp. 209–10.
37. "Surveillance and Containment Measures to Support IAEA Safeguards," *International Atomic Energy Agency Bulletin,* vol. 19 (October 1977), pp. 20–26.

the agency with assistance necessary for it to act as supplier, many U.S. policymakers were initially doubtful of the wisdom of relinquishing the kind of control which bilateral agreements were deemed to provide.[38] It was only when it later became apparent that the IAEA system might contribute to the credibility of impartial inspections, promote uniformity of safeguard standards, and make all of this available at a lower cost that the United States agreed that the agency should serve as the exclusive agent for safeguard administration.

This shift in policy was also partially the result of the belief that recipient countries would be more willing to accept inspections by an international organization of which they were a member than from the supplier countries themselves. Ironically, however, many of the governments with which the United States had cooperation agreements indicated a preference for the existing bilateral arrangement. Nevertheless, any failure on the part of the United States (the then-dominant nuclear power) to insist on IAEA safeguards as a condition precedent to receipt of fuel supplies would have been perceived as undermining the antiproliferation role of the IAEA.[39] The United States and other supplier countries began to insist successfully on recipient government acquiescence in IAEA safeguards. In 1961 Japan took the lead by becoming the first to voluntarily submit to IAEA safeguards. By 1977 a total of 550 nuclear facilities ranging from power plants to reprocessing, enrichment, and research and development facilities were under IAEA safeguards. Of these, 197 were subject to the INFCIRC/66/Rev.2 system.[40]

38. Under the International Atomic Energy Participation Act of 1957, the U.S. Congress authorized the president to make available to the agency up to 5,000 kilograms of U^{235}. And at the first IAEA General Conference in 1957, the U.S. Atomic Energy Commission pledged to match Soviet and British supply offers. However, support for a strong IAEA supply function soon waned in some U.S. policymaking circles as it was thought that bilateral arrangements would better serve the U.S. national interest by providing stronger U.S. control over the allocation and use of nuclear materials. See Donnelly, *Commercial Nuclear Power in Europe,* pp. 52–62.

For more on the bilateral controls issue see, for example, statement of Atomic Energy Commissioner Harold S. Vance in *Agreement for Cooperation between the United States and the International Atomic Energy Agency,* Hearing before the Subcommittee on Agreements for Cooperation of the Joint Committee on Atomic Energy, 86 Cong. 1 sess. (GPO, 1959), p. 23.

39. *Nuclear Power and Nuclear Weapons Proliferation,* vol. 1: *A Report of the Atlantic Council's Nuclear Forces Fuels Policy Working Group* (Washington, D.C.: Atlantic Council of the United States, 1978), pp. 63–64, 66.

40. "The International Scope of IAEA Safeguards," *International Atomic Energy Agency Bulletin,* vol. 19 (October 1977), p. 6.

Treaty on the Non-Proliferation of Nuclear Weapons

The evolution of IAEA safeguards did not cease with the development of the INFCIRC/66 system. The formulation of the guidelines was not an end in itself; rather, various attempts in the early 1960s to promote nuclear weapons disarmament (such as efforts on behalf of the Nuclear Test Ban Treaty of 1963) gave impetus to the search for an improved antiproliferation regime which would extend to the entire nuclear program of nonnuclear weapon states.

In December 1961 the United Nations adopted the so-called Irish resolution asking all states, and particularly the nuclear weapon states, to "refrain from relinquishing control of nuclear weapons," and to strive to secure an international agreement under which "states not possessing nuclear weapons would undertake not to manufacture or otherwise acquire control of such weapons."[41] Accordingly, on December 20, 1961, the Eighteen Nation Disarmament Committee (later the Conference of the Committee on Disarmament) was formed. Composed of five NATO members, five Warsaw Pact countries, and eight nonaligned nations under the cochairmanship of the United States and the Soviet Union, the ENDC considered several draft nonproliferation treaties until, finally, on June 10, 1968, a definitive text emerged. On July 1, 1968, the Treaty on the Non-Proliferation of Nuclear Weapons was opened for signature but did not enter into force until almost three years later.[42]

The NPT is based on five key provisions: article I commits nonnuclear weapon states not to manufacture, accept the transfer of, or otherwise acquire nuclear weapons. Article III requires all nonnuclear weapon states to agree to accept IAEA safeguards on all their peaceful nuclear activities. Article IV provides that all parties are guaranteed the right to engage in peaceful nuclear activities. Article V establishes an obligation for international sharing, on a nondiscriminatory basis, of any potential benefits that may be derived from peaceful applications of nuclear explosions. Article VI requires all parties to work for nuclear disarmament.

41. A/Res./1665 (XVI), December 5, 1961. See William B. Bader, *The United States and the Spread of Nuclear Weapons* (Pegasus for the Center for International Studies, Princeton University, 1958), pp. 35–43.

42. 21 U.S.T. 483. The "legislative" history of the NPT is discussed in Mason Willrich, *Non-Proliferation Treaty: Framework for Nuclear Arms Control* (Charlottesville, Va.: Michie, 1969), pp. 61–64.

Not surprisingly, the article III provision effectively requiring all parties of the NPT to refuse to supply nuclear materials to nonnuclear weapon states was the subject of long and difficult negotiations. For one thing, it threatened to be an impediment to the continued expansion of profitable trade opportunities in international nuclear commerce. For another, regional political concerns emerged. The member states of the European Atomic Energy Community (Euratom), for example, were reluctant to accept IAEA safeguards in place of the safeguard mechanisms established under the Euratom Treaty.[43] International safeguards were thought by them to be superfluous, and some feared that they might lead to an abandonment of Euratom with a consequent erosion of European unity. However, the Soviet Union, together with other non-Euratom countries, vigorously opposed the substitution of IAEA safeguards by those of Euratom as being incompatible with principles of an international system and as amounting to self-inspection by the states concerned.[44] As a compromise, the final draft of the treaty avoided the issue by permitting nonnuclear weapon states to negotiate safeguard agreements with the IAEA either individually or together with other nations, thereby allowing Euratom's regional safeguard capabilities to be taken into account.[45]

Furthermore, and more fundamentally, many countries were reluctant to agree to the treaty on grounds that the NPT inherently discriminated by denying to nonnuclear weapon states the right to undertake the explosive applications of nuclear energy, while at the same time preserving this opportunity for nuclear weapon states. Advanced nations such as Japan and West Germany were particularly concerned that as nonnuclear weapon states they would be at a commercial disadvantage in pursuing the peaceful uses of nuclear energy. Many developing countries were (and remain) resentful of the political inequities of an arrangement which imposes safeguard obligations on their nuclear activities while pre-

43. Articles 77 to 85 of the Euratom Treaty provide for an extensive safeguards system to be applied to the peaceful nuclear activities of all member states. The powers of the Euratom safeguards inspectorate generally exceed those of inspectors under the IAEA-NPT system; see Johnson, "Nuclear Power Proliferation: Problems of International Control," *Energy Policy* (September 1977), pp. 179, 187, and note 35. Note that Euratom has since negotiated a safeguard agreement with the IAEA which came into force in February 1977.

44. Willrich, *Non-Proliferation Treaty,* pp. 108–16.

45. See ibid., article III.4.

serving the status of the nuclear powers. In their view, the vague and general provisions of article VI of the treaty requiring the nuclear powers to work toward nuclear arms control measures constitute an inadequate quid pro quo for the more restrictive obligations which nonnuclear weapon states are required to accept.[46]

Although many may have been willing to accept this discrimination as it applied to nuclear explosive devices, others were reluctant to see its institutionalization in relation to peaceful uses of nuclear energy more generally. President Lyndon B. Johnson accordingly declared that the United States would not ask "any country to accept any safeguards that we are not willing to accept ourselves," and offered to place all U.S. nuclear activities under IAEA safeguards, except those having direct national security significance.[47] However, this was not to lead to the application of safeguards to all NPT parties because the Soviet Union, consistent with its traditional opposition to inspection, was unwilling to accept safeguards on its own peaceful program.

This issue remains directly relevant to the present nonproliferation debate. IAEA safeguards have not been applied to U.S., Soviet, and other nuclear weapon states' peaceful nuclear activities, although negotiations on a comprehensive agreement between Euratom, its member states, and the IAEA have been concluded.[48] Moreover, the developing and nonaligned states remain deeply resentful of what they perceive to be the continuing inequities of the NPT system, and most particularly of the failure of the nuclear weapon states to fulfill their article VI obligations. At the 1975 NPT Review Conference, noting that the nonnuclear weapon states have fully complied with all relevant provisions of the treaty, Yugoslavia, among other nonnuclear weapon states, vigorously protested the failure of nuclear powers to have reached any substantial agreement on ending the arms race.[49]

46. As the Indian government stated: "Institution of international controls on peaceful reactors and power stations is like an attempt to maintain law and order in a society by placing all its law-abiding citizens in custody while leaving its law-breaking elements free to roam the streets." Quoted from Willrich, *Non-Proliferation Treaty*, p. 124.

47. "Remarks at the Signing of the Nuclear Non-Proliferation Treaty, July 1, 1968," *Public Papers of the Presidents: Lyndon B. Johnson, 1968–69*, book 2 (GPO, 1970), p. 765.

48. See *Nuclear Power and Nuclear Weapons Proliferation*, vol. 2, p. 45.

49. *Review Conference of the Parties to the Treaty on the Non-Proliferation of*

The INFCIRC/153 Regime

Despite the difficulties encountered during its negotiation, the NPT entered into force on March 5, 1970. Shortly thereafter, the IAEA established a committee to develop a safeguard document which would serve as a basis for negotiating safeguard agreements between the agency and NPT signatories. On April 20, 1971, the board of governors approved the committee's draft recommendations and authorized the director general to use them as the basis for negotiating all article III safeguard agreements. Known as INFCIRC/153, or the Blue Book, these guidelines represented at the time an entirely new safeguard system, differing from its predecessor in scope, purpose, and implementation procedures.[50]

It is of fundamental significance that the INFCIRC/153 regime, since it was derived from the NPT, requires IAEA safeguards on *"all* peaceful nuclear activities" in the nonnuclear weapon states, whether or not requested by the state concerned (emphasis added). The INFCIRC/66/Rev.2 system, on the other hand, merely provides for the application of safeguards to agency projects, and where requested unilaterally or by the parties to a bilateral supply agreement. Thus under the NPT regime, all peaceful nuclear activities, whether imported or indigenous, must be placed under safeguards. Under the non-NPT system no such obligation is imposed.

In this respect, the INFCIRC/153 regime is a far more comprehensive system. It is also one whose broader scope is partly a reflection of its different purpose. As noted earlier, the non-NPT regime is intended to assure that any assistance provided by the agency or placed under its supervision is not used to "further any military purpose." The INFCIRC/153

Nuclear Weapons, final document, pt. 1, NPT/CONF/35/I, annex 2, pp. 32–33. Yugoslavia therefore joined Mexico, Nigeria, and Rumania in making specific demands for a pledge by the nuclear weapon powers to discontinue underground nuclear testing, to establish a special international regime, not to use or threaten to use nuclear weapons against nonnuclear weapon states, and to respect all nuclear-free zones. Also deplored was the apparent failure of the advanced nations to fully assist the developing countries on the peaceful uses of nuclear energy as stipulated in article V of the NPT. See William Epstein, "Failure of the NPT Review Conference," *Bulletin of Atomic Scientists* (September 1975), pp. 46–48.

50. "The Structure and Content of Agreements between the Agency and States Required in Connection with the Treaty on the Non-Proliferation of Nuclear Weapons," reprinted in Sanders, *Safeguards Against Nuclear Proliferation,* app. 3, pp. 73–95.

has the broader objective of assuring "the timely detection of diversion of significant quantities of *nuclear material* from peaceful nuclear activities to the manufacture of nuclear weapons or of other explosive devices or for purposes unknown, and deterrence of such diversion by the risk of early detection."[51]

The emphasis on the words "nuclear material" in INFCIRC/153 is not without purpose. By reason of the NPT article III directive that safeguards be applied to all nuclear materials, unlike the facility-specific approach under INFCIRC/66/Rev.2, INFCIRC/153 safeguards are based on material flow. The INFCIRC/153 system embodies somewhat tighter and more detailed implementation procedures, and provides greater guidance for the negotiation of safeguard documents.[52]

Under the INFCIRC/153 regime, safeguard procedures are centered around precisely defined material balance areas (MBAs), located at strategic or so-called key measurement points at which statistical measurement techniques are applied to random samples of material flow. Once a facility is in operation, access of the IAEA inspectors is limited to these areas. Unannounced inspections to conduct random samplings are permissible; however, in many instances prior notice is required. The frequency of routine inspections are set according to the volume of material passing through the facility at which the particular MBAs are located.

An important and novel characteristic of the INFCIRC/153 system is that the state within which safeguards are applied is required to prepare and maintain a national accounting system in respect to all nuclear material subject to safeguards. Independent verification is accomplished by verifying the location, identity, quantity, and composition of the safeguarded materials. Computer analysis and portable instrumentation, such

51. Ibid., par. 28, p. 78. As has been pointed out, the inclusion of the phrase "or for purposes unknown" relieves the IAEA inspectorate of the difficult burden of proving the manufacture of an explosive device from unaccounted-for material. The disappearance of substantial amounts of nuclear materials is ipso facto regarded as sufficient grounds for a finding of diversion. B. Sanders and R. Rometsch, "Safeguards Against Use of Nuclear Materials for Weapons," *Nuclear Engineering International* (September 1975), p. 682.

52. Both systems provide for the negotiation of so-called subsidiary arrangements between the agency and the state within which safeguards are to be applied. These documents are intended to complement the safeguard agreements by establishing in a separate instrument the technical and administrative rules under which safeguards are to be implemented. Under the INFCIRC/153 system, these rules have been far more standardized. Sanders, *Safeguards Against Nuclear Proliferation*, pp. 25–27.

as stabilized assay meters and various nondestructive assay instruments, assist in the verification of the accuracy of the inventory and other reports submitted by the facility operators.[53] This enables the monitoring of both changes in volume and isotopic content. Irregularities between book and physical inventories are first noted in a material balance report prepared by the operators. Any materials unaccounted for by independent verification must be reported to the agency inspectorate. Statistical and probabilistic evaluations of the quantities of unaccounted for materials serve as the basis for determining whether a diversion has occurred.[54]

The Adequacy and Effectiveness of IAEA Safeguards

An evaluation of the existing international safeguard system logically begins with a recognition that a number of countries have not ratified the NPT and are therefore not subject to its regime. Of the 111 nonnuclear weapon states that are parties to the NPT, sixty-eight had safeguard arrangements in force in May 1980.[55] However, among the nonparties to the NPT, twelve have significant nuclear activities in operation, under construction, or on the drawing board.

Of the following nonparties to the NPT, seven have safeguards administered by the IAEA on all or most of their peaceful nuclear activities: Argentina, Brazil, Chile, Colombia, Pakistan, South Africa, and Spain. As a nuclear weapon state, China is not required to accept agency safeguards and none are applied. Egypt is the only nonnuclear weapon state with significant nuclear activities to which no IAEA safeguards are applied. France accepts Euratom and IAEA safeguards on materials transferred under trilateral agreements. Of all the nonparty states, India has the largest number and variety of unsafeguarded facilities: two reprocessing plants, two fuel fabrication plants, and three reactors. Therefore, of these

53. "Application of Safeguards Procedures," *International Atomic Energy Agency Bulletin*, vol. 19 (October 1977), p. 10.
54. Warren H. Donnelly and Barbara Rather, *Nuclear Weapons Proliferation and the International Atomic Energy Agency: An Analytic Report*, Committee Print, for the Senate Committee on Government Operations, 94 Cong. 2 sess. (GPO, 1976), p. 115.
55. "NPT Newsletter," *International Atomic Energy Agency Bulletin*, vol. 22 (August 1980), pp. 100–01.

twelve, nine submit to IAEA safeguards effectively encompassing all or most of their significant nuclear activities.[56]

India, Israel, South Africa, and Spain, though engaged in significant nuclear operations, undertake activities not subject to NPT safeguards. As nonparties to the NPT and by their refusal to submit to the accompanying safeguard system, they may therefore lawfully maintain two separate sets of nuclear facilities: one set under safeguards, and another either imported without bilateral safeguard requirements or developed indigenously, independent of safeguards. At present, India is the only country with a dual nuclear power program, although Israel, Egypt, South Africa, and Spain have unsafeguarded nuclear research facilities.

As nonparties to the NPT, these countries are not subject to the INFCIRC/153 regime requiring all peaceful nuclear activities to be placed under safeguards. Only INFCIRC/66/Rev.2 safeguards need be applied, and these will only arise when and if safeguards are required as a condition precedent to exports of nuclear materials to these countries. Therefore, as the number of non-NPT states with significant nuclear power programs increases, it may be reasonably expected that the number of such dual power program states will also increase. In the absence of additional safeguard requirements, many non-NPT states will be in a position to acquire foreign nuclear technology, which, though transferred under INFCIRC/66/Rev.2 safeguards, will be available for use in indigenously developed, unsafeguarded facilities.

The problems of the nonuniversal scope of the NPT are compounded by certain arguable ambiguities within the treaty itself. Under article III.2 each party to the NPT undertakes not to provide nuclear assistance to nonparties unless such assistance is made subject to IAEA safeguards. However, the question arises as to which safeguard regime is to be required. Are safeguards only to be imposed with respect to the specific assistance provided (as under INFCIRC/66/Rev.2), or are they to apply to all the peaceful nuclear activities of the recipient state (as under INFCIRC/153)? Of course, the specific language of article III.2 calls for the application of such safeguards as are "required by this article", and this presumably includes the paragraph one directive that safeguards must be applied to "all peaceful nuclear activities." Unfortunately, as has

56. "The International Scope of IAEA Safeguards," pp. 2–8.

been pointed out, the treaty provides no mechanism for an authoritative construction of this provision.[57] Each nuclear supplier is therefore free to adopt its own interpretation. And as a consequence of any less than strict construction of article III, many importing countries are further permitted the opportunity to develop dual nuclear power programs in the manner just described. Happily, recent agreements among major suppliers on establishing common export policies may have the beneficial effect of closing this loophole. But in the longer term, as other nations develop their nuclear industries and compete for lucrative export markets, such arrangements may prove less effective.

One additional difficulty with the existing dual system relates to the important doctrine of pursuit. Article III.2 of the NPT effectively prohibits nonnuclear weapon states as well as nuclear weapon states from making any nuclear assistance available without accompanying safeguards. Implicit in this pursuit requirement is the notion that if consistently adhered to, such an obligation would result in a web of international safeguards encompassing a great many states, including many nonparties to the NPT. Paragraph sixteen of INFCIRC/66/Rev.2 establishes the foundation for a similar concept within the non-NPT system. Thus, it has been said that this provision implies the principle that the supply of any nuclear item should never further any military purpose and that therefore any nuclear material produced by means of such items should also come under safeguards.[58] As noted earlier, however, INFCIRC/66/Rev.2 merely provides guidelines for the negotiation of safeguard agreements. Its provisions are not mandatory; indeed, paragraph sixteen merely states that it would be "desirable" for each safeguard agreement negotiated to incorporate the principle of pursuit. Not surprisingly, not all agreements contain a provision to this effect.[59] And as a consequence, certain nonparties to the NPT may be free to export nuclear materials derived from safeguarded equipment and materials without accompanying safeguards.[60]

57. Paul C. Szasz, "The Inadequacy of International Nuclear Safeguards," *Journal of International Law and Economics*, vol. 10 (August–December 1975), p. 427.

58. Sanders, *Safeguards Against Nuclear Proliferation*, pp. 15, 97.

59. Ibid.

60. Of course, there are two dimensions to the concept of pursuit: one of time and the other of territoriality. The agency has evidently been very careful to include in its non-NPT agreements a provision for the continuation of safeguards after the

In regard more specifically to the problems of the NPT, it should be noted that under article X.I, the right is reserved by all parties to withdraw from the treaty upon serving three months' notice to the other parties and to the UN Security Council. The only restriction on withdrawal is that the withdrawing party must first decide that "extraordinary events, related to the subject matter of this Treaty, have jeopardized the supreme interests of its country," and must also include in its notice a statement to this effect. A party to the NPT can therefore withdraw at any time and refuse further controls under that particular regime.

For this reason, it has been pointed out that the function of the NPT is limited to giving timely notice of diversion, and can never realistically be expected to prevent the military application of nuclear energy. Any state that intends to violate its obligations under the treaty would be perfectly within its rights to withdraw and refuse controls; and indeed, would probably do so in the event that detection and exposure were imminent.[61]

If the purpose of NPT safeguards must realistically be limited to ensuring the "timely detection" of any diversion, and if the stated purpose of non-NPT safeguards is to assure that safeguarded facilities and materials are not used to further "any military purpose," how effective are these regimes in achieving these objectives?

There is, first of all, no consensus as to what constitutes "timely" warning.[62] However, it is worth noting that the computer-based accounting system applied under INFCIRC/153 is by one account capable of processing the necessary information in less than one week.[63] If a diversion

---

agreement has been lawfully terminated or in the event that it is terminated earlier than agreed upon. In this manner, safeguards will attach to successive generations of materials derived from safeguarded materials and equipment after the agreement has come to an end (ibid., pp. 21, 22). It is unclear, however, whether all agreements provide for the continuation of safeguards both in respect to derived materials produced for domestic consumption as well as such materials as may be intended for export. The concept of territorial pursuit is explicitly institutionalized only within the framework of the NPT under article III.2, where nuclear material and equipment may only be transferred abroad on the condition that the nuclear activity for which they are intended is also covered by safeguards.

61. Szasz, "The Inadequacy of International Nuclear Safeguards," p. 434.

62. See Lewis A. Dunn and Frank Armbruster, "Warning Time, Crisis Dynamics, and Nuclear-Weapon Proliferation," HI-2852-D, prepared for the U.S. Department of Energy (Croton-on-Hudson, N.Y.: Hudson Institute, 1978).

63. "Computer-Based Safeguards Information and Accounting System," *International Atomic Energy Agency Bulletin,* vol. 19 (October 1977), p. 15.

is promptly reported, the world community should therefore be apprised of it in a relatively short time.

But whereas the system might succeed in providing prompt detection, there is the further question of whether it can detect the diversion of "significant" amounts of materials. As noted earlier, the IAEA relies on both system and statistical analysis in its evaluation of national accounts. These procedures, however, are complemented by a probability analysis to ascertain the confidence level within which significant quantities of missing materials can be detected. If there is a high probability that the detection of missing materials is feasible, the agency will then compare the amount detected with the so-called threshold amount of nuclear materials needed for weapon production.[64] In other words, both the amount of lost materials and the probability that it can be accounted for provides the basis for the agency's determination as to whether there has been a diversion.

Although the accounting system appears to have succeeded thus far, the IAEA inspectorate already foresees several practical problems in its future implementation. Among those cited is the probable need to increase the threshold amount, in view of anticipated increases in materials unaccounted for.[65]

Yet whatever the shortcomings of the NPT regime, the non-NPT system is likely to be comparatively less effective. To begin with, both the IAEA statute and INFCIRC/66/Rev.2 refer to, but do not define, the meaning of "military" and "peaceful" purposes. Is the detonation of a nuclear explosive necessarily in furtherance of some military purpose? What are the peaceful purposes for which safeguarded materials may legitimately be used?

The significance of these questions was most dramatically revealed on May 18, 1974, when India detonated a nuclear device, declaring in its aftermath that it was a peaceful nuclear experiment, not intended for weapon development, and that it was therefore not in violation of its international commitments. As if in anticipation of this argument, article III.1 of the NPT expressly characterizes the production of nuclear ex-

64. Donnelly and Rather, *Nuclear Weapons Proliferation and the International Atomic Energy Agency,* p. 111. The maximum permissible limits of threshold amounts are 8 kilograms of plutonium and 25 kilograms of uranium annually.

65. Ibid., p. 116. See also "International Symposium on the Safeguarding of Nuclear Material," *Nuclear Engineering International* (December 1975), pp. 1021–24.

plosives a proscribed nuclear activity. Yet safeguard agreements under the non-NPT regime have only relatively recently explicitly prohibited the use of nuclear materials and equipment for the purpose of developing nuclear explosives.[66]

Beyond this legal issue, there are some important practical and technical problems in applying non-NPT safeguards. It will be recalled that INFCIRC/66/Rev.2 safeguards are based on individual facilities, rather than on materials flow. In practical terms, this distinction is not particularly significant in once-through reactor programs where all enrichment is undertaken abroad and where spent fuel is stored in at-reactor cooling ponds. In fact it is generally conceded that facility-based safeguards are relatively easily applied to most reactor types.[67] In the operation of light water reactors the fuel vessel is closed except during the annual refueling period. Since the vessel can be sealed and discrete fuel elements counted, containment techniques can be applied relatively successfully. As long as the spent fuel rods are left in cooling ponds, surveillance and inspection can further ensure that no diversion has occurred.

Unfortunately, it is considerably more difficult to apply facility-specific safeguards to enrichment and reprocessing installations. To be effective, safeguards on any fuel-handling facility must be able to monitor material flows. The complexity of the operations involved makes it possible for diversion to occur at any stage in the operation. High radiation levels render large sections of reprocessing plants inaccessible. Currently, the inspection techniques at enrichment facilities are limited to input-output monitoring.[68] In each fuel cycle operation, not insignificant quantities of materials can be trapped in the hardware or vented in the waste streams. Although a large-scale diversion might be readily observed by inspection and camera surveillance, the detection of a small diversion requires more precise measurements. The computerized statistical analysis of material flows under INFCIRC/153 is therefore far more reliable than the techniques available under the non-NPT regime.

66. Sanders, *Safeguards Against Nuclear Proliferation,* pp. 10, 11.

67. This is particularly true for light water reactors because these must be shut down for refueling and require enriched fuel of very precise isotopic specifications. However, the safeguarding of on-load reactors, such as the Canadian CANDU reactor, is substantially more difficult. Such reactors may be refueled while in operation and can use unsafeguarded natural uranium in the fuel. Office of Technology Assessment, *Nuclear Proliferation and Safeguards,* p. 208.

68. Ibid., p. 209.

More fundamentally, it is generally agreed that the invocation of sanctions under either regime is not likely to be an effective deterrent, and that only the threat of detection, accompanied by the opportunity of other states to undertake countermeasures will be of any practical utility.[69] Thus, although timely detection is not an explicit objective of INFCIRC/66/Rev.2 system, it may legitimately be evaluated by its inherent capacity to provide adequate warning time.

Unhappily, there is a peculiar institutional constraint which inhibits the capacity of the non-NPT regime to serve this function. Under the INFCIRC/153 system, the director general can certify to the board of governors that it is unable to verify that no diversion has taken place when an NPT state obstructs the application of safeguards.[70] However, under the non-NPT system the board of governors need only be informed of an actual diversion.[71] Furthermore, in respect to NPT safeguards, the burden of proof that no diversion has occurred is placed squarely on the operator. For these reasons, there is likely to be far less warning time under INFCIRC/66/Rev.2 safeguards than under the NPT system.

Ultimately, any assessment of the effectiveness of IAEA safeguards is largely a matter of imperfect judgment. For one thing, it is very difficult to evaluate the procedures with precision since the protection of proprietary information obligates the agency not to disclose the results of its inspections.[72] But more fundamentally, the mere fact that the agency has never disclosed a diversion has been said to be an inadequate measure of effectiveness.[73] Many have not been convinced that a country can be prevented from circumventing safeguards if it is willing to assume the risk of detection, incur the expense, and take the trouble to do so.[74] It should again be emphasized that in the absence of supplier safeguard requirements there is nothing to prevent a non-NPT state from duplicating plants and equipment already in its possession nor is there anything to prevent

69. Szasz, "The Inadequacy of International Nuclear Safeguards," pp. 433–34.

70. INFCIRC/153, par. 19, reproduced in Sanders, *Safeguards Against Nuclear Proliferation*, p. 77.

71. IAEA, *Statute*, article XII.C. Note that neither the statute nor INFCIRC/66/Rev.2 provide for notification to the board on any obstruction.

72. INFCIRC/66/Rev.2, par. 13; INFCIRC/153, par. 5, in Sanders, *Safeguards Against Nuclear Proliferation*, pp. 73–74, 96.

73. U.S. Comptroller General, *Role of the International Atomic Energy Agency in Safeguarding Nuclear Material*, ID-75-65, report to the House Committee on International Relations (General Accounting Office, 1975), p. 27.

74. Ibid., p. 20.

it from exporting replicated technologies without accompanying safe-guards.

No less troublesome is the delicate political environment within which NPT safeguards are applied. The fact that the nuclear weapon states have failed to produce meaningful results in arms control and disarmament does not augur well for the future of international safeguards. The willingness of nonparties to join the NPT and to refrain from the covert manufacture of nuclear weapons could become increasingly dependent upon the perceived determination of the great powers toward fulfilling their article VI obligations. Moreover, there already is some indication within the IAEA general conference that the developing countries are becoming resistant to further spending on safeguards. Some member states are perhaps legitimately fearful that safeguards may come to dominate the agency's programs, thereby diminishing its capacity to provide technical assistance.[75]

Lest the many difficult problems confronting the IAEA precipitate a premature erosion of confidence and support of international safeguards, there is much that must and can be done to improve the existing regime. Technological improvements such as the early introduction of advanced material accounting systems may prove helpful.[76] Problems of financial support and manpower recruitment have also been recognized as areas in need of greater attention. Closing the gap between the NPT and non-NPT regime is certainly a matter of paramount importance. Happily, measures are already under way toward standardizing bilateral safeguard agreements and publishing agency evaluations of safeguard procedures.

Yet there is no denying that the realities of the present situation may soon reduce international credibility in the existing system. The IAEA safeguard mechanisms already may have been stretched to the limits of political acceptability. In the absence of wholly new, though complementary, institutions, much of the answer may continue to be found in the policies of the major nuclear exporting states.

75. Allen V. Astin and others, "The International Atomic Energy Agency: An Appraisal with Recommendations for Future United States Policy," report to the Secretary of State of the Panel to Review Activities of the IAEA, February 4, 1972, p. 24.
76. The in-plant dynamic material control system (Dymac) which is currently being developed in the United States is widely regarded as one of the most promising new safeguard technologies. The system is expected to provide near real-time material control by making nearly continuous measurements of all materials being stored, transferred, or processed.

The Export Policies of the Major Suppliers

RALPH T. MABRY, JR.

THIS APPENDIX presents summaries of the national nuclear capacities and export policies of the major nuclear supplier nations. It also describes the efforts of these and several other nations to coordinate their export policies through the London nuclear suppliers' group.

National Nuclear Capacities and Export Practices

United States

The United States has been and remains today the world's foremost supplier of nuclear materials and equipment. It leads all other countries in both power reactor exports and enrichment services supplied.[1] Until quite recently, the United States so dominated the international market in nuclear materials that even its principal competitors—France and West Germany—relied principally upon the United States for enriched fuels.

Because of its primacy in the nuclear supply market, the United States has been able to exercise a leading role in proliferation control. As noted

1. See Stockholm International Peace Research Institute, *SIPRI Yearbook 1977: World Armaments and Disarmaments* (Cambridge: MIT Press; Stockholm: Almqvist and Wiksell), pp. 43–45; *Development, Use and Control of Nuclear Energy for the Common Defense and Security and for Peaceful Purposes: Second Annual Report,* H. Rept. 1347, 94 Cong. 2 sess. (Government Printing Office, 1976), p. 85.

173

earlier, from 1946 until the early 1950s, the United States firmly denied international access to its nuclear technology, and even scientific exchanges with Britain and Canada were suspended. But as it became apparent that this strategy would fail both in denial and control, the United States shifted its policy emphasis from one of denial to active promotion of the peaceful uses of atomic energy. The Atoms for Peace proposal paved the way for the export of nuclear equipment. In 1954 Congress rewrote the restrictive Atomic Energy Act of 1946 to authorize the Atomic Energy Commission to provide enrichment services to foreign nations under bilaterally negotiated nuclear cooperation agreements.[2] The United States now has cooperation agreements with more than twenty nations and groups of nations that permit U.S. assistance in nuclear research and power reactor programs. Although individual agreements may differ in detail, they uniformly authorize the supply of nuclear materials and equipment, the imposition of restrictions on the transfer of materials and equipment, and the application of safeguards by the International Atomic Energy Agency or the United States.[3]

A noteworthy feature of U.S. nuclear cooperation policy under the Atoms for Peace program is the exclusion of enrichment technology and facilities from the area of permissible cooperation. The position of the United States has always been that enrichment technology is too directly applicable to military uses to permit its disclosure. But whereas cooperation in establishing enrichment facilities has been denied, the United States has tried to provide assurances that it can be relied upon as a dependable source of enriched fuels. Underlying this important characteristic of U.S. nuclear export policy is the theory that the best way to discourage independent development of full fuel cycle capacity is to offer a dependable supply of fuel on attractive terms.[4]

As if to assure the recipient nations that U.S. policy on fuel supply was not intended to establish and maintain a monopoly on fuel services, the United States originally sought no commitment from importers to refrain

2. Atomic Energy Act of 1954, 68 Stat. 1050, sec. 144(a) 1.

3. Warren H. Donnelly and Barbara L. Rather, *United States Agreements for Cooperation in Atomic Energy: An Analysis,* Committee Print, prepared for the Senate Committee on Government Operations, 94 Cong. 2 sess. (GPO, 1976), app. 1.

4. *Nuclear Power and Nuclear Weapons Proliferation,* vol. 1: *Report of the Atlantic Council's Nuclear Fuels Policy Working Group* (Washington, D.C.: Atlantic Council of the United States, 1978), p. 78.

from engaging in sensitive fuel-handling activities. Implicit in this posture was the notion that any such requirement would have been politically unacceptable to the recipient nations and have the undesirable effect of encouraging rather than discouraging the pursuit of indigenous fuel cycle capability. U.S. bilateral cooperation agreements implicitly permitted the use of non-U.S. enriched fuels in U.S.-supplied reactors. Moreover, enrichment contracts specifically provided for the right of the recipient to terminate the agreement should it wish to be supplied from another source.

In the early years of nuclear cooperation, U.S. agreements provided for facility-specific safeguards to be applied only to the materials and equipment specifically exported. Unless they had adhered to the Treaty on the Non-Proliferation of Nuclear Weapons, the beneficiaries of U.S. assistance remained totally free to undertake independent nuclear programs. U.S. policy thus perpetuated the inadequacies inherent in the "duality" of the international safeguard system.

The cooperation agreements also contained important provisions pertaining to spent fuel reprocessing. Typically, any alteration in the form, content, or reprocessing of U.S.-supplied nuclear material or material produced through its use was only to be undertaken in facilities that both parties determined could be effectively safeguarded. Under early agreements, although the recipient received title to transferred materials, the United States reserved the right to designate the facilities within which produced fissionable materials could be stored, and to purchase any amounts in excess of the importing country's needs. If this purchase option was not exercised, the recipient nation was entitled to retain the excess or transfer it to third countries upon U.S. approval.[5]

With the declassification of reprocessing technology in 1958, a general liberalization on the exchange of nuclear information in the mid-to-late 1950s, and increased reliance on international safeguards, the possibility of a proliferation of sensitive fuel cycle facilities prompted an informal ban on U.S. exports of reprocessing technology in the mid-1960s. Later, in 1972, the U.S. nuclear regulations were amended to prohibit the transfer of reprocessing technology.[6] But with the detonation of a nuclear device by India in 1974, still further export controls were deemed necessary.

5. Donnelly and Rather, *U.S. Agreements for Cooperation in Atomic Energy*, p. 44.
6. 10 C.F.R., pt. 110, now pt. 810.

Accordingly, from 1975 to 1977, Congress enacted a number of legislative measures intended to further U.S. nonproliferation objectives and tighten nuclear export requirements.[7] Finally, and most recently, Congress enacted the Nuclear Non-Proliferation Act of 1978.[8] This act actually constitutes a major amendment to the Atomic Energy Act of 1954. Unless otherwise stated, all section references to the NNPA are to the amended sections of the 1954 act.

The NNPA is a complex piece of legislation providing for a number of administrative actions and requiring a variety of international negotiations intended to further U.S. nonproliferation goals. It consists of six parts dealing respectively with fuel assurance, strengthening IAEA safeguards, establishing the criteria and administrative organization of U.S. nuclear export policy, revising U.S. agreements for nuclear cooperation, providing for nonnuclear energy assistance to other nations, and setting up the administrative mechanism within which the substantive provisions are to be implemented. Most pertinent to this discussion are the provisions relating to U.S. export requirements.

Section 127 specifies six export criteria: (1) IAEA safeguards must be applied to all U.S. nuclear exports and to any materials derived therefrom;[9] (2) no nuclear exports or materials derived from them may be used for the manufacture of any nuclear explosive; (3) adequate physical protection must be maintained for all exports and any materials derived therefrom; (4) prior U.S. approval must be obtained for the retransfer of U.S. exports and any materials produced through the use of U.S.-exported materials; (5) no reprocessing or any alteration of the form or content of any exported U.S. nuclear material or material produced through its use may be undertaken without prior U.S. consent; and (6) no U.S. enrichment, reprocessing or heavy water production technology may be exported unless the aforementioned conditions are applied to any derived nuclear materials or equipment.

7. Most notable is the International Security Assistance and Arms Export Control Act of 1976 (90 Stat. 729) which, among other things, conditions military and economic aid to countries providing or receiving material or technology relating to enrichment and reprocessing upon their willingness to accept certain nonproliferation commitments.

8. 22 U.S.C. 3201.

9. More specifically, each U.S. export agreement must stipulate that the recipient will permit the application of such safeguards as required by article III.2 of the NPT. However, it is not clear whether that means the application of INFCIRC/153 safeguards.

By virtue of section 126(a), the foregoing criteria were made immediately applicable. The Nuclear Regulatory Commission was prohibited from issuing a nuclear export license for transfers where these criteria or their equivalent were not met. As a practical matter, since all nations with which the United States had agreements for cooperation met these criteria by the time the act entered into force, no immediate export embargoes were effectively imposed.

Congress recognized, however, that the IAEA and Euratom failed to meet the provisions of paragraphs four and five.[10] In this limited instance, therefore, section 126(a)(2) provides for a two-year delay within which they may renegotiate their agreements. Presumably, however, unless the president makes a determination that the failure of the IAEA and Euratom to comply would be seriously prejudicial to the achievement of U.S. nonproliferation objectives, they would face embargoes.

A seventh additional criterion is established under section 128. As a condition of continued U.S. exports, *nonnuclear weapon states,* at the time of export, must maintain IAEA safeguards with respect to *all* their nuclear peaceful activities (emphasis added). An eighteen- to twenty-four-month grace period is provided within which this criterion need not be applied. The requirement is further tempered by the authority of the president to waive its application. Note, however, that Congress is given two months within which to disapprove of the waiver by means of a congressional veto exercised by a concurrent two-thirds resolution in both houses.

Section 123 of the act specifies nine requirements that the president must vigorously seek to include in all new cooperation agreements. Unlike the provisions in sections 127 and 128, these are not criteria on the basis of which exports are to be approved or disapproved, but contractual commitments that must be undertaken by each country that wishes to enter into an agreement for cooperation with the United States. These conditions go somewhat beyond those informally agreed upon by the London nuclear suppliers' group in January 1978 and include: (1) a guarantee that full-scope safeguards will be maintained in respect to all nuclear material and equipment exported or produced through the use of exported material and equipment; (2) maintenance of IAEA safeguards on all nuclear materials in all the peaceful nuclear activities of the nonnuclear wea-

10. See, generally, *Nuclear Non-Proliferation Act of 1977,* S. Rept. 95-467, 95 Cong. 1 sess. (GPO, 1977).

pon states; (3) a guarantee that none of the nuclear materials and equipment transferred or materials produced through their use will be used for any nuclear explosive device; (4) a stipulation that the United States will have the right to require the return of any items transferred if the cooperating state detonates a nuclear explosive device or terminates an IAEA safeguard agreement; (5) a guarantee that no retransfer of exported materials or facility and material produced through their use will be made without prior U.S. consent;[11] (6) a guarantee that adequate physical security will be maintained; (7) an agreement not to undertake the reprocessing or enrichment of exported nuclear materials or of materials derived from transferred equipment or material without prior U.S. approval; (8) a guarantee that no weapon-grade materials will be stored in any facility that has not been approved by the United States in advance; and (9) a guarantee that any nuclear items produced or constructed by use of transferred sensitive nuclear technology will be subject to all the preceding requirements.

In regard to current agreements, section 405(a) of the new act explicitly provides that none of the foregoing conditions need be applied. The United States is therefore clearly not precluded from honoring its existing agreements. However, section 404(a) of the new act requires their immediate renegotiation with a view toward incorporating all of the nine conditions set forth in section 123.

In addition to the section 127 export criteria, the United States imposes what may be categorized as post-export controls. Under section 131, the Department of Energy, with certain specified exceptions, may not enter into any so-called subsequent arrangements for reprocessing or for the subsequent retransfer of recovered plutonium until a determination has been made that this will not result in a "significant increase of the risk of proliferation." In making this determination, "foremost consideration" must be given to the question of whether the reprocessing or retransfer will occur under conditions that will "ensure timely warning to the United States of any diversion." Otherwise stated, the United States will assess the capacity of the applicable safeguards to give "timely warning" and where they are found to be deficient, the requisite approval will be denied.

Finally, as a further nonproliferation measure, section 129 specifies actions which would trigger a cut-off of U.S. nuclear exports. Under this

11. This requirement may be interpreted to apply to a retransfer of nuclear material not of U.S. origin but used in U.S. reactors.

provision, nonnuclear weapon states would be denied U.S. exports if they were found by the president to have (1) materially violated a U.S. agreement for cooperation; (2) assisted a nonnuclear weapon state in undertaking any nuclear activities having a direct significance to the manufacture of nuclear explosive devices; (3) materially violated an IAEA agreement; or (4) engaged in any activities having direct significance for the manufacture or acquisition of nuclear explosive devices.

In regard to the nonproliferation effects of these new export requirements, it should be noted that by requiring the non-NPT parties to agree to place all their peaceful nuclear activities under safeguards, these nations will have effectively accepted safeguards essentially equivalent to those administered under the NPT. Of course a nonparty could place all of its nuclear facilities under INFCIRC/66/Rev.2 safeguards and still meet U.S. full-scope requirements. However, the act nevertheless makes an undeniably significant contribution to closing the dual-system loophole discussed above.

In practical terms, much of the success of these measures will depend upon the willingness of the nuclear importers to agree to the new terms. The initial response of certain countries, such as France, has not been entirely encouraging. Moreover, some nonnuclear weapon states may ultimately decide to forsake U.S. exports, seek alternative sources of supply, or even develop wholly indigenous materials and facilities. In any event, any assessment of the new export requirements would probably be premature at this time and will certainly depend in some measure upon the export policies of other supplier nations.

Canada

Canada was one of the first countries to engage in nuclear energy research and development, having collaborated with the United States and Great Britain in atomic research during World War II. Among its most significant contributions to nuclear technology is the commercial development of the heavy water moderated CANDU reactor which, unlike its light water counterpart, operates on unenriched natural uranium. In mid-1979 twenty-seven CANDU reactors were in operation, under construction, or planned. Only three were outside Canada, however.[12] In

12. "World List of Nuclear Power Plants," *Nuclear News* (August 1979), pp. 68–87.

addition to its reactor exports, Canada is a major supplier of natural uranium.

The Canadian reactor industry is currently dominated by Atomic Energy of Canada, Ltd. (AECL) and Canada General Electric. CANDU reactors have been sold to India, Pakistan, Argentina, and South Korea. Taiwan and India have been provided with research reactors. Canada also has cooperation agreements with Euratom, the IAEA, and fourteen individual countries.[13] No reprocessing or enrichment services are provided, and consequently Canadian nuclear exports are confined to the reactor, heavy water, and uranium markets.

The responsibility for export policy is shared by four governmental institutions. The Department of External Affairs is responsible for the negotiation of all agreements for cooperation and safeguard requirements. Nuclear export permits are issued by the Department of Industry, Trade and Commerce, with the concurrence of the Atomic Energy Control Board (AECB) which decides upon the sufficiency of the safeguards to be applied. AECL is responsible for the promotional aspects of the Canadian nuclear industry and provides reactor design and engineering assistance to private hardware manufacturers.

Most will agree that Canada has historically maintained a strong anti-proliferation export policy. In 1974, when India detonated a nuclear explosive with plutonium derived from a Canadian-supplied pilot reactor, the Canadian government immediately suspended all nuclear cooperation. And in 1976, as it was unable to induce New Delhi to agree to strengthened safeguards, the government imposed a permanent embargo on exports of nuclear material and equipment to India.[14] Shortly thereafter, in 1977, Canada also placed a moratorium on uranium exports to nations unwilling to accept the AECB's toughened export requirements.[15]

The Canadian government has also been involved in trilateral negotiations with the United States and Australia with a view toward establishing common uranium export policies.[16] The United States, Canada, and Australia have recently agreed to require acceptance of the NPT as

13. Argentina, Australia, Finland, West Germany, India, Iran, Japan, Korea, Pakistan, Spain, Sweden, Switzerland, Indonesia, and the United States.
14. *New York Times,* May 19, 1976. For its effects, see *Far Eastern Economic Review* (April 16, 1976), p. 55.
15. Ron Glen, "Impact of Canadian Ban on Uranium Sales," *Nuclear Engineering International,* February 1977, p. 5.
16. See *Wall Street Journal,* April 7, 1977.

a condition to uranium exports. The first agreement to supply natural uranium under these conditions was recently negotiated with Finland.[17] Much of the current Canadian export policy can be traced to the December 22, 1976, announcement that shipments of Canadian reactors and uranium to nonnuclear weapon states would be denied to all countries that failed to ratify the NPT or accept international safeguards over their entire nuclear programs.[18] This policy supplemented earlier export requirements, including peaceful use agreements, physical security commitments, and retransfer restrictions. The current Canadian position, however, requires "standby safeguards" to be implemented in the event NPT safeguards expire or are abrogated. The Canadian government now supports the prohibition of nuclear exports to all states that have not ratified the NPT or otherwise agreed to INFCIRC/153 safeguards.

United Kingdom

Great Britain has a long history of nuclear research and development. It was one of the first countries to detonate a nuclear explosive device and in 1953 was the world's first nation to operate an industrial-scale reactor. Since then the government has pursued a policy of expanded civilian nuclear power. In 1979 the United Kingdom had 6,400 megawatts, electric of nuclear generating capacity and is expected to have 9,400 MWe by 1985.[19]

Despite intensive efforts by the British nuclear power industry to increase its share in international nuclear trade, Britain has not fared well in foreign reactor sales. Only two reactors have been marketed overseas, one to Italy and one to Japan.[20] No sales of reactor components have been made since 1970, and the last export of a complete British reactor took place in 1957.

Part of the reason for the unsuccessful commercial performance of British reactors is the early penetration of the European and world market

17. *New York Times,* July 21, 1978.
18. *New York Times,* December 23, 1976.
19. OECD Nuclear Energy Agency and the International Atomic Energy Agency, *Uranium: Resources, Production and Demand* (Paris: OECD, 1979), p. 29.
20. *Nuclear Proliferation Factbook,* Joint Committee Print, prepared for the House Committee on International Relations and the Senate Committee on Governmental Affairs, 95 Cong. 1 sess. (GPO, 1977), pp. 266–67.

by the United States.[21] Another stems from the fact that the United Kingdom has relied almost exclusively on the commercial deployment of Magnox and advanced gas-cooled reactors, both of which have gained a reputation for poor technical performance.[22] The U.S.-origin light water reactor now dominates almost 90 percent of the world market. It has only been since 1979 that the British government has inched toward renouncing its historic resistance to LWR development.

The United Kingdom has been much more successful both in the development and sale of fuel-handling services. An irradiated Magnox fuel reprocessing plant has been in operation since 1964. British Nuclear Fuels, Ltd., a wholly owned subsidiary of the U.K. Atomic Energy Authority (UKAEA), now operates the facility and is also engaged in conversion and enrichment activities.[23] Almost all of Britain's commercial enrichment work is undertaken within the framework of the Urenco-Centec organization, a tripartite industrial enterprise formed in 1971 by the United Kingdom, the Netherlands, and West Germany. The collaboration of these countries in the development of the centrifuge enrichment process has been supported by an aggressive marketing program. It has been estimated that Urenco has secured orders for some 26 million separative work units and has succeeded in obtaining letters of intent for enrichment services worth some £200 million.[24] Major customers are located in Japan, West Germany, Spain, France, and the Netherlands.

The reprocessing activities of BNFL have been shrouded in controversy—a controversy that has been of particular importance to British nuclear export policies. As the possible consequence of the failure of Great Britain to compete successfully with other major suppliers in the market for nuclear equipment and materials, attention has focused on the market for fuel handling services. British policy on the application of IAEA safeguards is therefore arguably of less practical significance than the proliferation implications of its policy on local reprocessing of foreign-origin spent fuels. The issue of the reprocessing in Britain of foreign fuel has provoked a stormy national debate which has extended beyond the

21. See, generally, Henry R. Nau, *National Politics and International Technology: Nuclear Reactor Development in Western Europe* (Baltimore: Johns Hopkins University Press, 1974).

22. See *Défense et Diplomatie*, vol. 2 (December 22, 1977), p. 3.

23. *Financial Times*, December 19, 1979.

24. U.S. General Accounting Office, *Overview of Nuclear Export Policies of Major Foreign Supplier Nations*, ID-77-60 (GAO, 1977), app. 3, p. 43.

environmental considerations to concern for its possible proliferation impact.

Historically, most reprocessing in the United Kingdom has been confined to Magnox fuel reprocessing at the Windscale and Calder works in Sellafield, Cumbria. In 1968 a section was added to reprocess oxide fuel. However, in 1973, partly because of technical difficulties and partly because of an accidental release of ruthenium[106] in the oxide fuel handling section of the plant, the facility was ordered closed. Magnox fuel reprocessing has since continued, but in 1976, the British Royal Commission on Environmental Pollution, chaired by Sir Brian Flowers of the UKAEA, urged a postponement of any nuclear power expansion until a full environmental impact assessment had been made.[25] The report also called for an indefinite deferral of deployment of fast breeder reactors.

Official government policy, nevertheless, remained strongly in support of nuclear expansion. Negotiations had been underway with Japan and other nations for sales of reprocessing services valued at an estimated £700 million by 1990.[26] Consistent with its objective to provide reprocessing services capable of servicing non-Magnox fuel, in 1977, BNFL applied for permission to construct a 1,200-ton-per-year thermal oxide reprocessing plant (Thorp) at the Windscale site. Pursuant to local authorization requirements, an inquiry was conducted to determine, among other things, whether the plant should be built and, if so, whether it should be permitted to handle foreign fuels.[27]

The findings of the Windscale inquiry resulted in a major victory for the government and has since served as a cornerstone of its nuclear policy. Extensive consideration was given to the proliferation implications of the proposed project. Opponents of the Thorp plant argued that to be economic, the expanded oxide fuel reprocessing capacity would need to accept substantial foreign reprocessing contracts, and the return of the recovered plutonium to nonnuclear weapon state clients would inevitably increase the risk of proliferation. Due note was also taken of U.S. policy preference for an indefinite postponement of commercial reprocessing and plutonium recycle.[28]

25. *New York Times,* September 23, 1976.
26. Richard Masters, "What Sort of Inquiry into British Reprocessing?" *Nuclear Engineering International* (March 1977), p. 4.
27. United Kingdom Town and Country Planning Act of 1971, sec. 23; and Hon. Mr. Justice Parker, *The Windscale Inquiry,* vol. 1: *Report and Annexes 3–5* (London: Her Majesty's Stationery Office, 1978).
28. Parker, *The Windscale Inquiry,* pars. 6.21, 6.22, and 6.23, p. 19.

However, citing President Jimmy Carter's acknowledgment of the pressures created by the fuel assurance issue and declining spent fuel storage capacity, it was concluded that the reprocessing of foreign-origin irradiated fuels was perfectly harmonious with nonproliferation objectives. The evidence presented was interpreted to suggest a pressing international need for expanded reprocessing capacity in order to meet spent fuel storage requirements. The denial of reprocessing services was perceived as creating an "immediate" incentive for nonnuclear weapon states to develop indigenous facilities.[29] To deny such services would therefore enhance the risk of proliferation. Indeed, a refusal to accept foreign fuel would be a "breach of the spirit if not the letter of the NPT."[30]

The report received a resounding endorsement in Parliament. In March 1978 the House of Commons voted by a 130-vote margin to allow construction to go forward. The authorization in no way restricted the operation of the plant to the reprocessing of British fuels.[31] In the course of the debate, the secretary for environmental affairs indicated that, in the government's view, the return of reprocessed plutonium under international safeguards was an adequate deterrent to diversion.[32] The Foreign Office indicated, however, that due consideration would be given to the U.S. request that a final decision be deferred until the International Nuclear Fuel Cycle Evaluation was completed.[33] It is generally expected that work on the Thorp storage ponds will soon be under way, although the actual construction of the facility will probably not begin before 1981.

France

The French industrial nuclear energy program ranks as one of the most extensive in the world. The government's current energy strategy is to place considerable emphasis upon nuclear power as the foremost future energy source. In 1979, France had 12,000 MWe of nuclear generating capacity. By 1985, it is expected to have 39,000 MWe.[34] Although the conventional once-through LWR fuel cycle is currently accepted, long-range plans call for the use of plutonium in fast breeder reactors. A dem-

29. Ibid., pars. 6.21, 6.33, pp. 19, 21.
30. Ibid., par. 17.6, p. 85.
31. *New York Times,* March 3, 1978.
32. "The Windscale Debate," *Atom,* no. 259 (May 1978), p. 143.
33. Ibid., p. 144.
34. *Uranium: Resources, Production and Demand,* p. 29.

onstration 250-MWe liquid metal fast breeder reactor, known as Phénix, has been in operation since 1974; work on an industrial scale 1,200-megawatt, thermal prototype (the Super Phénix) is already under way. It has been estimated that by 1985 as much as 23 percent of France's domestic energy requirement will be met by nuclear power.[35]

In support of this ambitious program, France has developed the most complete LWR-FBR fuel cycle capability in the world. In addition to commercially exploitable, indigenous uranium resources, natural uranium ore has been reliably available from Gabon, Niger, and Canada, among other countries. Gaseous diffusion enrichment plants have been in operation since the early 1960s. Construction of an enrichment facility with an annual capacity of 10.8 million separative work units at Tricastin by the French-controlled Eurodif organization is well under way.[36] Currently there are two operational reprocessing plants in France: the UP_1 at Marcoule and the UP_2 at La Hague. In 1976, in keeping with anticipated near-term reliance on LWRs, the UP_2 facility was modified to accommodate oxide fuel reprocessing. Two new plants (UP_{3a} and UP_{3b}) are being planned for operation in 1985 and 1986, respectively.

The expansion of domestic nuclear capacity has been accompanied and complemented by an aggressive export promotion program. The first French reactor was exported to Belgium in 1969. In 1976 Iran and South Africa submitted letters of intent to purchase two reactors each.

Although 90 percent of the enriched uranium production of the Eurodif plant is scheduled to be allocated to the shareholders, the balance is slated to be split among Japan, Switzerland, and West Germany. Thus far, this large commitment to co-owners has prevented Eurodif from offering large quantities of enrichment services to nonpartners. However, slippages in national nuclear programs of shareholders are expected to create secondary market opportunities.[37]

In the wake of the controversy surrounding the Windscale plant, the shutdown of the multinational Eurochemic facility in 1974, and the indefinite deferral of reprocessing in the United States, France has emerged as the only country in the world capable of offering near-term commercial reprocessing services. The commercial opportunities implicit in this capa-

35. Jean-Paul Silve, "Fuel Cycle Industry Combines Private and Public Enterprise," Nuclear Engineering International (December 1976), p. 55.
36. The other Eurodif co-owners include Italy, Belgium, Spain, and Iran.
37. Nuclear Assurance Corporation, International Data Collection and Analysis, Task 2, EN-77-C-01-5072, prepared for the U.S. Department of Energy (Atlanta: Nuclear Assurance Corp., 1978), p. 35.

bility have not been overlooked. As a result of an aggressive pursuit of the international market for reprocessing services, France has succeeded in obtaining half of the reprocessing contract that BNFL had been negotiating with Japan.[38] Smaller contracts have been signed with Belgium and Sweden, and most recently with West Germany.

At one time, France was also prepared to export reprocessing technology. Agreements were negotiated in the mid-1970s for the sale of reprocessing facilities to South Korea and Pakistan. Although trilateral safeguard agreements for the application of IAEA safeguards were concluded for each recipient in 1975 and 1976, respectively, the proposed sales provoked strong international, and, most especially, U.S. criticism. Indigenous reprocessing capacity for Korea or Pakistan was widely viewed as not justified by any technical or economic necessity. Accordingly, in early 1976, partly as a result of U.S. diplomatic pressure, the South Korean project was dropped.[39] Likewise, after several years of indecision, the Pakistani deal was in effect canceled.[40]

Partly as a consequence of the international controversy which the export contracts provoked, in September 1976, the Inter-Ministerial Council on Nuclear Export Policy was created.[41] The council, chaired by the president, includes the prime minister and the ministers of Foreign Affairs, Defense, Economy and Finance, Industry and Research, Foreign Trade, and the administrator of the Commissariat à l'Energie Atomique (CEA).[42] On October 11, 1976, the council adopted six guidelines on the export of nuclear materials and equipment that have since remained in force.[43]

38. *Nuclear Engineering International* (November 1977), pp. 4–5.

39. *New York Times,* January 30, 1976.

40. As recently as September 1977, the French government was firm in its determination to go forward with the agreement although it had earlier agreed not to export sensitive nuclear technologies to nonnuclear weapon states. See *New York Times,* June 1, 1977, and September 9, 1977; and *Washington Post,* April 23, 1978.

41. See Bertrand Goldschmidt, "A Historical Survey of Nonproliferation Policies," *International Security,* vol. 2 (Summer 1977), p. 82; *New York Times,* September 13, 1976.

42. The Commissariat à l'Energie Atomique is responsible for controlling all French nuclear activities from research to defense. As such, it has played a major role in the development of French nuclear policy. Since 1975 fuel cycle activities have been entrusted to the Compagnie Générale des Materières Nucléaires (Cogema).

43. *Wall Street Journal,* October 12, 1976. The guidelines are reprinted in GAO, *Overview of Nuclear Export Policies,* app. 2, pp. 35–36.

Each proposed export is evaluated by reference to these principles which, briefly summarized, begin by acknowledging nuclear power as necessary to the energy needs and development of a number of countries. Accordingly, the French government is committed to cooperate in the development of the peaceful nuclear programs of other nations, guarantee the fuel supply of the power plants it exports, furnish fuel cycle services and transfer such technologies as may be required. Commercial competition in international nuclear markets must not, however, favor the proliferation of nuclear arms. The approval of exports must reflect the commitment of the French government to reinforce such safeguards as are imposed on exported items, and to bring French export policies in line with any relevant international agreements. The guidelines conclude by declaring that although it will consult with supplier and importing countries on the application of these principles, France fully intends to formulate and maintain its own export policies.

At the time of their promulgation, these principles were regarded as a major, if subtle, shift in French export policy.[44] When, on October 11, 1978, the council issued a brief statement concerning a moratorium on future sales of reprocessing plants, this evaluation appeared to have been reconfirmed. However, it was subsequently announced that the guidelines would in no way affect the contract that had already been executed with Pakistan. It was only after substantial international pressure that France finally advised the Pakistani government that it would only supply a plant of a type whose end product contained a mixture of uranium and plutonium unsuitable to the production of nuclear weapons—an offer which Pakistan refused.

France's refusal to sign the nonproliferation treaty provides an important explanation to the very general and rather vague character of the September 1976 guidelines. The French government has consistently expressed its sympathy for the principles of nonproliferation. It has continuously pledged to adopt export policies consistent with those of the signatories to the treaty. As a general rule, the application of the IAEA safeguards has supplemented bilateral requirements; the reactor export arrangement with South Africa includes IAEA safeguards.[45] A separate bilateral agreement provides for the continuation of those controls. Yet

44. *New York Times,* September 13, 1978.
45. GAO, *Overview of Nuclear Export Policies,* p. 36.

France remains steadfast in its refusal to become a party to the NPT and formally commit itself to a detailed position on nonproliferation (as has the United States, for example, through the Nuclear Non-Proliferation Act of 1978).

This difference in approach may be partly attributed to France's early commitment to acquiring a national nuclear weapon capability. Anglo-American cooperation in the formative years of nuclear development has been a persistent source of irritation to the French who were largely excluded from this special partnership. The 1962 Nassau Agreement was resented for similar reasons, but most especially because it was perceived as a minimization of European (as distinct from Anglo-American) cooperation in security matters.

Correspondingly, a prevalent view among French strategists in the early 1960s was that the United States could not be fully relied upon in the event of a nuclear attack. To a greater or lesser degree, it has since been frequently argued that the proliferation of nuclear weapons would help to assure international stability even if smaller nations, such as France, were unable to launch a massive nuclear retaliation.[46] The French have therefore contended that the United States in particular has been mistakingly obsessed with the dangers of nuclear weapon proliferation.

In refusing to sign the NPT, it has been argued—in a fashion closely paralleling the arguments of many developing nations—that world disarmament and *not* proliferation was the crux of the problem, and that the implicit assumption that smaller nations were any less likely than the superpowers to act responsibly with nuclear weapons was the height of arrogance.[47] Not surprisingly, the NPT has also been perceived as manifesting a misplaced emphasis on arms control and, more cynically, as an attempt by the superpowers to preserve the prestige and power which goes along with their monopoly positions.

West Germany

In 1979 West Germany had 9,600 MWe of nuclear generating capacity. By 1985 it is expected to have 20,200 MWe.[48] Although legal

46. See, generally, Pierre Gallois, *The Balance of Terror: Strategy for the Nuclear Age* (Houghton Mifflin, 1961).

47. Wilfrid L. Kohl, *French Nuclear Diplomacy* (Princeton University Press, 1971), pp. 167, 168, 261–62.

48. *Uranium: Resources, Production and Demand*, p. 29.

battles have slowed the growth of the domestic nuclear program in recent years, it is generally anticipated that West Germany will place significant reliance on nuclear power as a future energy source. A fast breeder reactor prototype, the SNR-300, is currently under construction and is scheduled for commissioning in 1984. Through commercial firms, West Germany holds a one-third interest in the Urenco-Centec enrichment organization. A pilot reprocessing plant located at Karlsruhe is the only such facility in operation. A second, larger reprocessing plant, to be built by the West German partner in United Reprocessors, Ltd., was scheduled for operation in the late 1980s, but has been deferred indefinitely because of local opposition.

Due to relatively closed nuclear markets in Europe and North America, much emphasis has been placed on facility exports to countries outside Europe and North America. The first West German nuclear reactor exported was ordered from Argentina in 1968. Only two West German reactors are currently in operation abroad: one in Argentina and another in the Netherlands. Under the direction of the giant Kraftwerk Union, AG, at least seven nuclear power plants are under construction in Austria, Brazil, Iran, Spain, and Switzerland.[49] The most controversial sale has been the export agreement negotiated with Brazil in 1975.

The Brazilian deal provides for the construction of an enrichment facility, a fuel fabrication plant, as many as eight 1,300-MWe reactors, and a pilot reprocessing plant.[50] If fully implemented, the $5 to $8 billion project would give Brazil full fuel cycle capability. As such, it could serve as a foundation of a nuclear weapons program—the first in Latin America—and would present a proliferation risk made particularly alarming by the fact that Brazil is not a party to the NPT.[51]

News of the agreement provoked a wave of criticism in the United States, both from the press and within official government circles.[52] Al-

49. *Nuclear Proliferation Factbook,* p. 279.

50. For details see Norman Gall, "Atoms for Brazil, Dangers for All," *Foreign Policy,* no. 23 (Summer 1976), p. 160; see also William W. Lowrence, "Nuclear Futures for Sale: To Brazil from West Germany, 1975," *International Security,* vol. 1 (Fall 1976), pp. 147–66.

51. The provisions of the Treaty of Tlatelolco establishing a nuclear free zone are not binding until all Latin American states are a party and the other states concerned have acceded to the two protocols. Although the treaty allows for the waiver of this restriction, Brazil has not complied, with the result that the treaty remains inapplicable.

52. *New York Times,* editorial, June 13, 1975; *Washington Post,* June 1, 1975.

though the Bonn government has since declared that West Germany would no longer export sensitive nuclear technologies to nonnuclear weapon states, it has consistently refused to cancel the deal with Brazil.[53] Now that the South Korean and Pakistani deals have been abandoned, West Germany is the only supplier with a still-standing commitment to export sensitive fuel cycle facilities to a nonnuclear weapon state.

There have been a number of factors underlying the reluctance of West Germany to rescind. Among them has been the desire not to undermine the country's credibility as a business partner.[54] Some have also implied that for all its moral posturing, the United States has opposed the Brazilian deal on less than altruistic grounds. It has been suggested, for example, that the agreement has been perceived by Americans as a challenge to U.S. export performance in what has traditionally been regarded as a sacrosanct sphere of Yankee economic influence. Evidently, at least a few West Germans have felt that the United States has been willing to use its nonproliferation policy to protect its share of the international nuclear market.[55]

But more fundamentally, the West German government has insisted that the agreement does not risk the proliferation of nuclear weapons and that it complies with West Germany's obligations as a party to the NPT. It has been argued that the integration of industrializing nations like Brazil into the network of international nuclear cooperation furthers nonproliferation objectives by providing an opportunity to apply international safeguards.[56] And it has also been argued that the IAEA tri-

53. *New York Times,* June 18, 1977.

54. In an interview on West German television (channel ZDF) on April 21, 1977, Chancellor Schmidt was asked whether in spite of the controversy surrounding the Brazilian agreement, West Germany must "absolutely defend this high-technology in international competition." Schmidt responded, "It must above all defend being seriously considered as a supplier in the future. If we wish to preserve our export opportunities, i.e., the opportunity of preserving our export jobs, we must, above all, stand by agreements that we have signed. That applies to Brazil as much as it does relative to the treaty on the nonproliferation of nuclear weapons. . . . Ultimately the German economy and a larger part of our work force, all of us, live by the fact that we export the most modern technology."

55. Compare Karl Kaiser, "The Great Nuclear Debate: German-American Disagreements," *Foreign Policy,* no. 30 (Spring 1978), p. 88; and Gall, "Atoms for Brazil, Dangers for All," p. 167.

56. See *New York Times,* July 7, 1975, letter to the editor by Dr. Niels Hanson, Chargé d'Affaires, Embassy of the Federal Republic of Germany.

lateral agreement under which the deal was struck actually exceeds NPT requirements.[57]

West Germany was an active participant in the meetings of the London nuclear suppliers' group. In fact, the licensing regulations set forth in its Atomic Law prohibit the issuance of a materials export license which does not comply with its international obligations; and the Foreign Trade Act places special requirements on the export of such trigger list items as have been agreed to by the London nuclear suppliers' group.[58] As a matter of practice and policy, IAEA safeguards have always been required as a condition to nuclear exports.

As already noted, West Germany is now on record as favoring a moratorium on any further export of sensitive technologies. On the basis of the Brazilian agreement, it may be legitimately concluded that should such exports nevertheless occur they would be subject to IAEA safeguards.[59] Prior West German approval would be required for any retransfers and they would also be subject to IAEA safeguards. The importer would furthermore be required to promise not to manufacture any nuclear explosive device and to maintain safeguards, should the agreement be terminated.

Soviet Union

In mid-1979 the Soviet Union had 11,875 MWe of nuclear generating capacity and an additional 12,920 MWe was under construction.[60] Recent press reports suggest that the USSR is firmly committed to nuclear power as a future energy source.[61] The fast breeder is expected to play a major role. Two test breeder reactors are currently in operation, and a 1,500-MWe liquid metal fast breeder reactor is being designed.[62]

57. Ibid.; Kaiser, "The Great Nuclear Debate," p. 89.
58. See GAO, *Overview of Nuclear Export Policies*, app. 1, p. 24.
59. The agreement is reproduced in Warren H. Donnelly and Barbara Rather, *Nuclear Weapons Proliferation and the International Atomic Energy Agency*, Committee Print, prepared for the Senate Committee on Government Operations, 94 Cong. 2 sess. (GPO, 1976), app. 11.
60. *Nuclear News* (August 1979), pp. 86–87.
61. *New York Times,* January 14, 1977.
62. *Washington Post*, October 5, 1978. The first Soviet breeder reactor went "hot" in 1969, placing the USSR alongside France as a world leader in FBR experience. See Gloria Duffy, "Soviet Nuclear Exports," *International Security*, vol. 3 (September 1978), pp. 83–111.

The Soviet Union is known to have full fuel cycle capabilities. It supplies its own uranium requirements, but there is no data available on the extent of its reserves. Although the Soviets have gained extensive experience in enrichment and reprocessing technology through their military programs, their commercial enrichment and reprocessing capacities are not known.[63] The Soviet Union has sold 26 reactors abroad, the first having been ordered by East Germany in 1956.[64] Since then contracts have been negotiated with Hungary, Bulgaria, Czechoslovakia, Poland, Rumania and, in 1975, Cuba. Thus far, all but two reactor exports have been to Communist countries. In 1969 and 1971 two reactors were ordered by Finland. The Finnish government admits to having been attracted by the low-interest financing terms it was offered and is reportedly interested in acting as intermediary for Soviet nuclear exports to other countries.[65] More recently, the Soviet Union has offered to build a reactor in the Philippines that would replace a facility being built by Westinghouse.[66] And in October 1978 an agreement was successfully concluded to provide a 300-MWe reactor to Libya.[67]

The Soviet Union has been a long-time supporter of the international safeguard regime. As a party to the NPT and, as noted below, an active participant in the London nuclear suppliers' group, it has required the application of full-scope safeguards to all of its nuclear exports.[68] Since Libya is also a party to the NPT it may legitimately be expected that INFCIRC/153 safeguards will be applied to its reactor as well. Although Cuba is not a party to the NPT, on the basis of past Soviet practice it would seem unlikely that construction on the Cienfuegos reactors will begin before trilateral full-scope safeguards have been accepted.

Whereas the Soviet Union has not exported any sensitive fuel cycle facilities, it is believed capable of allocating some 3 million SWUs per

63. The current emphasis on breeder development would seem to suggest an intention to expand reprocessing capacity for civilian use. Although the extent of civilian reprocessing actually taking place may not be known, there appears to be no excess capacity for international development. See *Nuclear Proliferation Factbook*, pp. 284–85.

64. U.S. Central Intelligence Agency, *Nuclear Energy*, ER 77-10468 (August 1977), p. 43.

65. *Washington Post*, September 29, 1978.

66. *Wall Street Journal*, February 15, 1978.

67. *Washington Post*, October 4, 1978.

68. See *International Atomic Energy Agency Bulletin*, vol. 19 (October 1977), p. 2.

year of its enrichment capacity to non-Communist countries.[69] No reprocessing services are provided to other countries, and Soviet agreements with other Communist countries require the return of all spent fuel. Should there be a change in policy on reprocessing, it would seem highly improbable that any material transfers would be made without accompanying safeguards.

Japan

Japan has one of the largest civilian nuclear programs in the world. In 1979 Japan had 15,000 MWe of nuclear generating capacity. By 1985 installed nuclear generating capacity is projected to increase to 26,000 MWe.[70]

The light water reactor is currently the mainstay of the domestic reactor industry, having been developed under licenses from U.S. firms. Only one gas-cooled reactor of the Calder-Hall design has been imported. However, uncertainties over future nuclear fuel supplies have stimulated interest in other reactor types. Serious consideration has been given to the purchase of CANDU reactors.[71] An advanced thermal reactor designed to operate on either uranium or plutonium fuel is nearing completion. Moreover, the Japanese government has favored the deployment of the fast breeder reactor, having recently concluded a trilateral accord with France and West Germany for cooperation in FBR technology.

In support of a fast breeder program, and for related reasons of fuel assurance, Japan has made a steady and persistent effort to develop full fuel cycle capability. An experimental enrichment facility using the centrifuge process went into operation in 1974. The Power Reactor and Nuclear Fuel Development Corporation (PNC) is currently building a pilot enrichment plant at Ningyo. Commercial scale enrichment is expected to begin in the late 1980s.

In 1974, with the assistance of an experienced French firm, PNC completed the construction of a 210-ton-per-year pilot reprocessing plant at Tokai-Mura. Testing began late in the same year but was interrupted in 1977 when the United States refused to grant permission to

69. CIA, *Nuclear Energy*, p. 37.
70. *Uranium: Resources, Production and Demand*, p. 29.
71. *Asian Wall Street Journal*, June 29, 1978.

reprocess spent fuel of U.S. origin. Bitter differences between the two
countries ensued, but were at least temporarily resolved by a September
12, 1977, agreement under which reprocessing operations were permitted
to resume for a period of two years. The two governments agreed that
any recovered plutonium would be stored pending a determination of the
technical feasibility of alternative fuel cycles as well as such different reprocessing technologies as coprocessing—a process which yields a mixture of uranium and plutonium oxides not directly usable in nuclear
weapons.

A 2,000-ton-per-year reprocessing plant is presently under consideration.[72] However, despite continuing efforts to achieve fuel cycle independence, the Japanese government fully expects to be dependent on
other nations for fuel services in the foreseeable future. Firm contracts
have been negotiated with the United States and Eurodif for enrichment
services through 1985. Even during the course of negotiations on the
Tokai-Mura operations, discussions were under way with the British and
the French for the supply of reprocessing services. Contracts have since
been executed with Cogema in September 1977, and with BNFL in May
1978.[73]

The development of the nuclear industry in Japan has therefore not
reached the point where serious consideration is being given to a corresponding development of export market opportunities. As of September 1978 no nuclear facilities, materials, services or technology had
been marketed abroad.[74] This is not to suggest that potential opportunities will be ignored. In fact, as part of a 1973 bilateral agreement for
technological and scientific cooperation with the Soviet Union, consideration is being given to the sale of Japanese pressurized water reactor
components, possibly in exchange for Soviet enrichment services.[75] However, it does not appear likely that Japan will undertake any significant
nuclear exports for some time to come.

Reportedly, Japanese officials are most particularly committed not to
export enrichment and reprocessing technologies, and apparently in 1977

72. Construction will begin by 1985 and the design is expected to take into consideration the creation of a fuel cycle park which would include a plutonium fabrication plant, *Nuclear Engineering International* (June 1978), p. 7.
73. *New York Times,* May 25, 1978.
74. Nuclear Assurance Corporation, *International Data Collection and Analysis,*
Task 2, p. 37.
75. *Nucleonics Week,* July 7, 1977, p. 10; *Japan Economic Journal,* July 19,
1977, p. 3, and September 9, 1977, p. 3.

even sought to assure the United States of their intentions not to do so.[76] Of course, as in the case of France and West Germany, it may legitimately be wondered whether the sought-after growth in the domestic nuclear industry will require the support of an aggressive nuclear export strategy. Clearly the Japanese are perfectly capable of becoming significant and credible suppliers of nuclear technology. However, as a member of the London nuclear suppliers' group, it may just as clearly be expected that Japan will exercise considerable restraint in its nuclear exports.

As has been suggested, Japan's nuclear export procedures are still at the very early stage of formulation.[77] The Ministry for Trade and Industry, which is responsible for the international promotion and licensing of exported materials and equipment, has yet to develop standard regulatory and licensing criteria for nuclear exports. No system or procedures for approving retransfers of exported items has been established. However, Japan is a party to the NPT; and the United Nations Bureau of the Ministry of Foreign Affairs, which has been responsible for the development of Japan's international nuclear policy, has been working to institutionalize the trigger list export guidelines of the London nuclear suppliers' group.

The London Nuclear Suppliers' Group

Under article III of the NPT, the parties agreed not to provide nuclear assistance without accompanying IAEA safeguards. In recognition of this obligation, on August 22, 1974, a number of nuclear suppliers, including Australia, Denmark, Canada, West Germany, Finland, the Netherlands, Norway, the Soviet Union, Great Britain, and the United States, filed two memorandums with the director general of the IAEA setting forth uniform procedures for the transfer of nuclear materials and technology.[78] The procedures included a so-called trigger list of items that would not be sold without being placed under IAEA safeguards.

76. Richard P. Suttmeier, "Japanese Reactions to U.S. Nuclear Policy: The Domestic Origins of an International Negotiating Position," *Orbis,* vol. 22 (Fall 1978), pp. 653, 654.

77. GAO, *Overview of Nuclear Export Policies,* app. 5.

78. The letters of transmittal and accompanying memorandums were distributed by the IAEA as INFCIRC/209 and INFCIRC/209/Add.2, reproduced as appendix 1 in Benjamin Sanders, *Safeguards Against Nuclear Proliferation,* Stockholm International Peace Research Institute Monograph (Ballinger, 1975), p. 58.

Nine months later, in May 1974, India detonated a nuclear device and a year thereafter, West Germany agreed to supply sensitive fuel-cycle facilities to Brazil. These developments, no less than the French agreements with South Korea and Pakistan, served as a painful reminder of the deficiencies of the existing nonproliferation regime. It also became apparent that international competition for the sale of nuclear equipment and fuel-cycle services might actually tempt individual countries to be less than strict in their safeguard requirements. Accordingly, it became increasingly evident that nonproliferation objectives would be furthered if the nuclear supplier nations would consult among themselves and agree on procedures to regulate the export of nuclear materials and equipment.

In the spring of 1975, largely at the behest of the United States, a group of the major exporters of nuclear equipment agreed to meet in London in the first of what has been a series of meetings designed to coordinate national policies on the transfer of sensitive technologies. The initial participants included the United States, Britain, West Germany, France, the Soviet Union, and Canada; Japan and Italy were "technically" represented as threshold exporters.[79]

Because of threats of withdrawal by France and the Soviet Union if the proceedings were made public, the first and subsequent meetings of the group were held in relatively tight secrecy. Much of what is known about the progress of the negotiations has therefore been limited to apparent leaks to the press.[80] But from these it would appear that the following four major issues loomed largest in the discussions: (1) the desirability and practicability of requiring full-scope safeguard agreements of all nonnuclear weapon states; (2) whether the spread of sensitive fuel cycle facilities should be prohibited and/or placed under international controls; (3) the adequacy of the IAEA safeguard system and the effectiveness of new safeguard technology; and (4) whether the group should convene in a regular, formal fashion.

By early 1976 a general consensus began to emerge. The number of participants was gradually expanded to include Czechoslovakia, East Germany, the Netherlands, Poland, and Sweden, after having been ini-

79. *New York Times,* June 18, 1975.

80. A relatively good idea of the development of the London meetings can be reconstructed from newspaper accounts. See, for example, *New York Times,* June 26, 1975; September 23, 1975; November 22, 1975; January 4, 1976; February 24, 1976; June 2, 1976; November 9, 1976; April 28, 1977; and January 12, 1978.

tially restricted to fewer members in an effort to facilitate agreement on certain broad principles. Finally, and most recently, in January 1978, the fifteen nations agreed on common criteria for transfers of items on an accompanying trigger list.[81]

Briefly summarized, the trigger list includes:

—*Source and special nuclear material,* that is, natural and enriched uranium, thorium, and plutonium in excess of specified quantities.

—*Nuclear equipment,* nuclear reactors capable of producing more than 100 kilograms of plutonium per year and specified reactor components.

—*Nonnuclear material,* including heavy water, spent fuel reprocessing facilities, and plants for the fabrication of fuel elements.

As a condition to the transfer of any trigger list item, each recipient state must be required to:

—Formally pledge that no nuclear explosive devices would be constructed.

—Place all transferred material and facilities under effective physical protection.

—Place all transferred items under IAEA safeguards. Explicitly specified are facilities for reprocessing, enrichment, and heavy water production. Any facilities of the same type as may be replicated by the recipient country must also be under IAEA safeguards.

—Undertake not to operate or modify an enrichment facility capable of producing uranium enriched to more than 20 percent without the prior approval of the supplier country.

—Agree not to retransfer any trigger list item except under the foregoing conditions.

In addition to requiring the preceding as a condition to nuclear exports, each supplier agreed to:

—Exercise restraint in the transfer of sensitive facilities, technology, and material.

—Promote the acceptance of multinational, regional fuel cycle centers.

—Recognize the importance of including in agreements on the supply of trigger list items appropriate provisions for mutual agreement between supplier and recipient on arrangements for reprocessing, storage, use or retransfer of weapon-usable material.

81. The guidelines are reproduced in Atlantic Council, *Nuclear Power and Nuclear Weapons Proliferation,* vol. 2, p. 63.

—Promote international cooperation in the exchange of physical security information and the protection of nuclear material in transit.

—Make special efforts in support of effective implementation of IAEA safeguards.

—Maintain regular consultations on matters connected with the guidelines. And in the event of violations, suppliers should agree upon an appropriate response, with due regard being given to the termination of nuclear transfers to the recipient state.

Both the negotiations and the export guidelines finally agreed upon represent a major accomplishment. In respect to the specific criteria established, the agreement has made more explicit the responsibilities of the suppliers under the NPT. Moreover, it has strengthened the barriers against the proliferation of enrichment and reprocessing technology. Beyond this, the deliberations of the conference may have helped to persuade the French to give up their plans to transfer sensitive technologies to South Korea and Pakistan. And the symbolic significance of the meetings should not be underestimated as they represent the first significant attempt to bring the suppliers to a common understanding on nuclear exports. At the same time, this latest accord has gone a long way in assuring that bilateral arrangements between suppliers and recipients will assume a minimum of uniformity.

Yet for all of these achievements the agreement is not without certain important shortcomings. Most significantly, the accords that have been reached thus far are merely a "gentlemen's agreement."[82] Much of the language used is merely normative rather than mandatory. Any member can withdraw at any time and since the guidelines do not amount to a treaty, no member is legally bound to comply.

Furthermore, several actual or potential exporters did not participate: most notably, India, Argentina, and South Africa. To what extent they were purposely excluded is not publicly known. But if the initial reason was to facilitate agreement on a general understanding, that particular reason had outrun its purpose long before January 1978.

A fundamental shortcoming is the absence of a consensus to require full-scope safeguards. The London guidelines call for the imposition of safeguards only in respect to imported nuclear material, equipment, and facilities, or facilities derived therefrom. Unlike the NPT, there is no re-

82. Frank Barnaby, "A Gentlemen's Nuclear Agreement," *New Scientist,* vol. 73 (February 24, 1977), p. 469.

quirement that IAEA safeguards be applied to all the peaceful nuclear activities of the recipient state. Indigenously designed and constructed facilities are not included.[83]

Finally, having conducted the negotiations in secrecy and wholly outside the institutional framework of the IAEA, the parties demonstrated a lack of confidence in the IAEA which might weaken its effectiveness. Also, the very formation of the group runs the serious risk of being perceived by the developing countries in particular as a cartel-like conspiracy to further their dependence on the industrialized countries. As such, it could not only complicate North-South negotiations on the distribution of the world's wealth, power, and technological capability, but could also fuel existing resentments concerning the discrimination inherent in the NPT.

83. As noted earlier, in December 1976 Canada unilaterally announced its intention to require full-scope safeguards as a condition to Canadian nuclear exports. It later joined with the Soviet Union in an unsuccessful attempt to get the London conference to do so as well.

Summary of Proceedings
of the Bellagio Conference

NINETEEN scholars, government officials, and officials of international organizations from thirteen countries met in Bellagio, Italy, from March 28 to 31, 1980, to consider possible new forms of international cooperation in nuclear energy activities. Such cooperation would be designed to facilitate the continued peaceful use of nuclear energy without increasing the risk of a further spread of nuclear weapons.[1]

The conference was sponsored by the Brookings Institution. The Rockefeller Foundation provided conference facilities and accommodations for participants in its Bellagio Study and Conference Center. The Fritz Thyssen Foundation and the Alfred P. Sloan Foundation helped to meet conference expenses.

A draft Brookings study on possible new forms of international cooperation in nuclear energy was made available to participants as background for their deliberations.

The Bellagio Conference was the first international meeting on the problems of civil nuclear energy to be held after the conclusion of the International Nuclear Fuel Cycle Evaluation (INFCE) one month earlier. The conference therefore provided a good opportunity to consider what concrete actions should be taken in the post-INFCE period. The

1. An effort has been made to consider comments by participants on an earlier draft of this summary. Participants have not, however, been asked to concur in the summary, and its contents are solely the responsibility of the conference rapporteur.

timeliness of the Bellagio Conference was increased by the fact that the second conference to review the operation of the Treaty on the Non-Proliferation of Nuclear Weapons (NPT) met in August 1980. Moreover, a United Nations conference on the peaceful uses of nuclear energy is expected to convene by 1983.

In order to promote a free exchange of views, most of the discussion at the Bellagio Conference was not for attribution. (The only exceptions were the presentations introducing agenda items.) In addition, it was understood that participants spoke only for themselves and not for their governments or for the organizations with which they were affiliated.

Trends in Civil Nuclear Energy

In opening the first session of the conference, the chairman, Karl Heinz Beckurts, noted that nuclear power is now a smaller energy option than had once been believed. Even the low INFCE projections of nuclear generating capacity may be too high. Sensitive fuel cycle facilities have spread more slowly than was anticipated only five years ago. This can be explained by the slower growth of the world economy, the political problems of the nuclear energy industry, and changing views of developing countries toward nuclear power.

The nuclear energy industry needs to regain a favorable climate of opinion, which requires establishment of a better international regime. The positive results of INFCE provide a starting point. (The fact that everyone claims victory in INFCE shows, however, that not all problems have been solved.) A pragmatic, evolutionary approach is appropriate. Current assets, such as the NPT, should not be abandoned. Nuclear power must be fitted into the existing economic framework.

Discussion

The Swedish referendum on nuclear power, which was held only a few days before the Bellagio Conference, was taken as an example of the way in which this source of energy has become a political issue in a number of countries. Interpreting the results of the Swedish referendum is not easy. On the one hand, 57 percent voted against phasing out nuclear power in ten years. But on the other hand, 80 percent voted against expanding the present nuclear program. The vote, moreover, reflected more than public views of nuclear power; positions on other issues, such as public ownership of electric utilities, and attitudes toward political parties and institutions were also recorded. In a fundamental sense, the referendum was an upheaval by the political periphery against the power structure. It was therefore similar to the earlier Austrian referendum on nuclear power and to the Norwegian referendum on the Common Market.

The "green" parties, which oppose nuclear power, are becoming a significant factor in West German politics. They have the support of about 5 percent of the total electorate and 20 percent of young voters. Political problems have not, however, affected nuclear power to the same extent everywhere. Strong nuclear programs are going forward in France, Japan, and the Soviet Union.

The slower growth of nuclear energy may provide an opportunity for constructive action. In the past, the apparent inevitability of a rapid expansion of nuclear power and the excessive claims made for it created emotional responses. Time may now be available to reduce the symbolism of nuclear energy and deal with it as a matter of rational choice. If time is not used effectively, however, expectations of the eventual phaseout of nuclear power could grow. Moreover, some minimum rate of growth is needed to attract the scientists and engineers required to maintain the nuclear option.

Uranium Supply and Demand

In his oral presentation and in a paper that he prepared for the conference, Stanley R. Hatcher concluded that the demand for uranium is likely to exceed the production attainable from known resources before the end of the century. If additional resources are to be found and further production capability created, increased exploration is needed. This is a matter of some urgency, since the normal lead time from discovery to production is around fifteen years.

Uranium production is subject to political and environmental constraints, but the most important constraint is the availability of capital. If, as is quite possible, there is an oversupply of uranium until around the mid-1990s, the price of uranium could fall below the level needed to induce investment in new production facilities. The desire of enrichers to operate their plants at a high percentage of capacity could, however, exert a stabilizing influence on the uranium market.

Regional and national imbalances in uranium supply and demand cause consumers to be concerned about assurance of supply and producers to be concerned about stability of markets. Insecurity of supply could lead to a more accelerated introduction of the breeder reactor.

Discussion

The difficulty in comparing dynamic demand estimates with static resource estimates, as is customary in discussions of the uranium market, was noted. Errors in estimating the rate of decline in production from known resources can be crucial. In comparing supply and demand, it should not be assumed that a perfect world market for uranium exists. Regional and national imbalances are the main problem today. In the next century, a shortage of uranium may be the problem.

The uranium industry needs long-term planning, but the planning base at present is poor. The largest suppliers and consumers are, however, industrialized nations that should be able to project future supplies and requirements.

The demand for uranium depends ultimately on the long-range contracting procedures of utilities, which in turn depend on existing and planned nuclear generating capacity. It is now customary for utilities to order fuel in the fourth or fifth year of reactor construction. In view of the fifteen-year lead time in uranium mining, however, fuel should be ordered ten years earlier than it now is.

The willingness of the uranium enrichers to exert a stabilizing influence on the uranium market was questioned. There will be substantial excess enrichment capacity during the 1980s, but enrichers will shut down if they cannot cover marginal costs. It will be easier for enrichers using the centrifuge technology to adjust plant capacity to actual demand than for those using the gaseous diffusion method. Some enrichers will maintain higher levels of operations by enriching uranium tails.

The cost of mining uranium varies widely from country to country. U.S. costs are higher than Canadian and Australian costs. U.S. costs may increase, because the number of feet of drilling required to find additional reserves is increasing. Exploration costs in some other areas are, however, falling.

Opinions differed concerning the future development of the uranium market. One view was that uranium producers would behave like oil exporters. Another was that the price of uranium would be that of the highest cost producer, which today is the United States.

No support was expressed for a commodity agreement to stabilize the uranium market. In the unlikely event that such an agreement could be negotiated, prospects for administering it successfully would be poor.

Some participants favored a consultative arrangement to exchange information on uranium supply and demand. One suggestion was that the Uranium Institute be used for the purpose, pending other arrangements. The fact that governments are not directly represented in the Institute and most U.S. utilities do not belong would, however, limit the usefulness of this approach.

Another suggestion was to entrust consultations on the uranium market to the International Atomic Energy Agency (IAEA). The possibility of the agency's assuming some tasks relating to the provision of information on the uranium market has been discussed in the IAEA, but problems were anticipated in obtaining and disseminating adequate data on a commodity as politically and economically sensitive as uranium. One participant believed that these problems could be solved, but expressed reservations concerning the IAEA as an information clearinghouse on the uranium market. Another thought that the real question was whether the IAEA would take the central role in fuel assurances and terms of trade. If so, an IAEA role in consultations on the uranium market could fall naturally into place. If not, such a role could be sterile.

Measures to Deal with Interruptions of Fuel Supplies

Philip J. Farley presented highlights from the paper on dealing with interruptions of fuel supplies that he had written for the conference. Among various measures discussed, a safety network (cross-guarantees by suppliers and/or mutual help arrangements among utilities), dedicated stockpiles, and a nuclear fuel bank seemed most worthy of consideration. New institutions should not be created, however, unless they are clearly needed.

Whether nonpolitical interruptions of nuclear fuel supplies (accidents, sabotage, strikes, commercial disputes, and so forth) will be frequent or serious enough to justify elaborate advance arrangements may be questioned. Ad hoc adjustments to such interruptions may be sufficient. Political interruptions, especially those occasioned by proliferation concerns, raise another question. Would substitute fuel supplies be available that were not subject to the same constraints as caused the interruptions?

Reliance on the market to the maximum extent possible is likely to be more effective than new cooperative arrangements. The role of governments should be to facilitate the functioning of the market, rather than to create new institutions. Priority should be given to resolving current differences concerning nonproliferation controls on nuclear trade and fuel cycle operations. A consensus on a nonproliferation regime is needed within which the market can efficiently and reliably balance supply and demand.

In effect, the solution to the problem of assurance of fuel supply at the front end of the fuel cycle depends on working out the nonproliferation problems of the back end of the cycle. This will take time. An evolutionary approach is therefore indicated.

If such an approach fails, a duel supply system could arise. Some countries with indigenous uranium, or access to suppliers of uranium and enrichment services that do not impose tight safeguards and fuel cycle restrictions, might become self-sufficient nationally or as a group. A dual supply system would be inefficient and might impose additional political strains on the international nuclear energy industry.

Discussion

The discussion dealt almost entirely with the nature of the fuel assurance problem and general approaches to it. Little was said about specific measures to cope with interruptions in fuel supplies.

Assurance of fuel supply is part of a larger problem: assurance of supply of material, equipment, and services for the entire nuclear fuel cycle. Moreover, suppliers are as interested in assurance of demand as consumers are in assurance of supply.

Several areas of concern were identified: nonpolitical interruptions, political interruptions for other than nonproliferation reasons, and nonproliferation interruptions. Opinions differed concerning the ability of the market to handle nonpolitical interruptions. Some argued the utility of swap arrangements, but noted the possible need for new credit facilities to enable less developed countries to take advantage of such arrangements. Guarding against political interruptions was viewed as especially difficult. Greatest attention was devoted to nonproliferation interruptions.

Several participants saw little connection between civil nuclear energy and the spread of nuclear weapons. By implication, they questioned the imposition of nonproliferation conditions by nuclear suppliers. If such conditions are imposed, these participants and others argued that they should not be set by the suppliers alone. A stable new regime for nuclear energy must be multilateral. Suppliers must abandon unilateral rights. Consumers, as well as suppliers, must be involved in negotiations on the terms of supply.

Several participants cited approvingly the statement by the director general of the IAEA that irrevocable safeguards should mean irrevocable assurance of supplies. Unilateral policy changes by suppliers were strongly criticized. Suppliers should not think that only they are concerned with the proliferation problem.

Some kind of new international regime for nuclear energy is virtually inevitable, because the alternative is a chaotic situation that would interfere with the development of nuclear energy. The question is whether the new regime will be acceptable to both suppliers and consumers. A favorable outcome appears likely because consumers would not accept a nuclear OPEC, and suppliers could not maintain one. Creating a new regime will be a long, difficult process, but recognizing that mutuality is the only approach would be a big advance.

Some participants saw the formation of the London nuclear suppliers' group as a mistake, since it violated the principle of mutuality. The INFCE, in which suppliers and consumers worked together, was compared favorably with the suppliers' group, which excluded consumers. One participant noted that the guidelines issued by the suppliers' group had the effect of requiring safeguards on a heavy water plant in Argentina, but not in Switzerland or Germany. Another participant asked whether the suppliers' group guidelines had the hidden purpose of maintaining a line between industrialized and developing countries.

Several participants supported the London nuclear suppliers' group and its guidelines. One of them suggested that the guidelines could be improved by recasting them as assurances that supplies would be forthcoming, if certain conditions were met.

The only specific measure to deal with fuel supply interruptions that aroused much interest was one form or another of the emergency network. Very little support was expressed for creating a nuclear fuel bank in the near future. The international nuclear fuel authority called for in the U.S. Nuclear Non-Proliferation Act of 1978 (NNPA) was, without challenge, described as dead.

Some participants were pessimistic concerning prospects of reaching agreement on a system of cross-guarantees. They noted that while governments would be the guarantors, private firms were the actual suppliers in many countries. They also feared that the NNPA would interfere with the functioning of the cross-guarantees. Others were more optimistic. On the specific problem of the NNPA, they noted that it could be amended or its provisions superseded by an international agreement.

Storage of Spent Fuel

Mitsuo Takei summarized his discussion paper on the problems of spent fuel management. He also drew on a longer paper presenting background data on the same problems. Special attention was devoted to Japan and other East Asian countries.

The spent fuel problem is clouded by uncertainty. The future growth of nuclear generating capacity is uncertain and, as a consequence, so is the magnitude of spent fuel arisings. Additional uncertainties exist concerning the construction and operation of reprocessing plants and the development of away-from-reactor (AFR) facilities for the storage of spent fuel.

Problems still exist between Japan and the United States on the reprocessing of U.S.-origin spent fuel in Japan and on its transfer to France and the United Kingdom for reprocessing. Transfers are now being approved by the U.S. government on a case-by-case basis. These transfers will presumably be judged compatible with nonproliferation goals, when the international plutonium storage system under discussion in the IAEA has been established.

The storage of spent fuel is principally a problem of the industrialized countries. The development of small and medium-sized reactors is a more urgent requirement for the developing countries than providing additional means of storing or otherwise disposing of spent fuel. Japan's experience in developing a small reactor for merchant ships can be useful in designing a small power reactor. The IAEA might appropriately study storage systems for developing countries and serve as an intermediary in arranging for their construction.

The industrialized countries will need more AFR storage space, either on their own territory or elsewhere. A system under which fuel suppliers would buy back spent fuel should be considered. The United States has proposed that a regional spent fuel storage center be established on Palmyra Island in the Pacific Ocean. The Japanese government has agreed to study this proposal, but has not taken a public position on its merits. The Japanese nuclear community is uncertain concerning both the purpose of the U.S. proposal and its feasibility.

Discussion

Inevitably, several hundred thousand tons of spent fuel will require some kind of storage by the end of the century. Possibilities include storage at reactors, in national away-from-reactor facilities, and in international facilities. Return to the fuel-supplying country has also been proposed. Opinions of participants differed concerning the potential importance of storage by reprocessors. One view was that the two principal reprocessors, British Nuclear Fuels, Ltd. and Cogema, were not interested in expanding their spent fuel storage capacities and would not accept spent fuel that was not to be reprocessed. Another held that, whatever their declared policies, the installations of BNFL and Cogema are in fact becoming spent fuel storage centers for Western Europe and Japan.

The spent fuel storage problem is not difficult from the point of view of magnitude, technology, or cost. It has been estimated that all spent fuel arising by the year 2000 would cover a football field in a pile only three feet high. This amount of spent fuel could be stored at reactors, if all of them had ponds able to take ten years of spent fuel arisings.

Storing spent fuel is not technically difficult. Racks at reactors can be altered to increase the capacity of storage ponds. Wet AFR storage facilities can be built. Storage in spent fuel transporters is also an attractive possibility. The danger of creating so-called plutonium mines may have been overstated. With the passage of time, spent fuel does become easier to handle. After 100 years, however, a single fuel element emits 500 rads of radiation at a distance of one meter—enough to kill in half an hour.

Storing spent fuel is relatively cheap. An AFR storage facility would cost $25 to $50 per kilogram of capacity. Operating costs would be $2 to $5 per kilogram annually. Storing spent fuel appears to be cheaper than reprocessing it and storing separated plutonium. Reprocessing could be economically advantageous, however, if there were a market for separated plutonium at a high enough price. Such a development depends on the recycling of plutonium in power reactors.

Recycling in today's thermal reactors appears unlikely. The economic case for doing so is uncertain, and in any case all available plutonium may be needed for the fast breeder reactors. Some participants believed, however, that the option of thermal recycle should be retained in the event that the deployment of breeders is delayed and as a means of gaining added security of energy supplies. The accumulation of large stocks of separated plutonium would be undesirable.

Some countries would be interested in using international facilities for the storage of spent fuel, but only if reprocessing was not thereby foreclosed. They would want assurance that spent fuel could be withdrawn, or the value of its contained plutonium realized.

An expert group established by the IAEA to study international spent fuel management has tentatively concluded that an international spent fuel storage system comparable to the proposed international plutonium storage system (IPS) is not needed at this time. The group is considering criteria for spent fuel storage sites, but will not become involved in the selection of specific sites.

No optimism was expressed concerning the willingness of fuel suppliers (other than the Soviet Union) to take back spent fuel. In the late 1960s, Sweden sold spent fuel from its first reactor to BNFL, but was never able to make another similar arrangement. More recently, Yugoslavia offered to return spent fuel to the United States with reimbursement for its plutonium content, but received no reaction.

Increased AFR storage on a national basis is the most likely development. Some participants saw no disadvantages in this, provided safeguards were applied, and regarded international storage arrangements as not worth the trouble. Others saw some economic and nonproliferation advantages in international storage. One suggestion was to use international storage of spent fuel as an incentive to promote membership in the international plutonium storage system.

Reprocessing

Ian Smart opened the session on reprocessing by summarizing the paper he had prepared for the conference. His longer paper on multinational arrangements had also been distributed to participants.[2]

Reprocessing will grow and spread, and the world will have to learn to live with it. One reason for reprocessing is the belief—which is not shared by everyone—that it is an essential step toward the acceptable management of spent fuel. Another reason for reprocessing is the desire for increased security of energy supply. From this point of view, investing in indigenous reprocessing capacity is comparable to developing high-cost indigenous fuels as a substitute for imported oil.

Given the rate of spent fuel accumulation, scope for more reprocessing capacity clearly exists. At some point, investment in away-from-reactor storage facilities for spent fuel will compete with investment in the additional reprocessing capacity that will be needed for breeder deployment or possibly for thermal recycle.

There are essentially two approaches to reducing the proliferation risk in reprocessing: technical and institutional. The most promising technical measure would combine physical isolation of reprocessing with location together of reprocessing and fabrication of mixed oxide fuel facilities. The institutional approach would involve some kind of multinational arrangement for reprocessing.

Multinational arrangements for reprocessing are complicated, contentious, and inevitably speculative. Multinational reprocessing must reconcile four criteria: restraint, viability, symmetry, and parsimony. Restraint (limiting fear of nuclear weapons proliferation) and viability (providing effective industrial and commercial energy benefits) are of primary importance.

On commercial as well as nonproliferation grounds, nonnuclear weapon states participating in multinational arrangements might be asked to give up independent national reprocessing. In return, they should be offered commercial and technical benefits. Economies of scale would

2. United Kingdom Department of Energy, *Multinational Arrangements for the Nuclear Fuel Cycle*, Energy Paper 43 (London: Her Majesty's Stationery Office, 1980).

provide commercial benefits, but it might also be necessary to locate some multinational reprocessing plants in low-cost areas (which could mean developing countries). The transfer of sensitive technology that multinational reprocessing might involve need not be a problem if plutonium is put under international control.

Multinational reprocessing can be justified only if it results in economic as well as nonproliferation gains. Nevertheless, reprocessing does create proliferation apprehensions that should be allayed. Reprocessing will take place. The problem is how to make it safer.

Discussion

A realistic estimate of reprocessing capacity by the year 2000 is needed. Only a few countries may be involved. Ninety percent of the spent fuel arisings will probably be in the industrialized countries. Spent fuel may have to be transported to reprocessing plants over long distances from only a few developing countries. The cost of transporting spent fuel, however, is relatively insensitive to distance.

Different views were expressed concerning the economies of scale in reprocessing. One view was that large reprocessing plants are much more efficient than small plants. Another view was that small plants can be built cheaply in some developing countries. A third view was that reprocessing costs depend less on capital expenditures than on the percentage of capacity remaining idle.

Multinational reprocessing arrangements were seen by one participant as a means of making a "large plant" policy more acceptable. Another participant argued that the possible merits of multinational reprocessing and a policy favoring large plants should be considered separately.

Several participants questioned the feasibility of requiring countries that joined multinational reprocessing arrangements to renounce national reprocessing. One participant, however, saw this requirement as a reasonable commercial condition.

Considerable attention was paid to the difficulties that must be overcome in organizing multinational reprocessing arrangements. Joint investment without joint management would probably not be acceptable today, but joint management is difficult. International collaboration in advanced technology is hard enough when it is not mixed up with other problems, such as nonproliferation.

Other practical problems are agreement on a site for a multinational plant and disposal of the radioactive waste after reprocessing. Also, if location of a reprocessing plant with a plant to fabricate mixed oxide fuel is viewed as desirable, the relationship between the two plants would have to be settled. Would they be under the same ownership and management?

One approach might be to start with a multinational facility for the storage of spent fuel and add a multinational reprocessing plant on an adjacent site later. The problems of managing a storage facility are simpler than those of a reprocessing plant. Also, the need for additional storage capacity may be more urgent.

International Plutonium Storage System

Katherine Larson presented the key points in her paper, "International Plutonium Storage: the Establishment of a Scheme within the International Atomic Energy Agency."

In December 1978 the director general of the IAEA convened an expert group to study the possible creation of an international plutonium storage system (IPS) within the agency. The group has reached the stage of working on a draft agreement to establish such a system within the framework of the IAEA. No conclusions have been reached and many issues remain to be discussed. The general outlines of an IPS have, however, emerged.

The IPS would be based on article XII.A.5 of the IAEA statute, which authorizes the agency, in connection with the application of safeguards, to require the deposit with it of "any special fissionable materials" in excess of what is needed for research or use in reactors.

The IPS would be voluntary and thus probably would not involve all members of the agency. Although the board of governors of the IAEA would have to approve the scheme, the group of experts is considering the creation of a commission, subordinate to the board, that would help it carry out the scheme. It is foreseen that day-to-day operations would be conducted by agency personnel.

All separated plutonium under safeguards would be registered with the agency. Excess plutonium would be deposited in a facility designated an international plutonium store. The precise definition of "excess" has not yet been determined by the group of experts, although it will conform to the requirement set forth in the statute that all plutonium not needed for research or use in reactors be deposited.

International plutonium stores would not be banks, but checkrooms. Depositors would retain title to plutonium deposited, and IAEA personnel at the stores would take custody over it. The stores would, however, be nationally owned and operated. They would probably be located at reprocessing and fuel fabrication plants, although other locations have not been excluded.

The expert group has not yet established procedures for the release of deposited plutonium. Decisions on release could be made by either agency personnel or the commission. In either case, a specialized arbitration mechanism might be required to settle disputes. The expert group has not considered banning the release of plutonium for recycle in thermal reactors, since the statute would appear to permit release for use in all reactors. Nor has the group thus far tackled the question of suppliers' rights over deposited plutonium.

Discussion

Several participants spoke in favor of the IPS. One called the IPS the centerpiece of a new regime, although not necessarily the first step toward creating it. Another saw the IPS as the means of developing an international regime that would work, thereby avoiding the rise of a dual supply system.

Whether the major suppliers would accept the IPS is uncertain. Their policies toward it would obviously depend on the extent to which it met their proliferation concerns. In the view of some participants, the willingness of the suppliers to give up their rights of prior consent over plutonium subject to the IPS would be crucial to the success of the scheme.

How many fuel-importing countries would join the IPS is also uncertain. The attitudes of developing countries toward the IPS would be influenced by the extent to which attention was simultaneously paid to their desire for greater assurance of fuel supplies. Some developing countries might insist that all plutonium, including military plutonium, be included, or at least registered, in the IPS.

For many importing countries, the incentive for joining the international plutonium storage system is essentially to retain access to the larger part of the world market for nuclear supplies. Holdouts would be subject to the more onerous unilateral policies and procedures of suppliers, such as those embodied in the U.S. Nuclear Non-Proliferation Act of 1978.

As the scheme now stands, thermal recycle of plutonium would be permitted. The economic incentive for thermal recycle, although it would provide added security of energy supplies, would be weak. Most plutonium would probably be held for use in breeder reactors.

Doubts were expressed concerning the willingness of India, Israel, and South Africa to join the IPS. The participation of these countries, however, was not viewed as essential to getting the system started. Moreover, the IPS could be expected to establish a code of conduct that would influence the behavior of even those countries that did not join it.

Rules of Trade

Onkar Marwah made the opening presentation on the problem of achieving a consensus on the rules of trade in sensitive nuclear materials and technology. This problem should be considered in the context of key INFCE findings: no single fuel cycle is appropriate for all countries (the breeder reactor is a legitimate objective for some countries), and the goals of nonproliferation and assurance of supply are complementary. Energy, commercial, and security considerations interact, and all are relevant to the question of the rules of trade. Few scientific and engineering secrets about nuclear weapons remain. There are cheaper and more efficient ways of building a nuclear bomb than diverting civil nuclear facilities to military use.

Most nuclear generating capacity will continue to be in the industrialized countries for the rest of the century. Only six or seven developing countries have nuclear power facilities, or will acquire them in the near future, and only a few of those countries have shown an interest in developing integrated nuclear facilities. It is therefore only necessary to obtain the cooperation of a small number of countries on the rules of trade.

Several kinds of restraints on the trade in nuclear materials and technology have appeared since the Indian test explosion in 1974: multilateral restraints (the guidelines of the London nuclear suppliers' group), bilateral restraints (the Australia-U.K. agreement), and unilateral restraints (the U.S. Nuclear Non-Proliferation Act of 1978). All of these restraints are subject to reinterpretation. Restraints apply to both fission-

able and nonfissionable materials (heavy water, graphite, pumps, etc.).
It is impossible to predict which technology will be declared sensitive.

A number of questions must be answered with respect to the rules of
trade:

—How far can unilateral rules be applied? At what stage should there be
negotiations between suppliers and consumers?

—What are the trigger list items whose denial would inhibit the spread
of nuclear weapons?

—Should exceptions to the rules of trade be tacit or explicit?

—What guarantees should be extended against unpredictable changes in
rules, political sanctions, and discrimination by suppliers in favor of some
clients?

—How can new suppliers of nuclear equipment and services, such as
India, Brazil, and Argentina, be integrated into the international nuclear
trading system?

In working for a consensus on the rules of trade, several countries
could be ignored. Except for the light water reactors at Tarapur, India
is basically beyond the reach of sanctions, and the Tarapur reactors can
be modified to use mixed oxide fuel. Argentina and Brazil will soon be in
the same position as India. South Korea and Taiwan have special relationships with the United States, and Pakistan is already working for an
independent nuclear capability.

The realistic course with respect to the rules of trade is to maintain
the guidelines of the London nuclear suppliers' group, tacitly tune out the
awkward states, and encourage some of them to abstain voluntarily from
nuclear weapon programs. Achieving a consensus involves creating a
framework in which countries can be drawn to the existing rules of trade,
not devising new rules.

Discussion

Several participants argued that it would be wrong to focus on only a
few countries in developing a new regime for nuclear energy. Eleven developing countries have nuclear power programs, and the number may
increase to sixteen or seventeen. These countries cannot be ignored, especially if a market for nuclear materials and equipment is to be maintained for the industrialized countries. The developing countries are much
more imporant than their share of nuclear generating capacity would suggest.

De facto full-scope safeguards were proposed as the minimum objective of the rules of trade. Eleven non-NPT countries have accepted safeguards, and eight of that number have de facto full-scope safeguards. The desirability of full-scope safeguards was not questioned, but the need for the IPS that goes beyond existing safeguards was noted. Safeguards and the IPS would be linked, since safeguards would be required over plutonium released by the IPS.

Establishment of rules of trade should be seen as an evolutionary process with no definite end. A formal code of conduct would be hard to negotiate. Some elements would be implicit. The approach should be managerial, rather than contractual. Continuing adjustment to changing circumstances would be necessary.

The differing interests of the developing and industrialized countries were again brought out. Because their civil nuclear industries are at an earlier stage, the developing countries are primarily interested in the front end of the fuel cycle, especially in assurance of supply. The industrialized countries place greater emphasis on problems of the back end of the fuel cycle, such as the management of spent fuel and the control of separated plutonium.

Despite this difference, it was pointed out that the IPS could benefit the developing countries by changing relationships between suppliers and consumers. For example, suppliers might be more likely to give fuel supply assurances and transfer technology to countries that joined the IPS than to countries that did not.

A committee of the whole to consider post-INFCE problems was created at the June 1980 meeting of the board of governors of the IAEA, but the committee's initial terms of reference focused on the problem of assurance of supply. This proposal reportedly enjoyed wide support among developing countries and the nations of Western Europe, but the United States was said to have strong reservations. Several conference participants saw the committee of the whole as a good—and possibly the only practical—way to initiate international discussions on the rules of trade.

Conclusions

No effort was made to agree on recommendations or formal findings. The deliberations of the conference appeared, however, to support several propositions. Little interest was displayed in certain other concepts.

Considerable support was shown for the international plutonium storage system. Prospects for creating the IPS would, however, depend on its adequately meeting the proliferation concerns of suppliers and on concurrent efforts to deal with the supply assurance problem of the developing countries. Willingness of suppliers to relinquish their rights of prior consent over plutonium subject to the IPS could be essential to the success of the scheme.

Strong support was expressed for giving assurance of supply as much attention as nonproliferation objectives. The need for more predictable and less arbitrary policies by suppliers was emphasized. Some value was seen in an international emergency network, including cross-guarantees of fuel supplies.

The desirability of beginning discussions on the rules of trade in nuclear materials, equipment, and technology was generally accepted. Creation of a committee of the whole of the IAEA board of governors was regarded by some, but not all, participants as the best way to get these discussions under way.

Little interest was shown in the creation of new international or multinational institutional arrrangements. The IPS was the only clear exception. Very little support was expressed for the early establishment of an international nuclear fuel bank. International storage of spent fuel and multinational reprocessing arrangements were not ruled out, but the difficulties in both of these ventures received at least as much attention as their advantages.

A major value of the conference lay in the opportunity that it provided for an informal exchange of views on important international problems. In closing the conference, the participants unanimously expressed their appreciation for the skillful way in which the chairman had guided their deliberations.

Conference Participants

Karl Heinz Beckurts *Kernforschungsanlage, Jülich (conference chairman)*
Antonio Carrea *Comisión Nacional de Energía Atómica, Buenos Aires*
Abram Chayes *Harvard Law School*

Juan Eibenschutz *Comisión de Energéticos, Mexico City*
Philip J. Farley *Stanford University*
John E. Gray *International Energy Associates Limited, Washington, D.C.*
Stanley R. Hatcher *Atomic Energy of Canada, Ltd.*
Katherine Hope Larson *International Atomic Energy Agency*
Byoung Whie Lee *Atomic Energy Commission, Seoul*
Måns Lönnroth *Secretariat for Future Studies, Stockholm*
Onkar Marwah *Graduate Institute of International Studies, Geneva*
Milan Osredkar *Institute Josef Stefan, Ljubljana*
Manfred Popp *Bundesministerium für Forschung und Technologie, Bonn*
Günter Schuster *Commission of the European Communities*
Domingo L. Siazon, Jr. *Embassy of the Philippines, Vienna*
Ian Smart *Consultant on international energy affairs, London*
Mitsuo Takei *Institute of Energy Economics, Tokyo*
Ronald Walker *Australian Foreign Service*
Joseph A. Yager *Brookings Institution (conference coordinator and rapporteur)*

Index

221

Nonproliferation and U.S. Foreign Policy

Joseph A. Yager
Editor

Checking the proliferation of nuclear weapons—a long-time objective of U.S. foreign policy—has become increasingly difficult as more and more countries acquire the technological expertise to produce them. The difficulty is compounded by the spread of facilities for enriching uranium and reprocessing spent nuclear fuel.

This book examines the present and possible future incentives for and against the acquisition of nuclear weapons by a number of countries. The authors find that the countries studied differ greatly in their approach to nuclear issues and in their susceptibility to U.S. influence. These differences and the fact that other foreign policy goals often take precedence make it almost impossible for the United States alone to carry out a consistent and effective nonproliferation policy. The best hope seems to lie in the creation of new international arrangements for civil nuclear energy and in the promotion of a more secure international environment in which countries that now feel threatened will have less reason to obtain nuclear weapons.

The authors have chosen for analysis countries that are capable of building nuclear weapons within a relatively short time and that may have some incentives for doing so. Joseph A. Yager discusses Japan, South Korea, and Taiwan; Richard K. Betts, India, Pakistan, Iran, and South Africa; Henry S. Rowen and Richard Brody, the Middle Eastern Arab states and Israel; and William H. Courtney, Argentina and Brazil. Introductory and concluding chapters are provided by the editor.

438 pp./1980/cloth and paper